# FREUD ON RELIGION

*Key Thinkers in the Study of Religion*
Series Editor: Steven Engler, Mount Royal College, Canada

*Key Thinkers in the Study of Religion* is a series of compact introductions to the life and work of major figures in the study of religion. Each volume provides up-to-date critical evaluations of the place and value of a single scholar's work, in a manner both accessible to students and useful for instructors. Each volume includes a brief biography, analyses of key works, evaluations of criticisms and of overall impact on the field, and discussions of the work of later scholars who have appropriated or extended each key thinker's approach. Critical engagement with each key thinker's major works makes each volume a useful companion for the study of these important sources in the field. Intended for undergraduate and introductory graduate classrooms, the series aims to encapsulate and evaluate foundational contributions to the academic study of religion.

This series is sponsored by the North American Association for the Study of Religion (NAASR), an affiliate of the International Association for the History of Religions.

**Published**

*Bastide on Religion: The Invention of Candomblé*
Michel Despland

*Bourdieu on Religion: Imposing Faith and Legitimacy*
Terry Rey

*Derrida on Religion: Thinker of Differance*
Dawne McCance

*Dumont on Religion: Difference, Comparison, Transgression*
Ivan Strenski

*Ernesto de Martino on Religion: The Crisis and the Presence*
Fabrizio M. Ferrari

*Freud on Religion*
Marsha A. Hewitt

*Lévi-Strauss on Religion*
Paul-François Tremlett

**Forthcoming**

*Clifford Geertz on Religion*
Willem Hofstee

*Eliade on Religion*
Okuyama Michiaki

*Evans-Pritchard on Religion*
Daniel L. Pals

*Peter L. Berger on Religion: The Social Reality of Religion*
Titus Hjelm

*Rudolf Otto on Religion*
Gregory D. Alles

*William James on Religion: Belief, Experience and Plurality*
Jeremy Carrette

# Freud on religion

Marsha Aileen Hewitt

ACUMEN

*Dedicated to the memory of Aileen Snape Hewitt (1921–77).*

First published in 2014 by Acumen

Acumen Publishing Limited
4 Saddler Street
Durham
DH1 3NP, UK

ISD, 70 Enterprise Drive
Bristol
CT 06010, USA

www.acumenpublishing.com

ISBN: 978-1-84465-797-1  (hardcover)
ISBN: 978-1-84465-798-8  (paperback)

British Library Cataloguing-in-Publication Data
A catalogue record for this book is available from the British Library.

Printed and bound in the UK by 4edge Ltd., Essex.

# Contents

# Preface

It is by now taken for granted that Sigmund Freud has had an enormous impact on modern Western culture. Psychotherapy, psychiatry, literature, religion, philosophy, art, education and many other fields have in some way felt the profound influence of his thought. After Freud, human beings cannot sensibly regard their feelings, thoughts or motivations as fully transparent to themselves. Common cultural taglines, such as "the devil made me do it", contain deep Freudian insights about the nature of the individual's sense of will and subjective agency, and strongly suggest that conscious awareness is not the master of the mind's domain. After Freud, it no longer makes sense not to call ourselves and others into question on any number of levels. Every question regarding our motivations, perceptions of reality, fantasies, feelings and dreams is inherently a *psychoanalytic* question. Perhaps where Freud has had the most influence in popular culture is in the ways we think about dreams. Since the publication of Freud's *The Interpretation of Dreams* (*Die Traumdeutung*) over 100 years ago, there has been an explosion of scientific research as well as popular interest in the process and meaning of dreams.

The depth and pervasiveness of the influence of psychoanalysis and its reverberations within our discursive cultural frameworks, interpersonal relationships and individual sense of self were brought home to me powerfully and surprisingly in a remarkable exchange some years ago between my little grandsons. One night, as I was putting them to bed, the conversation about the day's events and the boys' observations on life in general turned to the subject of "bad dreams". Both were eager to talk about bad dreams they had experienced, at times competing with each other in their descriptions of the various scary monsters they had encountered there. Sean, barely four years old at the time, recounted a "really scary dream" where "a bad guy" crept into his room with the intention of stealing his beloved Handy Manny doll. With great solemnity, Sean told us how frightened he was at the prospect of losing his cherished companion. Before I could utter a word of consolation, Josh, then only six, made the following observation: "Well, Sean," said he, in the "been-there, done-that" tone of the wiser older brother, "I think the reason you were so scared wasn't because the man was going to take away your doll. I mean, it's only a *doll*, right? Why be so scared of losing a *doll*? I think that really you were scared that the bad man was going to steal *you*, that makes more sense, right? Because after all, it's only a doll, and it's way more scary if someone takes *you* away than your doll!" After some silent pondering, Sean agreed this explanation was plausible.

Two things struck me about this stunning little vignette: one was that if *I* had heard a patient recount a dream like Sean's, I would have interpreted it in similar fashion. I would have focused on the manifest, expressed *feeling* of fear while following the patient's free associations to the *feeling* in order to understand the underlying latent dream thoughts. What struck me most forcefully, however, was the degree to which Freudian ways of thinking about our own minds have so deeply shaped the way people of all ages account for feelings, fantasies and dream life without even being aware of it. I remain confident that Josh, then six years old, had never read a word of Freud in his life. Yet he was able to think about his brother's dream *psychoanalytically*, in an automatic, taken-for-granted way that testifies to how deeply psychoanalysis has seeped into our cultural context and its ordinary discourses. There is nothing passé about Freud.

In his creation of a psychoanalytic theory that he repeatedly reminds us is derived from clinical experience, Freud cast a powerful light on the darkness of the mind and its hidden motives, demonstrating, to paraphrase Paul Ricoeur, that the desiring individual moves through life in disguise, pretending to himself and others to be something he is not, without even knowing it. In a decisive, narcissistic blow to cherished Enlightenment ideals, Freud demonstrated that consciousness and reason constitute a small, fleeting and vulnerable part of the mind. It is by now a commonplace truism that who we think we are is not always who we really are. Our minds are stubbornly opaque, inaccessible to the full transparency of rational inquiry. Freud tells us that our loftiest, most celebrated values and ideals are also not quite what they seem, originating as they do in the murky contradictions and terrifying conflicts of body-based needs and desires. Psychoanalysis gives us a language and frame of reference to make more enriched and fuller sense of ourselves. Whether we agree with Freud, or have even read him, the incontrovertible fact remains that he has decisively shaped and influenced the way we think about our own mental life, and that of others.

Freud has also changed the way we think about religion. It is widely and unquestioningly accepted that Freud was a cantankerous atheist who denigrated religion and belittled believers. A large number of Freud's interpreters and critics concur that he had no patience for religion, that he held believers in contempt, and that he dismissed their religiosity as infantile, ridiculing them for what he judged to be their inability and/or unwillingness to grow up. There are at least two major problems with this reading of Freud that I address in this book. The first is that this view of Freud is based almost exclusively on one of his books on religion, *The Future of an Illusion,* which is erroneously regarded by many as emblematic of Freud's entire published thinking on the subject. The second problem, while less obvious, is nonetheless connected to the first: that Freud's discussion of religion as rooted in an infantile state of mind is intended to insult or demean religious believers, as so many of his critics claim. Freud's psychoanalytic account of the internal, unconscious origins of religion is not in itself a judgement against religious believers. His description of the negative impact of religion on the level of the individual and society is a separate issue. Freud is not trying to promote atheism in his writings on religion. He is no Richard Dawkins or Christopher Hitchens. Identifying Freud's differentiated theory with one text misses the rich complexity and diversity of his thinking about that most persistent, stubborn and ubiquitous phenomenon found only among human beings: religion.

Writing yet another book on Freud's theory of religion is a daunting task, not only because of the vast literature already in existence on the subject, but also because it involves wading into unresolved fields of controversy that raged even in Freud's lifetime. Many of Freud's critics tend to fixate on Freud himself and his personal foibles as a way of undermining his theories of religion, rather than really paying attention to what he actually said. I am much less interested than many of Freud's critics to explain his atheism by speculating about his personal psychological conflicts or linking his unbelief in God with an unresolved Oedipus complex. I do not address the controversial studies on Freud's relationship with his father and mother, the influence of his Catholic nanny, his alleged knowledge and/or ambivalence about his Jewish heritage, or whether he could read Hebrew. These topics have been extensively and exhaustively covered, for better or worse, by others. I am not invested in defending religion or atheism as having anything to do with either healthy emotional functioning or psychological pathology. My task is both more modest, and perhaps more ambitious: to let the books as far as possible speak for themselves first and foremost as *psychoanalytic* works that make their own contribution to a theory of human being that has changed permanently the way we account for who we are.

Marsha Aileen Hewitt

Carmel-by-the-Sea, California

# Acknowledgements

My thanks to Steven Engler for inviting me to write this book and for his support for my approach to the topic. I am especially grateful for his consistently courteous and reliable responses to all my questions as I worked on this project. I benefited from a number of conversations with colleagues and friends in psychoanalysis and religious studies at various stages while I was writing this book, particularly James Di Censo. My thanks to John Kloppenborg and Stuart Pizer for reading portions of the manuscript. Their thoughtful comments helped me clarify some important aspects of my thinking, and I remain grateful for their generous encouragement. Thanks also to Josh Levy for our many enlightening discussions about Freud. I greatly appreciate his steady and positive interest in my work. Thanks to my wonderful graduate students, both in the Toronto School of Theology and the University of Toronto, who have read and debated Freud with me over the years; in particular, Nicholas Dion for his excellent research assistance when called upon. For Joel Ruimy, my deepest gratitude, not only for his superb editorial work on the manuscript, but for his infinite patience and loving support throughout the very long process of research and writing.

This book is dedicated to the memory of Aileen Snape Hewitt (1921–77): "a certain spiritual grandeur ill-matched with the meanness of opportunity".

# INTRODUCTION

# Freud and the psychoanalytic study of religion

I have never ventured beyond the ground floor and basement of the building. You maintain that if one changes one's point of view one can also see a higher floor, in which there live such distinguished guests as religion, art, etc. ... If I still had a lifetime of work ahead of me, I should dare to assign a home in my lowly little house to those highborn personages. I have already done so for religion since coming across the category "neurosis of mankind".

(Freud to Ludwig Binswanger, 8 October 1936)

## Thinking Freud thinking religion

A basic condition for the possibility of the study of religion is that some effort be made to establish its conceptual horizons, regardless of whether the theoretical orientation is comparative, historical, anthropological, psychological, sociological or phenomenological. This is a tricky enterprise because the term "religion" is itself the contested object of ongoing critical debate. One may go so far as to say that the relentlessly "full-scale questioning" that is taking place in the theoretical study of religion is almost "obsessively self-critical" (Hughes 2006: 127, 129). For many scholars, the category "religion" is by no means identical to any specific example or particular instantiation of the generic concept. There is "religion", and there is a vast array of diverse "religions;" the latter is not automatically or easily subsumed within the former. As Jonathan Z. Smith concludes in his survey of the colonialist, homogenizing and Western origins of the category, religion is

> created by scholars for their intellectual purposes and therefore is theirs to define. It is a second-order, generic concept that plays the same role in establishing a disciplinary horizon that a concept such as "language"

plays in linguistics or "culture" plays in anthropology. *There can be no disciplined study of religion without such a horizon.*

(Smith 1998: 281–2, emphasis added)

A number of scholars appear to agree. Pascal Boyer describes religion as a "convenient label" that (for him) covers "all the ideas, actions, rules and objects that have to do with the existence and properties of superhuman agents such as God" (2001: 9). Benson Saler asserts more generally that "[r]eligion is an abstraction … promulgated in our culture and supported by our experiences" (1993: 212–13). However, as Smith's historical review of the origins and evolution of the term "religion" implies, there are multiple problems that arise with any attempt to *define* it, at least in a strong sense. In the period of early colonialist European expansion, "religion" often referred to something the "savage" or "pagan" "other" had no inkling of or did not possess. This use of the term "religion" clearly helped separate the moral, godly and Christian from everyone else. Many contemporary scholars would agree that "monothetic", or "universalist-essentialist" conceptions of religion are untenable and insufficient to account for the diverse range of human beliefs and actions that are ordinarily described within the category "religion" (Saler 1993; McCutcheon 1995). Even the "clearest examples of what is normally meant by religion" like Judaism, Islam and Christianity cannot themselves be understood as constituting "monolithic and clearly bounded entities" (Saler 1993: 214, 200).

At the same time, any attempt to speak at all coherently about religion demands that we have some idea as to what we are talking about, what we think it is, and what basic elements or features may be considered central to and universally present in that peculiar range of human experiences and actions generally recognized as "religion". Efforts to identify universal characteristics that justify their inclusion in the conceptual construct "religion" need not inevitably imply that these characteristics are *definitive* in an essentialist sense that assumes there is an "essence of religion" (Segal 2006: 136). There is an important distinction between the idea of an inherent, unassailable absoluteness or essence of a phenomenon and features that may be considered as universally relevant to or commonly associated with it. The phenomenon "religion" can be recognized as having universal applicability to a wide range of culturally diverse expressions of shared human experiences by giving them meaning and coherence. In this sense religion is an organizing concept. Theorizing activity must demand that the relationship between universality and particularity be held both provisionally and lightly. Adopting this approach to theory construction is especially important to the way we think religion.

Establishing conceptual horizons that allow for clarity of understanding concerning what is meant by religion in a second-order discourse that attempts to *think* religion is not, then, necessarily the same as *defining* it. Whereas conceptual horizons can be constructed with enough flexibility to incorporate the expansion of data and changing insights dictated by new theories and field researches, definitions can too often betray a tendency to be theoretically static, conceptually limited, ideologically closed and therefore antagonistically competitive. Scholars of religion are by now only too familiar with the problematic nature of the concept "religion" and the diverse range of debates around how it should be defined. Decades ago, Joseph Kitagawa observed with astute simplicity that "No one has as yet proposed a satisfactory definition of the term 'religion' that is acceptable to everyone concerned" (in Penner & Yonan 1972: 111). His words remain as true today as they were then. However, complete agreement about definitions of religion and/or their inherent political legitimacy and implied power structures is not a necessary prerequisite for the construction of a flexible conceptual horizon or series of horizons that we can recognize as giving the phenomenon theoretical shape and coherent delineation. As Ann Taves sensibly points out, whether or not scholars decide to employ the term religion "should be decided on the basis of the questions we want to ask and the methods that are most appropriate for answering them, not on the history of the use of the term" (2006: 139).

In my view, anthropologist Melford Spiro's (1966) attempt to offer what he calls a definition of religion has proven flexible and durable enough to provide a satisfactory theoretical baseline for conceiving and *thinking* religion that a number of scholars continue to share and sometimes build upon in one way or another. Spiro identifies a universal characteristic of religion as pertaining to the human tendency to believe in "culturally postulated superhuman beings" who have the power "to assist or to harm man" (*ibid.*: 96, 91, 94). Given his assumption that religion is a humanly produced, historically and culturally diverse institution designed "for the satisfaction of needs", Spiro maintains that it further consists of "patterned interaction with culturally postulated superhuman beings" (*ibid.*: 96). Spiro's focus on superhuman beings as a "key variable" (*ibid.*: 91) in any definition of religion is responsive enough to be compatible with some efforts of more recent scholarship to conceptualize the nature of religion. For example, cognitively oriented theorists such as Lawson and McCauley have updated and reformulated Spiro's definition as beliefs in "culturally postulated superhuman agents" (McCauley 2004: 60). Pascal Boyer maintains that "Religion is about the existence and causal powers of non-observable entities and agencies. These may be one unique God or many different gods or spirits or ancestors, or a combination of these different kinds" (Boyer 2001: 7). Cognitive archaeologists David Lewis-Williams and Steven Mithen assume that beliefs in supernatural entities constitute a universal characteristic among human groups (Lewis-Williams & Clottes 2007; Mithen 1996, 1999). For Scott Atran, "Supernatural agency is the most culturally recurrent, cognitively relevant, and evolutionarily compelling concept in religion" (2002: 57). In spite of the persistent lack of agreement concerning definitions of religion, we may reasonably conclude that Harvey Whitehouse's description of religion as "any set of shared beliefs and actions appealing to supernatural agency" (2004: 2) is an acceptable key variable to a number of contemporary scholars of religion.

Freud's psychoanalytic study of religion belongs within the conceptual horizons outlined above in its shared concern as to how and why human beings come to have beliefs in otherworldly or superhuman beings, agents and/or entities of any kind. This is the central question that organizes and directs Freud's interest in religion. Psychoanalysis explores the deep motivational structures of the unconscious minds of individuals that result in the cultural productions of religions. Freud's theories of religion are best understood as an effort to construct a second-order discourse about religion from the perspective of the universal characteristics and operations of the human mind. This is why I deliberately refrain from using the term "cultural texts" with reference to Freud's writings on religion. Freud's remarks and observations on religion are not only dispersed throughout a wider range of his works not usually associated with the rubric "cultural texts"; more importantly, his ideas on religion are an inextricable part of the entire theoretical and conceptual structure of psychoanalysis itself. Donald Capps's observation that "Freud's writings on religion are, in fact, inseparable from his work as a whole" (2001: 2) is quite correct, and accords with a major premise of this book. Thus, without the concept of unconscious mental processes, which succinctly sums up what psychoanalysis is (Freud 1925a: 70), there could be no psychoanalytic theory of religion.

Despite Freud's own acknowledged cultural ethnocentrism (see Chapter 1), he is interested in religion more as a generic phenomenon than in the concrete beliefs, doctrines or ritual practices of any particular religion, although he inevitably addresses these when necessary in the course of extending and applying his ideas. He is most interested in unearthing the origins of religion as located in the unconscious psychic operations of human minds. Although Freud relied primarily on two representatives of Western monotheism, Christianity and Judaism, as his reference points for theorizing religion, his insights need not be dismissed as irrelevant or invalid because of this methodology. Here I have in mind Saler's (1993) proposal that the Western monotheisms Judaism, Christianity and Islam may be taken as valid "reference religions" for conceptualizing religion. This does not mean that all religions are to be subsumed within or forced to inhabit these monotheistic frameworks, or judged against their moral and epistemological norms. Saler writes:

> Those instantiations, called religions, include the Western monotheisms, our most prototypical cases of religion. They also include whatever else we deem to participate in the pool of elements to the extent of resembling the Western monotheisms in significant respects. And

how do we establish what is significant? By cogent analytical arguments about elements that we deem analogous to those we associate with our reference religions, the Western monotheisms. (*Ibid.*: 225)

I think it is fair to say that Freud would agree with Saler on this point.

Although psychoanalysis is a theory that is independent of religion, for Freud it can explain the unconscious motivations that give rise to religion and its place in the creation of culture. He would most certainly endorse Spiro's view that "to understand culture it is not sufficient to attend to cultural symbol systems and how they work; it is also necessary to attend to the mind and how *it* works" (1987: 162). One of the most important aspects of Spiro's concept of religion that assists in a fuller understanding of Freud rests upon the argument that religion centrally involves relationships with imagined superhuman others who have the power to help or harm human beings, and to whom human beings look for safety and the satisfaction of needs. Drawing directly upon Freud, Spiro also locates the origins of religious beliefs in human experiences as they are fashioned within family contexts. Fully aware that Freud's "ethnocentric conception of patriarchal fathers, and of gods reflecting this conception of 'father', is inadequate for comparative analysis", Spiro goes on to highlight what he sees as a more compelling dimension of Freud's theory. He writes:

> The theory … is that it is in the context of the family that the child experiences powerful beings, both benevolent and malevolent, who – by various means which are learned in the socialization process – can sometimes be induced to accede to his desires. These experiences provide the basic ingredients for his personal projective system … which, if it corresponds (structurally, not substantively) to his taught beliefs, constitutes the cognitive and perceptual set for the acceptance of these beliefs. Having had personal experience with "superhuman beings" and with the efficacy of "ritual", the taught beliefs re-enforce, and are re-enforced by, his own projective system. (Spiro 1966: 103)

This is the crux of Freud's critical theory of religion or, more precisely, Freud's theory of those internal mental operations and their developmental history within specific historical and familial contexts that give rise to subjective feeling states and cognitive capacities that can be understood within shared cultural networks as belonging to the category "religion". Although Freud used Christianity and Judaism as his "reference religions", his deeper interest lay in an analysis of the psychology underlying the pervasive, ubiquitous human phenomenon commonly known as religion. As applied to psychoanalysis, Freud would have agreed with Saler that as religion is a thoroughly human creation, "we need to expand our knowledge of human beings if we are to expand our knowledge of why and how they go about creating religions" (2004: 212). Freud's writings on religion are a significant part of his more comprehensive psychoanalytic project of expanding our knowledge about human beings.

Writing about Freud's theory of religion is a daunting and difficult task, partly because of the vast literature, still growing, about Freud and religion. Much of this literature is contentious, and rife with conflicting interpretations. A "Freud industry" (Falzeder 2007: 226) has certainly grown around his work on religion as well as psychoanalysis in general. Those critics who contend that Freud did little more than denigrate religion can find any number of quotations in his writings to support their view. Many statements can be taken from *The Future of an Illusion* (1927) or *Civilization and its Discontents* (1930a) as "proof" of his "dismissive" and "hostile" attitude to religion or his demeaning attitudes to religious believers. However, these readings need to be balanced in the light of other things Freud wrote about religion and religious believers. Freud is quite clear in his case study of the Rat Man, for example, that superstitious beliefs can exist within the rational minds of highly educated individuals (1909: 229–30). In Freud's view, the holding of religious beliefs is not synonymous with stupidity. Reading Freud on religion primarily in the key of an ill-tempered atheism misses the deeper, more complex aspects of his thought. As I argue throughout the pages that follow, Freud's critique of religion becomes distorted if it is restricted primarily to any specific text where he deals with the subject. The diverse range of his psychoanalytic inquiry into religion is not easily captured within a singular, homogeneous point of view.

There is then no "basic notion" or key of intelligibility (Ellenberger 1970: 463) whereby Freud's personality or his theory of religion can be easily or neatly explained. He was an atheist in the double sense that he did not believe in God and he had no direct, subjective experience that might be called mystical. Freud is unambiguously clear on these two points. Yet it does not automatically follow that he was invested in promoting atheism. For Freud, an explanatory scientific investigation into religion presupposes unbelief, in part because of its etic methodology. A number of contemporary scholars in the field of the academic or scientific study of religion would agree. Freud said many different things about why and how human beings are religious, and some of these things at times appear to be contradictory. He describes in detail the ways in which adherence to religious beliefs and their moral systems are individually and socially damaging. Yet Freud is also capable of recognizing how religion offers relief to the painful isolation of individual neurosis, and consolation in the face of inexplicable suffering. Moreover, he is keenly aware that religion is also the historical and intellectual vehicle for some of humankind's greatest cultural achievements. Freud cannot be said to simply "have it in" for religion. As I argue throughout this book, whatever Freud is saying about religion in any given text is centred around the specific set of issues he is attempting to address *in that particular text or set of texts.* My own approach reflects this reading of Freud. Each chapter or section is organized around a set of thematic and theoretical concerns that correspond to those addressed in Freud's writings, as I now set out to explain.

Although Freud was well aware that the greater part of mental operations are unconscious, and that the power of the ego is limited within "its own house, the mind" (1917a: 141), he nonetheless placed high value on human autonomy as providing the capacity for independent critical thought and moral action. As a theory and clinical practice, one of the chief goals of psychoanalysis is to encourage and foster the freedom of the individual to think for himself (Freud 1916: 433, 435; 1923b: 50; 1940: 175). Psychoanalysis attempts to identify and cultivate whatever trace or "scrap of independence" (1921a: 129) the individual may have in order to resist the pressures of familial and social conformity so that she can live a more enriched and authentic life. In what is perhaps the most succinct and hopeful description of the therapeutic goal of psychoanalysis that I have come across to date, Freud writes: "The neurotic who is cured has really become another man, though at bottom, of course, he has remained the same; that is to say, he has become what he might have become at best under the most favourable conditions". For Freud, such an achievement is "a very great deal" (1916: 435). The greatest impediment to intellectual and moral autonomy for all human beings in Freud's view was religion.

The theme of autonomy looms large in what is perhaps Freud's most (in) famous text on religion, *The Future of an Illusion,* which advances the thesis that religion is not only the enemy of critical thought and self-directed moral action but, even more egregiously, of science. As I argue in Chapter 1, *The Future of an Illusion* is his most Marxian and Feuerbachian text, one whose main purpose is to relocate theology within anthropology, and metaphysics within metapsychology. It is also a psychoanalytic reformulation and extension of Kant's famous Enlightenment dictum to think for oneself without the direction of others. As John Forrester correctly points out, "There is nothing more in tune with Freud's account of the childishness of religion than Kant's famous declaration" (2006: xxiv). Like Kant, Freud objects to "the grounding of religion as dependent on the ungrounded authority of others" (*ibid.*: xxiv). Religion is the antithesis of science in its epistemological approach that privileges myth and the unquestioned authority of doctrinal tradition over evidence acquired through independent rational inquiry. It is important to bear in mind that Freud has nothing so simplistic in mind as to replace religion with science as a different kind of religion that asserts one set of truth claims over the other.

Science, as Freud sees it, is necessarily committed to sustained self-interrogation and a willingness to change or abandon its theories, whereas doctrinal teaching is not. Freud's commitment to scientific investigation is less about its epistemological outcome than the establishment of careful research methodologies capable of yielding evidence-based knowledge that can be tested and contested. In Freud's view religion is not only an insufficient basis for morality and knowledge, its epistemological basis and methodology is utterly incompatible with science because it is the enemy of human autonomy. *The Future of an Illusion* goes much farther than simply pointing out the episte-mological and moral inadequacies of religion, however. Its far more important task is to provide a psychological explanation of religion through an in-depth analysis of its origins in the hidden motives and psychic forces of the human mind that call out for a nurturing, protective attachment relationship with a strong and dependable parent.

Chapter 1 provides a case study that illustrates the importance of attach-ment, in particular in *The Future of an Illusion*. Freud's account of the pathetic seventeenth-century painter Christoph Haizmann clearly demonstrates the compelling and powerful human need for proximity to a perceived parental protector, no matter how harmful that figure might be. I link this discussion to current attachment research, whose findings confirm the existence of biologi-cally and evolutionarily based needs for connection with other human beings that are present from birth. This explains, for example, why abused children often cling to the abusive parent: the threat of isolation and abandonment is more terrifying than the abuse itself. This insight is strongly suggested in Freud's account of Haizmann's desperate pact with a demonic father figure. That Freud understood the *relational* aspect of the need for a parental protector on earth, in hell or in heaven is often overlooked by his critics. Freud's argument that religious ideas are illusions born of the helpless dependency of earliest infantile experiences that remain preserved in the unconscious has nothing to do with an atheist agenda on his part or a desire to insult or humiliate religious believ-ers. As Peter Gay rightly points out, "The rule that the origins of an idea in no way determine its value – or lack of value – remains intact; certainly nothing Freud said in his papers on religion was designed to shake it. *But what mattered to Freud was just how much influence these origins could retain*" (1988: 531, emphasis added).

Chapter 2 delves more deeply into the psychoanalytic theories that are nec-essary to explain and understand Freud's increasingly complex treatment of the dynamics of religious beliefs. For Freud, gods, ghosts, spirits and demons are projections of repressed internal fantasies and mental states that contain psychic derivatives and precipitates of the external world and its authority fig-ures and institutions, particularly as represented by fathers real *or* imagined. The "projective character of the supernaturals" (Spiro & D'Andrade 1958: 459) has its origins in the parental introjects that populate the mind and are deriva-tives of the infant's real experience of real others with whom he has identi-fied and internalized. Freud situates and recasts the need for gods within the inherent human need for relationships with other beings. The longing for a protective and loving father-god is rife with ambivalence because of its inherent contradictions of love and hate. The child's ambivalent desire results in submission to paternal authority while fostering a sense of rebellion against it. The theme of rebellion against authority surfaces explicitly in *Totem and Taboo*. A discussion of this text, along with *Civilization and its Discontents* introduces new themes relating to Freud's theories of religion. The story of the rebellion against authority is psychologically complicated by the love and longing for the paternal authority figure, whom the sons also hate and set out to destroy.

Taking his inspiration from Sophocles' story of Oedipus, Freud describes the tragic outcome of a rebellion against paternal authority that succeeds in the destruction of that authority while ironically inscribing it with far greater power as it becomes psychologically internalized. The ancient primal father may be vanquished, but his authority is endlessly recreated throughout the generations in the minds of all human beings. Religious authority for Freud draws much of its power from the guilt and terror resulting from that original rebellion against the father that is endlessly repeated and psychologically passed down in the repressed memories of one generation to the next. The drama of Oedipus encapsulates a ubiquitous aspect of the human condition by giving intelligibility to "a universal law of mental life [that] had here been captured in all its emotional significance. Fate and the oracle were no more than materializations of an internal necessity" (1925a: 63). But there is more to this story, as Freud tantalizingly hints that behind the love and hatred for the father there exists a much older and very different experience of connection with the mother that may lie at the heart of unitive mystical experiences.

In Chapter 3, I present Freud addressing a very different set of concerns about religion in his last major work on the topic, *Moses and Monotheism*, which is discussed at length. In this remarkable, controversial and, to many, offensive book, Freud sets out to explain the origins of monotheism, the emergence of Judaism, the transmission of Jewish tradition and, perhaps most importantly, the formation and transmission of Jewish identity. He recapitulates his argument of the murder of the primal father outlined in *Totem and Taboo* to set the stage for his thesis that Moses, too, was murdered by his followers from Egypt, only to be reinstated centuries later as the revered founder of the Jewish religion and Mosaic law. Given its serial publication in the mid to late thirties, the historically unsupported idea that Moses was an Egyptian (or even existed at all) and that monotheism was therefore an Egyptian invention, was especially scandalous and clearly offensive, particularly since the author of these ideas was himself a Jew. But Freud's fierce independence of mind had a great deal to do with his Jewish identity, as he often insisted (1925a: 9). The serious problems contained in *Totem and Taboo* regarding historical accuracy and the means whereby unconscious ideas are culturally and psychologically transmitted remain unresolved in *Moses and Monotheism*. At the same time, Freud continued to insist, from *Totem and Taboo* through to *Moses and Monotheism*, that these issues are not ultimately important for his thesis. For Freud the real importance of his *Just So* stories accounting for the prehistory of humanity lies in the ways they can "bring coherence and understanding into more and more new regions" (1921a: 122) of the psychic development and cultural achievements of humankind. As far as Freud is concerned, the greatest achievement of humanity is the capacity for abstract thought and independent critical reason that constitutes the true legacy of Jewish monotheism.

In Chapter 4, I turn to a topic that is commonly treated with embarrassed dismissal or outright silence in the secondary literature on Freud, but nevertheless belongs in any discussion of Freud and religion: the occult. Freud had little time for or interest in the occult as it was understood and embraced in the popular culture of his day. However, Freud was very interested in telepathy (which is what he meant by thought-transference) and I discuss this dimension of his work in detail. In his view, thought-transference had nothing to do with the occult. Beliefs in spirits, life after death, clairvoyance and all other occult experiences address a similar set of psychological needs, as is the case with religious beliefs and practices. Occult and uncanny experiences are mental products as far as Freud is concerned. If, for example, minds have the capacity for non-verbal and unconscious communication, that phenomenon must be treated psychoanalytically, like any other mental product, and not like a supernatural event. Freud gives specific examples of thought-transference that demonstrate there is nothing mystical or other-worldly involved. In this respect the psychology of religion has much in common with the psychology of the occult: that people have religious or occult experiences does not mean that religious or occult phenomena exist. Both modalities of human experience contribute to Freud's exploration of the underlying unconscious mental processes, conflicts and fantasies that give rise to them. Freud was also interested in the minds of dreamers who claimed prophetic knowledge of future events and the mediums who communicated with ghosts in the same way he was interested in the minds of religious believers. In Freud's view, this area of investigation had nothing to do with occultism, "the black tide of mud" against which psychoanalysis was the "bulwark" (in Jung 1963: 150).

After much vacillation, in part because of his concern that psychoanalysis might be tainted by associations with the occult, Freud finally admitted to acknowledging the existence of telepathic communication. Again, as with his approach to religion, Freud attempted to explain telepathy in psychoanalytic terms, as a form of human communication operating outside the mechanisms of conventional verbal discourse. The possibility of thought-transference makes sense when situated within Freud's theory of the unconscious and its variety of communicative forms, as in altered states of consciousness such as nocturnal dreams or the mildly dissociated states manifest in ordinary mishaps (parapraxes) such as slips of the tongue or convenient "forgetting".

In Chapter 4, I note as well that contemporary psychoanalysis is paying increasing attention to this phenomenon. As contemporary psychoanalytic writers attempt to explain the variety of forms of unconscious communication that many experience from time to time in their own clinical work, they are constructing a more encompassing explanatory theory of interconnected subjectivities that they believe finds support in other disciplines, such as neuroscience and quantum physics. I discuss the pros and cons of these engagements at the end of the chapter, partly as a way of contrasting this more contemporary approach with Freud's. As I discuss especially with reference to the work of Elizabeth Lloyd Mayer, the idea of interconnected or "entangled" minds goes well beyond the more modest scope of Freud's interest in thought-transference to embrace a variety of noetic theories, such as remote viewing or the ability of the mind to manipulate events across great distances. Freud, ever on the alert against occult or mystical encroachments on his theory, addresses thought-transference within the bounds of psychoanalysis as a whole. And since the methodology grounding his account of unconscious communication as a phenomenon originating in the mind is in tandem with his analysis of religion, it needs to be included in any discussion of his psychoanalytic study of religion.

In Chapter 5, I address Freud's differentiated and complex treatment of love, which he later incorporated within the concept of Eros. There is a "tough-minded realism" (Gay 1988: xvii) to Freud's thought that permeates his theorizing, and this in itself seems to have generated a great deal of opposition, misapprehension and, often, angry repudiation of his ideas. Here I address what some critics describe as Freud's failure to recognize the primacy of relational needs, the importance of the mother in the developing life of the child, or the healing, transformative power of love as central to human emotional well-being. It is indeed the case that Freud scoffed at the Christian command to love the neighbour as amounting to little more than an idealized fantasy construct bearing little resemblance to the complicated, ambivalent nature of love as experienced by real human beings. Aggression is at the very least a derivative of Eros – if not an independent instinct in its own right – meaning in part that where there is love in Freud's view, there is hate as well. Not only his psychoanalytic investigations, but the harrowing experience of the First World War told Freud that the view of love as unalloyed by hate or directed towards others purely for its own sake belonged to the nursery rather than the world of real human beings (Freud 1930a: 120). Freud also argued that the Christian imperative to love abstract humanity concealed a deeper incapacity to love actual living human beings.

As I further argue in this chapter, Freud's repudiation of what he criticized as fantasy idealizations of love does not mean he did not recognize or value its inestimable importance for human well-being. Freud's clinical experience taught him the importance of transference love on the part of the patient for the analyst as a crucial part of the process. Love animates and carries the therapeutic action. The relational therapeutic context mobilizes the "patient's capacity to love and desire" (Phillips 2002: xix) as an instrument of emotional and psychological healing. In my analysis of Freud's life of Leonardo da Vinci, and his interpretation of Jensen's story *Gradiva,* I call attention to Freud's recognition of the central role of love in psychic health and the importance of maternal love in psychological development. This is another theme often overlooked by Freud's commentators. I also demonstrate how this skewed understanding of Freud's ideas of love can be traced back to the persistence of ancient religious prejudices that inform the anti-Judaism tradition that is historically embedded in Christian theology. I discuss the anti-Judaism that persisted for centuries within Christianity, and the ways in which it surfaces explicitly in Ian Dishart Suttie's attack on Freud in the 1930s. Suttie's distorted reading of Freud on love and the need for relationships with others is largely mediated by the religious prejudices inherent in a supercessionist Christian theology that sees itself as having reformed and replaced Judaism.

A careful reading of Suttie reveals that his strong objection to Freud is based on an "entire set of [religious] values" more than on a different understanding of psychoanalytic theory and practice (Gerson 2009: 30). Suttie appears to confront Freud from the position of a "pure-hearted Christianity" (*ibid.*: 33) against a morally bankrupt Judaism that privileges legal rigidity over love and relationship. The explicit anti-Judaism bias of Suttie has remained largely unrecognized or ignored in contemporary psychoanalytic accounts crediting Suttie with reinstating the centrality of love in psychoanalysis. However, it remains nonetheless latently operative within those assumptions about Freud as ignoring love, especially maternal love. Chapter 5 calls attention to this hidden but persistent religious bias that needs to be confronted consciously and deliberately, especially by those writers who uncritically credit Suttie with a positive influence on contemporary psychoanalytic theories. In this chapter, I bring to light the ways in which controversies concerning Freud's concept of love are haunted by this unacknowledged, ancient and persistent Christian anti-Judaism.

Freud was quite unabashed in declaring that "psychoanalysis is my creation … no one can know better than I do what psychoanalysis is" (1914a: 7). Things have changed in the decades following his death, with the emergence of several different psychoanalytic schools[1] that have taken psychoanalysis in a number of important, creative and innovative directions, both theoretically and clinically. While there are any number of important subsequent transformations that have been and will continue to be made to psychoanalysis that benefit its theoretical and clinical development, psychoanalysis inescapably remains Freud's creation, although he is not its owner. No version of contemporary psychoanalysis can dispense with the concept of the unconscious or overlook the unique importance of dreams and their indisputable contribution to therapeutic work. At the same time, Freud remains a deeply contentious figure who continues to "agitate the sleep of mankind", as Freud himself once remarked (in Gay 1988: xvii). Perhaps he is no more contentious and disturbing than when he writes about religion. On this topic, he appears to offend just about everybody, but as I hope will become clear in the chapters that follow, this has more to do with the way he is so often misread than it does with what he is trying to say. It should be readily apparent that he says a good many different things about religion that lead to different sorts of conclusions.

Freud's written texts create the impression that he wrote as he thought, seeing the "both/and" of mental phenomena more than the "either/or". Freud's texts are not finished products, as the numerous footnotes he added to later editions attest. He was not afraid to change his mind. He was able to acknowledge the negative and the positive impact of religion. At times, reading Freud is like reading someone who is setting to paper his thought processes as they unfold in his attempts to comprehend and articulate his "deep, intuitive knowledge of the human soul" (Ellenberger 1970: 467) and the deeply contradictory nature of the human mind. Freud placed a high value on his contributions to the psychology of religion (1925a: 66) because they allowed him to clarify his understanding of the unconscious origins of the highest developments of culture, and the parallels between religion and unconscious neurotic conflicts. These insights were hardly welcome in his own time, and they remain contentious today. Freud was well aware that "the underworld of psychoanalysis" (1914a: 66) can be an inhospitable place that is especially uncomfortable for those who idealize the human capacity for morality, spirituality and religion. Perhaps this is one reason for the widespread, public negative attitudes towards psychoanalysis that persist within and outside the academy.

This book sets out to think Freud thinking religion by focusing on his texts rather than his person. As much as possible, I treat him as a critical theorist of religion. My effort to "think Freud thinking religion" requires going beyond those texts that deal most directly with religion and, where relevant, into his general psychological theory dedicated to explaining the minds of human beings everywhere, past and present, religious or not. As contemporary scholars of religion not connected with psychoanalysis continue to insist, "the right place to look for the origins and causes of religion must be in the minds that create (and continually recreate) it" (Whitehouse 2004b: 71). As Freud engaged in the work of "thinking religion", he probed ever more deeply into the mental systems that support and produce religion but that are in themselves not religious. Freud would agree with contemporary scholars of religion that there are "no specific mechanisms in the mind" that are dedicated to religion (Boyer 2004: 30). Religion provided Freud with one very special – if not unique – avenue for his journey of discovery into the psychic depths of those unconscious processes.

# ONE

# Psychoanalysis as a critical theory of religion

> Religion is the record of the wishes, desires, and accusations of countless
> generations.                                          (Horkheimer 1972: 129)

Sigmund Freud's theory of religion "has evoked more controversy and con-
demnation than any of his other writings", writes Ernest Jones (1957: 349).
This observation remains as true today as it was more than fifty years ago. The
irony is that Freud does not write about *religion* as such. Rather, the real object
of inquiry in his work on religion is the human mind and those psychological
processes that result in and support the diverse cultural phenomena that many
commentators and scholars of religion associate with or identify as *religion*. As
a psychoanalytic theorist and clinician, Freud's interest in religion is explanatory and scientific, not theological. As far as he is concerned, a "scientific investigation of religious belief" necessarily presupposes "unbelief" (cited in Gay
1988: 637). In this respect Freud's psychoanalytic and differentiated theory of
religion is best situated within the intellectual tradition of psychological and
anthropological explanations of religion represented by figures such as Ludwig
Feuerbach (1804–72) and Karl Marx (1818–83). The shared goal of all three
theorists is to demystify religion and the sacred (Ricoeur 1970: 153) in order
to show that the basis of religion – its true "secret" – is anthropology. As far
as Feuerbach, Marx and Freud are concerned, gods are the non-conscious or
unconscious products of culturally mediated human minds. "Now God is the
nature of man regarded as absolute truth – the truth of man ... for the qualities
of God are nothing else than the essential qualities of man himself", writes
Feuerbach (1957: 19–20).

Religion is the psychological and cultural expression of the relation of humanity to its own nature, emerging out of and filling the "gap" that lies between the
individual and the human species (Harvey 1997: 28, 39). Feuerbach, whose
philosophy Freud "revered" (Grubrich-Simitis 1986: 287), was Freud's "favorite
thinker" (Gay 1988: 28). His influence reverberates throughout Freud's thinking

on religion (Stepansky 1986; Grunbaum 1987: 157; Wallace 1983; Gay 1987: 53) and is especially evident in Feuerbach's explanation of God as a psychological projection of humanity's own ideal qualities that become objectified in the image of an external, transcendent deity. "God", writes Feuerbach, "is only the nature of man regarded objectively" (1957: 270), the result of an alienation of the human spirit from its own true essence. He describes the psychological nature of human self-alienation that characterizes religion as a process where "[m]an denies as to himself only what he attributes to God ... Religion further denies goodness as a quality of human nature; man is wicked ... God is only good" (*ibid.*: 27–8). Feuerbach hopes that humanity will eventually become conscious of this truth, thereby restoring and reclaiming its own spiritual nature as fully human.

Marx, also inspired by Feuerbach's anthropological methodology, sharpens and summarizes his central thesis with the succinct statement, "*Man makes religion,* religion does not make man" (1975a: 175). Marx also emphasizes the psychological, spiritual and material enslavement of human beings by religion in his argument that its self-interested, political purpose is to mystify and conceal the truth that human suffering is largely self-inflicted. If the myriad forms of injustice in the world are human creations, they can be changed by human action. As far as Marx is concerned, religion keeps this truth of the human condition hidden from consciousness, thereby supporting and reproducing the exploitative and oppressive forces that result in misery and suffering for the vast majority of human beings. The false consolations and promises of religion manufacture little more than an "illusory happiness" that preserves and maintains the interests of an inhuman capitalist hegemony whose power and wealth are the direct products of exploitative practices it inflicts on the labouring classes. For Marx, it follows that the abolition of religion, along with its false promises of eschatological rewards, opens the way for the "real" (*ibid.*: 176) material happiness of actual living human beings. As far as Marx was concerned, people turn to religion for assurance that they will be compensated in eternity for what is lacking in their present lives. Religion's promise of salvation and eternal life draws its emotional power and psychological credibility from the contrasting conditions of miserable human earthly experience. Marx writes, "The demand to give up illusions about the existing state of affairs is the *demand to give up a state of affairs which needs illusions.* The criticism of religion is therefore *in embryo the criticism of the vale of tears,* the *halo* of which is religion" (*ibid.*: 176). Feuerbach and Freud would concur with Marx that a theocentric world is indeed an "inverted world" where religious narratives and myths are but "the general theory of that world" for which "the *human essence* has no true reality" (*ibid.*: 175). Freud reiterates this last point in particular with the assertion that religious myths were "projected on to the heavens after having arisen elsewhere under purely human conditions" (1913a: 292). Freud agrees with Marx and Feuerbach that mythologies are cultural products, man-made explanations of the human condition. "It is in this *human content* that our interest lies", he writes (*ibid.*, emphasis added). This last statement may be read as summing up Freud's entire approach to the psychoanalytic study of religion. Marx writes, in a remarkably prescient insight that could also describe most of Freud's naturalistic psychoanalytic methodology:

> The phantoms formed in the brains of men are also, necessarily, subli-mates of their material life-processes, which is empirically verifiable and bound to material premises. Morality, religion, metaphysics, and all the rest of ideology as well as the forms of consciousness corresponding to these, thus no longer retain the semblance of independence.
>
> (Marx 1976: 36–7)

The demystifying explanations by Feuerbach, Marx and Freud of religion share another concern: to liberate the human potential for existential autonomy from what they see as the debilitating grip of both external and internal heter-onomous authorities that alienate individuals from their capacities for moral agency and intellectual creativity. In this respect, their theories share a strongly implicit *ethical* interest. In so far as their critiques of religion aim to expose the ways in which the demands of this cultural and social phenomenon restrict and impoverish the human mind, the work of all three thinkers can be understood as further sharing an *emancipatory* interest. While Feuerbach and Marx express a less developed understanding of the complex interconnections between inter-nal and external forms of oppression, it was Freud who mounted a full depth-psychological account of the unconscious complexities of the psychodynamics of domination and submission within the individual mind. While Freud does not engage with Marx's critique of capitalism, he is critically appreciative of some aspects of Marx's thought (1933a: 176–82) with which his own think-ing at times bears striking similarity (Ellenberger 1970: 239–40). For example, Freud believed that a transformation in the relationship of human beings to property and possessions could be more effective in alleviating destructive social tensions than obedience to the dictates of religion or ethics (Freud 1930a: 143; Gay 1988: 548). Freud's work expands and deepens the explanatory range of both Marx and Feuerbach with respect to the psychodynamics of religious experiences, beliefs and actions, and their intersection with external material forces. In a theoretical move that is conceptually parallel to the anthropological philosophy of Feuerbach and Marx, Freud replaces metaphysics with a meta-psychology that identifies and interrogates the multiple affective components of the human being's need for a god that organizes the underlying internal dynamics of religious belief.[1]

In his examination of the cross-currents and intersections of psyche and society, and internal fantasy and external forms, Freud's critique of religion is best understood in terms of a psychoanalytic critical social theory. Furthermore, it is important to bear in mind that his efforts to explain the psychological forces underlying religious belief derive in significant measure from knowledge gained from his clinical work with patients. There is a strong connection that runs throughout Freud's work between theory and practice, where theoretical insights arise not only from observations made during clinical work, but also where the theory itself is directed to bringing about change. As both a theory and clinical practice, psychoanalysis hopes to effect new and different modes of thought and action in an individual life. This accounts for the often overlooked or forgotten fact that Freud did not conceptualize the individual mind as separate or isolated from its relationships with the external world. Individuals are social and relational beings for Freud. His longstanding preoccupation with cultural issues betrays a particular interest in the nature of the relationship between individual minds and society, which he broadened to include individual human (ontogeny) and species psychological development (phylogeny):

> My interest, after making a lifelong detour through the natural sciences, medicine and psychotherapy, returned to the cultural problems which had fascinated me long before, when I was a youth scarcely old enough for thinking … I perceived ever more clearly that the events of human history, the interactions between human nature, cultural development and the precipitates of primaeval experiences (the most prominent example of which is religion) are no more than a reflection of the dynamic conflicts between the ego, the id and the super-ego, which psychoanalysis studies in the individual – are the very same processes repeated upon a wider stage. (Freud 1935: 72)

While Freud's studies of culture and religion "originate in psychoanalysis", their scope extends "far beyond it" (*ibid.*), as will be seen in subsequent chapters. Virtually all his so-called cultural works address religion, probing the psychic intersections of the individual and society in a psychoanalytic theory of the world within the mind, and the mind writ large upon the world. Freud remained consistent in his view that individual psychology is *at the same time* a social psychology. "In the individual's mental life", he writes, "someone else is invariably involved, as a model, as an object, as a helper, as an opponent; and so from the very first individual psychology, in this extended but entirely justifiable sense of the words, is at the same time social psychology as well" (1921a: 68). As Russell Jacoby observes, "psychoanalysis rediscovers society in the individual" (1975: 79). As works of critical social theory, Freud's writings on religion illustrate how psychoanalysis "sink[s] into subjectivity till it hits bottom: society. It is here where subjectivity devolves into objectivity; subjectivity is pursued till it issues into the social and historical events that preformed and deformed the subject" (*ibid.*). The unconscious does not escape culture (Gay 1988: 338). What follows is a detailed analysis of those texts that most clearly demonstrate Freud's psychoanalytic critical theory of religion.

## Religion: individual and mass neurosis

In one of his earliest sustained treatments of the psychology of religion, Freud formulates an analogical relationship between religious belief and practice on the one hand and obsessional neurosis on the other by comparing and exploring their shared unconscious psychodynamics (Freud 1907a: 117). In a later work, he clarified that although religion functions like a "universal obsessional neurosis", the analogy does not "exhaust the essential nature of religion" (Freud 1927: 43). Moreover, he was well aware of the dangers involved in transplanting ideas that are "far from the soil in which they grew up". Nonetheless, and while bearing these cautions in mind, Freud insisted that there exists something of a resonance, or a "conformity", between religion and neurosis that bears investigation (*ibid.*: 42). What he means by this will be more fully elaborated in the next chapter; for now it is more important to consider Freud's view that the ritual actions of both religious believers and compulsive obsessional neurotics suggest the existence of a deeper and narrower range of universally shared internal psychological processes whose hidden or latent meanings are manifest in the diverse range of cultural forms. Freud argues that since the compulsive actions of neurotics and the ritual ceremonies of religious practitioners involve analogous "psychological processes" (1907a: 117), they should not be regarded as too sharply distinct (*ibid.*: 118). Although he does not elaborate the point further in the 1907 essay, Freud intriguingly postulates that "as a rule obsessive actions have grown out of ceremonials" (*ibid.*), suggesting that ritual action may be a more ancient substrate of the later psychic phenomenon of neurotic compulsion. The idea that internal, psychic conflicts and fantasies that pertain especially to religious feelings and desires have their origins in external events runs throughout Freud's work.

The surface dissimilarities between obsessive acts and religious rituals are attenuated or removed by psychoanalytic investigation, which demonstrates that both are "perfectly significant in every detail" and "serve important interests of the personality" (1907a: 120). It should be remembered in this context that for Freud (1915a), everything relating to human psychology has meaning and significance, including the most trivial bungled actions of daily life like slips of the tongue. This is especially true with regard to obsessive actions, where "everything has its meaning and can be interpreted" (Freud 1907a: 122). Religious ritual and the obsessional acts that are part of the neurotic's private idiosyncratic "religion" express features of the unconscious conflicts within human desire that are often experienced as dangerous to, and therefore forbidden by, the (largely unconscious) conscious mind. Neither the religious practitioner nor the obsessive neurotic are aware of the older layers of their minds that anchor their underlying motives and shape their unconscious fantasies, compelling them to perform their rituals no matter what their conscious beliefs about what they do may be (*ibid*.: 123). It is the *compulsive* nature of the practices that particularly interests Freud, the fact that they are not freely chosen but are *felt* to be necessary, and which seem to afford the believer a sense of protection and absolution. For Freud this is what betrays the presence of unconscious forces at work. These unconscious forces include the pressures exerted by a "guilty conscience" that stretch back to the early stages of psychological development. The persistence of primitive desires at odds with cultural standards perpetually arouses burdensome feelings of guilt that both resist and yet long for consolation and relief. Those guilty desires are often strongly rebuffed by culture's psychic representative and emissary, the "I" or "ego" (*das Ich*), as dangerous or forbidden, and are subject to the work of repression by religious believers and neurotics alike. With every impulse to transgression that is aroused "with each contemporary provocation", repressions must be reinforced or constantly renewed (*ibid*.).

However, the energy exerted by the repressed impulse finds expression in the form of manifest symptoms[2] that are present in the ritual practices of both religion and obsessional neurosis. The symptoms of regressive infantile wishful impulses that are encoded in ritual practice allow believers and neurotics alike a measure of self-regulation and reduction in the anxiety generated by unconscious conflict. However, this process is at best a compromise and therefore partial. In the effort to thwart unacceptable desire through its transformation in ritual or compulsive action, desire, not entirely repressed, finds expression in distorted form (Freud 1907a: 124–5). Religious and secular compulsive actions "fulfil the condition of being a compromise between the warring forces of the mind. They thus always reproduce something of the pleasure which they are designed to prevent; they serve the repressed instinct no less than the agencies which are repressing it" (*ibid*.). The psychodynamics common to religious ritual and neurotic obsession require the "renunciation of certain instinctual impulses" (*ibid*.: 125). Both obsessional neurotics and religious practitioners are plagued with a guilt that is connected both to persistent temptation and the "fear of divine punishment" that is its inevitable result (*ibid*.). The source of the guilty conscience common to both the neurotic and the believer lies in the biological substrate that undergirds and motivates desires that may be either sexual or "anti-social" and thus unacceptable to the moral demands of society and religion. "A progressive renunciation of constitutional instincts" belongs to "the foundations of the development of human civilization". The conclusion to this brief meditation on religion and neurosis blends Feuerbachian and

Nietzschean elements, as Freud observes that "it is surely no accident that all the attributes of man, along with the misdeeds that follow from them, were to an unlimited amount ascribed to the ancient gods. Nor is it a contradiction of this that nevertheless man was not permitted to justify his own iniquities by appealing to divine example" (*ibid.*: 127).

## *The Future of an Illusion*: religion against independent thought and moral freedom

Although Freud provides a number of concrete examples in his 1907 essay of compulsive and ritual actions, he uses them as illustrations to support his analysis of the psychological *processes* that underlie and give rise to both sets of behaviour. In a later work, *The Future of an Illusion* (1927), Freud offers a more extended and detailed account of the psychodynamics of religious beliefs. Unfortunately, and ironically, this text is one of Freud's most widely cited and least understood – or most misunderstood – works on religion. There is a common tendency in the secondary literature to treat this work as emblematic of Freud's entire theoretical critique of religion, which for many of his commentators amounts to little more than proof of his dismissive and personal hostility to religion. An excessively psychologizing concern with Freud's so-called atheism (Rizutto 1998) that seeks to rescue religion from what is seen as Freud's "reductive" and "pathologizing" analysis (Meissner 1984)[3] not only misses the point of what Freud is really addressing in this text; it also obscures some of the finer complexities of his thinking and the range of his critique. If one is to do proper justice to *The Future of an Illusion,* one ought not to read it as an atheist manifesto nor as exclusively representative of Freud's thinking about religion. *The Future of an Illusion* is *one* among several important works by Freud that deal with the subject of religion. Many of the commentators who focus so strongly on Freud's atheism and/or his personal biases towards religion are somewhat confused and unclear as to what Freud was mainly addressing in this particular text and the psychological phenomena he was attempting to illuminate. Granted, Freud makes no effort to conceal his evaluation that religion is on balance more harmful than beneficial for psychological well-being. However, his purpose in *The Future of an Illusion* lies in psychoanalytic investigation rather than in advocating for atheism. Freud is too well aware that efforts to "do away with religion" would be "senseless", "hopeless" and "cruel" (1927: 49). He also understood that religious beliefs are impervious to either "argument" or "prohibition" (*ibid.*). In the context of these statements, it is misleading to conclude that Freud would have any interest in replacing one set of beliefs with another.

This fact seems to have had little impact on Freud's more theologically or religiously minded commentators, who tend to be disturbed by what they see as Freud's efforts to discredit religion. This at times leads them to try to discredit Freud by defending religion. Jonathan Lear, for example, claims that Freud's work on religion is one of the "least valuable aspects" (2005: 192) of his corpus. Somewhat surprisingly, he goes on to assure his readers that Freud's views "need not give us a reason to abandon religious belief" (*ibid*.: 206). He appears concerned that merely by reading Freud, people will abandon their faith. For Lear, it is important to establish that Freud's approach to religion is mistaken so that new possibilities may open up for "a deeper psychoanalytic engagement with moral and religious commitment" (*ibid*.: 192). Again, this form of response is more defensive than intellectually argumentative in that it seems to be concerned with protecting religion as a positive source of morality and spiritual health rather than engaging with the substance of Freud's thought. The finer, more subtle points of Freud's analysis of the underlying psychology of religious beliefs and actions is missed. Theologically or religiously biased readings of Freud have the common tendency to single out *The Future of an Illusion* as a totalizing critique against religion itself, and in fairness, it is not impossible to see why. However, when this text is considered both within the context of Freud's writing on religion as a whole, and his general psychoanalytic theory, the picture becomes much more complicated.

Freud understood perfectly well that religious beliefs and devotion to gods could offer relief from the mental anguish caused by painful psychic conflicts and social isolation, at least for periods of time in an individual's life (1918: 114–15, 117). He also knew that individuals could find relief from the inhibiting and debilitating effects of obsessional neurosis by belonging to and participating in religious community life (1921a: 142). In other words, religion aids in the protection of sanity by offering socially acceptable ways of expressing neurotic compulsion through ritual action and psychological comfort with its consoling illusions. The "crooked cures" provided by religion have their place (*ibid*.). Again, these more subtle elements in Freud's thinking tend to be missed. Freud is either interpreted as unaware of the psychological benefits of religion or he is put on the couch, where his ideas are accounted for in terms of his alleged "conflicted" and "ambivalent" attitude (Kaplan & Parsons 2010: ix; Meissner 1984: 26, 41, 55, 78; Rizutto 1998) towards religion. These approaches include any number of ingenious speculations that discuss his relationships with and feelings towards his father and mother, his Catholic nanny, the death of his younger brother Julius when Freud was a toddler, his own Jewish identity, his knowledge of Hebrew and Yiddish, or his admiration for Moses. While these discussions unearth all kinds of interesting titbits about Freud's life that pose fascinating questions about his individual psychology, they fail to appreciate that each of Freud's texts on religion addresses a specific set of identified concerns and thematic interests relevant to each particular text. This crucial fact is missed utterly when his writings on religion are treated as a homogeneous theoretical set. *The Future of an Illusion* is *not Moses and Monotheism*, for example, and despite the similarities of some common themes, shared conceptual premises and psychoanalytic methodology, the focus of each book explores its own distinct field of inquiry.

The question of Freud's so-called atheism in his theory of religion is particularly vexing because it focuses on the wrong issue. As Paul Roazen (1989) observes in another context, Freud is too much of a "philosophically sophisticated" and "open-minded rationalist" to be motivated by personal atheism in mounting his psychoanalysis of religion. Although Freud did indeed describe *himself* as a "Godless Jew" (Gay 1987: 37) it does not follow from this self-deprecating and possibly playful statement that his works on religion are mere extensions of a personal atheism. *The Future of an Illusion* is a psychoanalytically oriented work of critical social theory that examines the impact of culture and its authority structures and values on psychological development through an analysis of the psychodynamics of religious beliefs and actions. It is a direct example of the ways in which an examination of culture illuminates the inner workings of the human mind. Freud's main concern in this text is for the most part epistemological, moral and political in its arguments concerning the adequate basis of knowledge and the proper sources of authority and moral agency. Freud also addresses the ways in which the negation of religion opens up new possibilities for human freedom within history. He has little interest in disputing theological truth-claims about the existence of God, or any other aspect concerning the "truth-value" of religious teachings (Freud 1927: 33).

The first two sections of *The Future of an Illusion* are devoted to a critical social-psychological analysis of the repressive and restrictive demands imposed by culture upon human beings, whose drive-based aspirations for pleasure and well-being are continually undermined and distorted by oppressive and exploitative social, economic and political forces. In a comment on the contemporary context of "European Christian civilization" (*ibid.*: 38) that bears strong resemblance to Marx, Freud discusses the cultural dialectic, where technological achievements have succeeded in harnessing the "forces of nature" for the production of goods for the satisfaction of human needs while political arrangements regulate access to those benefits by controlling their inequitable distribution. Freud observes that human beings themselves became commodities by virtue of their labour, and in the process became subject to a dominating elite who "imposed" civilization upon them through acquiring "the means to power and coercion" (*ibid.*: 6). While "mankind has made continual advances in its control over nature and may expect to make still greater ones", Freud continues, "it is not possible to establish with certainty that a similar advance has been made in the management of human affairs", a situation that may cause people to wonder if existing social arrangements are "worth defending at all" (*ibid.*: 7).

While human beings have no alternative but to live together in order to survive, they "feel as a heavy burden the sacrifices which civilization expects of them in order to make a communal life possible". Thus, in Freud's view, every individual is "an enemy of civilization" (*ibid.*: 6), which imposes increasingly severe forms of "coercion and renunciation of instinct" upon the majority in order to survive (*ibid.*: 7). Since human beings have strong destructive and anti-social tendencies that are a constant source of danger to the social order, and since these tendencies cannot be contained by externally imposed coercive measures alone, means must be devised for establishing culture's authority within individual minds. As will be discussed in greater detail below, this process begins in infancy, where human beings develop powerfully affective, intimate bonds with their parents, who are also the representatives of culture and its prohibitions on desire. In particular, the father is the chief representative of the laws and restrictions of external authority. In order to sustain culture, which is itself the best guarantee of species preservation, people must obey its dictates and submit to its steadily intensifying demands to renounce their own individual needs. While the individual may be the "enemy" of culture, culture is also increasingly the enemy of the individual. Freud writes that the "decisive question is whether and to what extent it is possible to lessen the burden of the instinctual sacrifices imposed on men, to reconcile men to those which must necessarily remain and to provide a compensation for them" (*ibid.*: 7). From the perspective of concerns such as these, religion as part of the "mental assets of civilization" (*ibid.*: 10) plays a key role in the internal regulation of human beings, whose willingness to accept various forms of privation is critical to the maintenance and preservation of the prevailing economic and political arrangements. Like Marx before him, Freud also sees that the compensations and illusions offered by religion play a key role in persuading people to accept and collude in these arrangements.

Religion as a product and representative of culture helps define the psychological identity of a people by distinguishing them antagonistically, Freud thinks, from outside "others", whose cultural achievements must be inevitably regarded as inferior. Moral codes, religion, artistic and technological achievements constitute cultural wealth, affording people some measure of narcissistic gratification that is regarded as worth protecting from internal as well as external threats. "The narcissistic satisfaction provided by the cultural ideal is also among the forces which are successful in combating the hostility to culture within the cultural unit", writes Freud, and these narcissistic benefits are enjoyed by both the "favoured classes" and the "suppressed" alike. Shared cultural pride establishes deep affective bonds between the oppressed and "their masters", who in turn are regarded as the embodiment of the former's ideals (Freud 1927: 13). The internal, affective identifications between the subjugated majority and their privileged overlords illuminate the question for Freud as to why certain cultures survived for so long "in spite of the justifiable hostility" on the part of "the large human masses" (*ibid.*). This psychic identification with idealized, masculine and paternal cultural leaders eventually takes the form of an internalized mental agency that represents the values of external authority. Freud called this extremely important psychic agency the "Above-I" (*Über-Ich*), or as it is more commonly known in English, the super-ego. Although this complex mental agency is widely associated with moral "conscience", it is and remains a largely unconscious part of the mind. Under certain conditions, it can become dangerously destructive to the individual in the cruelty of its punitive judgements. One of the most crucial roles of this "precious cultural asset" is to transform individuals from enemies of culture into its ardent upholders and defenders (*ibid.*: 11), even to their personal detriment.

The development of the super-ego is a contradictory and incomplete human achievement: on the one hand it encourages the formation of morality and sociality, but on the other it is an agency of authority as it fosters the tendency of individuals to submit to the pressures of external domination. However, if the subjugations and renunciations of culture aided by the super-ego are too painful to bear, violent social rebellion, with its lethal potential to destroy everyone, may be the unintended result. The main point in Freud's argument here is that the power of external authority, however unjust, is anchored in this psychic agency whose emotional source derives from the affectively charged, original loving or libidinal attachments between infants and their parents. Freud knows that an individual's awareness and understanding of the world, including relationships with it and with oneself, develops in and through affective connections with others from earliest infancy. The external social and political dynamics of domination and submission are reflected and structured within the very fabric of the human mind. The coercive restrictions and painful demands of society, exercised through its parental ambassadors, inhabit and haunt the individual psyche in its deepest and oldest recesses. The Freudian super-ego, saturated as it is with culture, represents the internal crossroads of psyche and society, that point of intersection where individual needs and social demands are so inextricably connected they become experienced as one. Individual and society are bound together in a deeply felt erotic or libidinal attachment that constitutes the condition of the infant's very biological survival. The memory-traces of that original state of helpless dependency on external providers remain lodged deep within the unconscious mind, finding expression in various forms of conformity to social rules and religious beliefs. Freud's concept of the super-ego here offers a fascinating insight into Herbert Marcuse's puzzled speculation as to why, in the history of human rebellion, restorations and fresh repressions inevitably follow and replace revolutionary success (1970: 38–9). From a Freudian perspective, while a given cultural formation may be overthrown, it can never be abolished as an organization of hierarchy and authority because the imperative to obey some form of social and political authority is a basic feature of the human mind. In a sense, the psychic dynamics of domination and submission necessarily emerge within early attachment relationships to the parental figures who ensure the survival of the human infant.

In *The Future of an Illusion*, Freud investigates the ways in which human beings create gods in terms of the "derivatives of their relations to their fathers" (Gay 1988: 328). For Freud, the single most important "item in the psychical inventory" of a culture is religion, which is both the creator and the repository of those cultural and individual illusions (1927: 14) that regulate social action and psychological attitudes. Religion is the cultural result of a biologically based emotional *need* for safety, security and protection for those who are terrorized by feelings of helpless vulnerability when faced with the brutal forces of inexplicable and unpredictable nature (*ibid.*: 15–16). Religion provides consolations for the narcissistic injuries to human self-esteem suffered as a result of impotent dependency and intellectual ignorance in the face of a terrifying and unpredictable natural world (*ibid.*: 16). Like Feuerbach before him, Freud also argues that religion offers a way to humanize nature and modify its impact. Religion provides explanations that allow believers to deal mentally with the dangerous conditions of existence that arouse powerful unconscious associations with the terrors of childhood that remain preserved within the mind.

In a historical period and cultural context where the domination of men was not considered to be nearly as problematic as it is today, and where male authority both in the family and society was "unquestioned" (Ellenberger 1970: 255), it is not surprising that Freud identified fathers as the primary providers for and protectors of their families and society. When it is further considered that he was writing in the context of a Christian culture whose divinities are embodied in the male figures of father and son, it is understandable that Freud would see the father as the internalized prototype for God. All three of the Abrahamic monotheistic religions, Judaism, Christianity and Islam, are organized primarily around male deities and their earthly male representatives. It makes sense in this cultural context that the gods of religion derive from the imagined or real experiences of paternal power and protection in infancy. The gods, Freud writes, have a "threefold task: they must exorcize the terrors of nature, they must reconcile men to the cruelty of Fate, particularly as it is shown in death, and they must compensate them for the sufferings and privations which a civilized life in common has imposed on them" (1927: 18). Over the long course of history and human development, the gods gradually become more distant and abstract. In the monotheistic religions, the gods become relegated to the moral "domain", where one of their main roles is to "even out the defects and evils of civilization". Eventually, the rules of culture are accepted as having a "divine origin" and become "elevated beyond human society" and "extended to nature and the universe" (*ibid.*:). Morality is born out of the need for protection against both the forces of nature and threats from other human beings. It is especially important to note that for Freud, religion derives from real experiences in the infantile relationships of human beings with their fathers, and so has a basis in an existential truth that is both preserved and distorted in the image of the father-god. Freud's goal is to analyse the roots of religious illusion that emerge from the bedrock of real psychic experience.

## Attachment theory

In order to fully appreciate Freud's argument that religious longing is the extended and distorted expression of an infantile desire for culture's desig-nated protector, the father, to provide safety for the utterly dependent infant, it is necessary briefly to consider contemporary attachment theory, which has become increasingly sophisticated and complex since its inception in the empirical studies of juvenile delinquency conducted by John Bowlby. His key insight, which remains a central tenet of the theory to this day, is that disrup-tions of the early infant–mother relationship are a major precursor to later mental disorders (Fonagy 2001: 6). A full theoretical explanation of the vast literature on attachment theory is beyond the scope of this chapter, but some of its central insights are relevant to Freud's theory of religion. As a biologically based, evolutionary developmental system, attachment is also a "psychologi-cal mechanism" in a larger system of adaptive behaviours designed to bolster survival and reproductive fitness. The survival value of attachment lies in its ability to enhance safety through proximity to the caregiver until the child is old enough to care for himself. Most important to this discussion, as Fonagy points out, is the idea that what the child seeks is not so much the attachment figure itself, but rather "a state of being or feeling" of safety that regulates the child's internal states and supports his cognitive development and general capacity for successful relationships with others and adult life in the world. "The goal that regulates the system is initially a physical state, the maintenance of a desired degree of proximity to [the mother]. This physical state is later supplanted by the more psychological goal of a feeling of closeness to the caregiver" (Fonagy 2001: 8). An emotional state of "felt security" is the goal of the attachment sys-tem, not "distance regulation" (*ibid.*: 13). Since the feeling of safety and security is paramount, they are not necessarily restricted to a particular caregiver; nor does the attachment figure need necessarily to be physically close. While the attachment system quiets down over the course of psychological development, it can be reactivated in frightening and stressful situations. The need to restore a sense of felt security can be achieved through personal relationships with figures conjured by the mind, such as gods.

As I have argued elsewhere (Hewitt 2008: 66–7), Freud anticipates some of the central tenets of what is now known as attachment theory in his argument that the origins of religion lie in the infant's need for a parental figure who becomes gradually internalized within the developmental processes involved in the formation of identity of self/other and the world at large. Contemporary evolutionary psychology lends powerful support to Freud in its view that the human brain is "wired" to "seek protectors" everywhere (Atran 2002: 69). It is a short step in the mind from the larger-than-life father protector of childhood experience to the fantasized, superhuman father-god of religion who also protects and consoles against the terrors of life. In a passage that could have been written by Freud, Scott Atran argues that "[a]ll religions follow the same structural contours. They all invoke supernatural agents to deal with emotionally eruptive existential anxieties, such as loneliness, calamity, and death" (*ibid.*: 266). For evolutionary psychologist and attachment theorist Lee Kirkpatrick, God is "an exalted attachment figure" (1999: 805) who mitigates or resolves unbearable feelings such as anxiety, isolation, and depression (*ibid.*: 816–17). The evolutionary imperative that dictates the need for a personal relationship with an attachment figure who guarantees infant survival underscores and supports the later need for a personal relationship with a god who offers protection and comfort in times of crisis or threat. In adulthood, the attachment system is activated in conditions of stress precipitated by frightening events, illness, separation or the fear of loss (*ibid.*: 807). Kirkpatrick claims that religious belief offers a "unique window into attachment processes of adulthood" (*ibid.*: 804). Although Freud could not have had a theory of attachment as we know it now, his analysis of the psychodynamics of religious belief clearly illustrates the power of early *attachment relationships* in shaping thought and action across the individual's life-span. "Like Freud's theory", writes Kirkpatrick, "attachment theory focuses on human concerns about comfort and protection, and God is psychologically represented as a kind of parent figure" (2005: 19).

The nature or quality of early attachment relationships will determine the ways in which the child establishes internal working models of self and world that will organize his relationships with others throughout his life. Some of the most important conclusions of attachment research include the findings that attachment bonds constitute self–other relations in all known cultures, and that the self exists only in relational contexts (Hewitt 2008: 68; van IJzendoorn & Sagi 1999). The degree to which a child becomes securely or insecurely attached to its caregivers plays a vital role in her later capacity for both managing powerful emotions and making adequate distinctions between internal fantasy and external reality, which in turn establishes possibilities for thinking critically about the emotions of others as distinct from one's own (Fonagy *et al.* 2002). Kirkpatrick's attachment studies (Kirkpatrick & Shaver 1990; Kirkpatrick 1999, 2005), applied to religious belief, suggest the existence of significant correlations between the different attachment styles of interpersonal relationships and attachment relationships to gods (Granqvist 2006; Hewitt 2008: 69). Long before the appearance of attachment theory, Freud understood that the emotional dynamics of infant–parent relationships are later transferred to religion, meaning that "certain ties of affection" connect the believer to religious teachings (1927: 47). The feelings of safety and security belonging to the early attachment relationships of infancy are activated in the religious experiences of adulthood, where they continue to provide a vital resource for the regulation of powerful affect. For Freud, one of the major benefits of religious belief involves what current attachment literature calls affect regulation, which refers to the capacity for conscious awareness and identification of one's feeling states, the ability to hold and contain them, and the capacity to distinguish between the feeling states of self and other. Although contemporary attachment theorists make no judgements concerning the psychological value of religious beliefs, both they and Freud recognize that mature emotional development includes the individual's ability to recognize and regulate unformulated feelings of helpless dependency that may be aroused in times of crisis and intense internal disruption. For Freud, the capacity for affect regulation signals the developmental achievement of autonomy and self-reflective awareness that can distinguish and hold a sense of the boundaries between fantasy and reality.

For Freud as well, religion provides important psychological insights into the attachment dynamics that underwrite the need for parental love and protection that he strongly associates with the father. In the absence of a reliable primary attachment figure in childhood, individuals will go so far as to conjure or hallucinate their own, which is how Freud interprets the father-gods of religious belief. In this way, fantasy may overwhelm reality to the extent that it resists appeals to evidence-based knowledge about oneself and the world. The thesis that unbearable feelings of vulnerability and loss are powerful motivators of religious beliefs is poignantly illustrated in Freud's (1923a) analysis of the "demonic possession" of a seventeenth-century painter, Christoph Haizmann, who made a pact with the Devil in exchange for material and emotional security. Freud treats the story of this pact as a psychoanalytic study of the painful desperation and depression ("melancholy") that the painter experienced upon the death of his father. Although the main focus of Freud's account is to explain the psychodynamics of spirit possession where "demons are bad and reprehensible wishes, derivations of instinctual impulses that have been repudiated and repressed" (*ibid.*: 72), the contours of the emotional devastation that can result from serious personal loss here are fully apparent. The abject emotional state ("*hunc miserum omni auxilio destitutum*") of "a man who fails in everything and who is therefore trusted by no one" (*ibid.*: 103) fuels Haizmann's desperate attempt to gain security (104) to the extent that he is willing to risk his salvation (*ibid.*: 104). However, when all these efforts failed, he ultimately turned to the church, and with the intercession of the Virgin Mary (*ibid.*: 73), the exalted heavenly Mother, he was released to the care of yet another parental agency in "the pious Fathers of the Church" (*ibid.*: 104).

The story of Haizmann's experience of social isolation, terrifying vulnerability and helplessness upon the death of his father demonstrates from a psychoanalytically informed attachment perspective how the devastation of loss reactivates and intensifies (*ibid.*: 105) the longing for a father – any father – to provide a safe haven against material and emotional danger. The Devil offered Haizmann the promise of *belonging* to him even after death (*ibid.*: 83). Freud explains Haizmann's choice of the Devil as his "direct" father-substitute in terms of the ambivalence that "governs" both the father–child relationship and the relationship "of mankind to its Deity" (*ibid.*: 85). Haizmann's psychological development did not resolve his ambivalent feelings towards his father in a more balanced emotional integration. Instead, he split these opposing emotional impulses and organized them along the contextual, cultural lines of conflict between binary supernatural figures, where they found shape and coherence in the images of both the Devil and God (*ibid.*: 86). Such an outcome is explained by Freud on the grounds that the father perceived in infancy is the "individual prototype of both God and the Devil", since both "were originally identical". It is then "not to be wondered at that [the child's] hostile attitude to his father, too, which is one of hating and fearing him and of making complaints against him, should have come to expression in the creation of Satan" (*ibid.*: 86). The "melancholic depression" that Haizmann experienced upon the death of his father is not unusual, Freud avers, especially in cases where the son feels "strong love" (*ibid.*: 82, 87). However, given what Freud infers is an unresolved ambivalence towards the father in Haizmann's case because of his pact with the Devil, the son's capacity for mourning and ultimate acceptance of his father's death is impaired by a depression that conceals an underlying hatred (*ibid.*: 87). Not surprisingly, the Devil was unable to give Haizmann the comfort for which he was so desperate. Haizmann finally found the security and care he needed by entering a Holy Order (*ibid.*: 104).

Freud's interpretation of Haizmann's pact with the Devil is a clear and succinct "case history" (*ibid.*: 80) that illustrates the ways in which the universal feelings of helpless vulnerability and dependency in infancy can extend into adulthood as a result of insecure attachment relationships. Haizmann's longing for a protective and consoling god is a variation on the common human need for divine protection and consolation so eloquently expressed in Psalm 23. Haizmann's case further illustrates the ways in which desire for a personal relationship with a protective deity, demonic *or* divine, originate in what would now be described as the individual's earliest attachment experiences. However, the story of Christoph Haizmann's pact with the Devil and subsequent rescue by the Holy Mother and the fathers of the church is also a story of the abdication of autonomous agency in the face of overwhelming grief and fear. Haizmann's capacity to make his own way in the world was impaired by psychological conflicts resulting at least in part from an unresolved ambivalence towards his father that made it impossible for him to live the life he wanted. The deeper significance of Haizmann's pact with the Devil and his later reconciliation with the church, however, lay in his even greater need to submit to an external authority that promised material and emotional security. This is the more important theme concerning religion that shapes Freud's interpretation of the Haizmann story. Freud explores this theme in much greater detail a few years later in *The Future of an Illusion*.

## The abdication of autonomous thought and moral agency

Freud rejects the idea that religion provides an adequate basis of epistemology and morality. He argues consistently and repeatedly that religious knowledge represents the antithesis of evidence-based critical thought, moral freedom and individual authenticity in its insistence that believers unquestioningly accept its dogmas and obey its moral dictates. The declared truths of revealed religion rest on the power of thoughtless assertion rather than reasoned, evidence-based argumentation, revealing the world as believers wish it to be, not as it is. Religious truth claims are supported by thoughtless appeals to ancestral authorities, which are backed up by retributive institutional power. "There is no appeal to a court above that of reason", Freud maintains (Freud 1927: 28), meaning that religious believers must authenticate their "inner experience" with evidence and argumentation that makes sense to others who do not share their private experience. Psychoanalysis provides a plausible way of translating the truth of interior experience into publicly acceptable form by releasing it from religious mythology and relocating it within the psychodynamics of infant–parent relationships. He further suggests that these psychological dynamics originate in prehistoric familial contexts, a story he fully elaborated in his earlier *Totem and Taboo* (1913b), but only briefly repeats in *The Future of an Illusion*. The "primal father", he writes, "was the original image of God, the model on which later generations have shaped the figure of God. Hence the religious explanation is right … religious doctrine tells us the historical truth[4] … though subject … to some modification and disguise" (1927: 42). Thus, for Freud religion is also based on an unconscious memory of a prehistoric relationship that is recapitulated and repeated in the early history of each individual and re-enacted in religious beliefs and actions. God, religious traditions, institutions and teaching authority coalesce in the differentiated symbolic image of an ancient paternal power who is revered and feared, and loved and hated, by religious adherents who have never worked through their own life experiences of helpless impotence. They remain trapped within their own internalized dynamics of need and desire, and domination and submission, that endlessly repeat the Oedipal conflicts that mark the original father–son relationship. This is what Freud means when he writes in another passage powerfully evocative of Marx that religious illusions express "the oldest, strongest and most urgent wishes of mankind. The secret of their strength lies in the strength of those wishes" and the longing for justice in an unjust world (1927: 30). From the perspective of attachment theory, religious beliefs in superhuman deities are the psychic precipitates of a biologically based, evolutionarily endowed motivational system organized around species survival.

## "Education to reality": the epistemological imperative

While Freud acknowledges the historical value of some religious beliefs and the ways they may have "contributed much" to culture by "taming ... the asocial instincts" (Freud 1927: 37), the welfare of humanity will be better served when they are removed as "the reasons for the precepts of civilization" (*ibid.*: 44). In place of genuine knowledge about the world, the "absurdities" (*ibid.*: 48) of religious teachings offer narcotic-like compensatory emotional consolations (*ibid.*: 49) for the burdens imposed by civilization that are paid for by limiting the capacity for critical thought, which in turn undermines the education of children. Here Freud is concerned with the distorting effects on the developing personality of "modern" pedagogical practices, whose twofold aim is to retard sexual development and promote the influence of religion. The result is a permanently impaired intellect that has been forced to "accept uncritically all the absurdities that religious doctrines put before him" (*ibid.*: 48) and abandon his own potential for real knowledge of the world by denying the contradictions and inconsistencies of religious explanations of reality. If human beings are educated for reality (*ibid.*: 49) in ways that encourage rather than prohibit independent, critical thought, they at least have the opportunity to accept that moral systems are of their own making as they consciously begin to understand themselves as the agents of history rather than its passive, frightened and suffering objects. The psychological restorative process that overcomes the alienation of distorted consciousness also affords individuals the chance to take charge of their own unruly and dangerous impulses. Our only hope for "controlling our instinctual nature", Freud argues, is through the exercise of our intellect, which is not necessarily a gender-determined capacity. Here Freud insists in an interesting aside that while it is "disputable" and "doubtful" that women are intellectually inferior to men, it is possible that they may have become so as a result of sustained cultural pressures and demands that restrict and distort their sexual and intellectual development. The distorting pressures that are brought to bear on both women and men result from the rules of culture that require unquestioning psychological and social obedience and submission to the prevailing authorities. These mediate and shape the human being's psychological development so powerfully that "we cannot really tell what in fact" a person is like (*ibid.*: 48). Freud concludes his study of religion in *The Future of an Illusion* by insisting that genuine knowledge of the world, including authentic moral action and intellectual, mental freedom, are to be found through the exercise of evidence-based, independent and critical scientific rather than religious reason.

Freud is sometimes accused of either substituting his own "religion" of science in place of the Christian faith, or of treating psychoanalysis as a new religious faith with himself as its secular pontiff. However, as Rempel correctly points out, such charges "ignore both Freud's own example of constant revision and lifelong plasticity of ideas, and his own clear and often repeated qualitative distinction between the nature of *his* beliefs and values and those of religious believers" (1997: 235). Freud explicitly states any number of times that his theories are not offered as absolute truths but, as Rempel again observes, "provisional hypotheses awaiting revision" (*ibid.*: 235). As we have seen, Freud does not advocate the use of scientific rationality because it has the capacity to disclose absolute truths. Rather, with its appeal to evidence, its reliance on critical inquiry, and perhaps most important, its willingness to revise or discard its own theories in the light of better ones, science provides the best possibilities for human beings to become educated to reality (Freud 1927: 49). Thus it is important to bear in mind that for Freud, science remains open to critical self-examination and transformation, especially in so far as it involves the reliance upon intellect, feeling and imagination. This concept of truth is made explicit in a quotation Freud approvingly cites from Leonardo da Vinci: "For in truth great love springs from great knowledge of the beloved object, and if you know it but little you will be able to love it only a little or not at all" (1910a: 74). For Freud, the insights derived from science are not intended merely to replace one set of unassailable truths with another, because this would leave the rigid method of thinking that is the product of an arrogant mind alienated from itself untouched. Freud's psychoanalytic concept of the mind does not allow him to sever imagination and reason, which is why he respects the truth value of art. The artist, unlike the religious adherent, has the freedom to shape his intuitions and fantasies into "truths of a new kind, which are valued by men as precious reflections of reality" (1911: 224). Art can open up pathways to truth via imaginative and enriched ways of thinking, with its *invitation* to suspend disbelief temporarily without *abandoning* reality, which religion requires. Freud rejects the authoritarian absolutism implicit in any and all "intellectual constructions" that purport to solve "all the problems of our existence uniformly on the basis of one overriding hypothesis", with "no question unanswered" (1933a: 158). Freud sees the quest for absolute knowledge as motivated by wishful desires that belong most appropriately to illusions borne of "intuition" (*ibid.*: 159).

With this idea Freud makes a distinction between meaning and truth, the latter understood as belonging to scientific inquiry, which asserts that "there are no sources of knowledge of the universe other than the intellectual working-over of carefully scrutinized observations – in other words, what we call research – and alongside of it no knowledge derived from revelation, intuition or divination" (*ibid.*: 159). As we have seen, science for Freud is not a closed system of knowledge like religion. It offers no consolations for the deprivations and hardships of existence. The value of science for Freud lies in its method of investigation and research that is characterized by a "relentlessly critical" thought process that must be always ready to change its views in light of new insights carefully derived from evidence. Freud was aware that a scientific mentality is necessarily grounded in stable, affectively regulated mental states capable of withstanding anxieties associated with the inability to know or explain various dimensions of human experience. Science can only consciously engage in establishing provisional and "rough approximation[s] to the truth" that are refined and revised in an ongoing process that constantly struggles "to gain some knowledge about the reality of the world" (Freud 1927: 55). Scientific inquiry is a source of "intellectual pleasure" (Freud 1911: 224) as thought moves beyond the individual mind in an effort to connect with the external world. In this sense, thinking and its conclusions, resulting in judgements, belong to a larger life energy or libidinal activity that is part of the work of Eros: "judgment affords us … an insight into the origin of an intellectual function from the interplay of the primary instinctual impulses". It operates "according to the pleasure principle" and bifurcates along the lines of affirmation or expulsion, connection or rejection (Freud 1925b: 238–9). "Affirmation" is a substitute for "unification" in Freud's view and it "belongs to Eros" (*ibid.*: 239). Eros motivates and drives creative work forward by transforming and differentiating desire towards the external world, and this results in the creation of culture. Considered together with the quote from da Vinci cited earlier, Freud regarded the search for knowledge as a pleasurable and loving activity linking and connecting the inner and outer worlds of human experience. In this very important sense, it may be said that in Freud's view, psychoanalysis constitutes an "ethic" of truth geared to fostering knowledge of one's mind by clearing away neurotic distortions. In other words, Freud's entire psychoanalytic project may be considered as a sustained effort in the "education to reality" (Blass 2006: 345). Freud's concept of scientifically generated knowledge is not a narrowminded enterprise confined solely to the study of empirically demonstrable material facts; as Blass correctly observes, this would "paradoxically limit our encounter with reality" (*ibid.*: 350).

Although Freud's argument carefully differentiates between knowledge and meaning, and illusion and reality, he neither denigrates nor dismisses the individual's search for meaning. Illusions, in Freud's view, are not synonymous with error; they could lead to truth. In an important clarifying statement that deserves to be quoted at length, Freud writes:

> This does not in the least mean that these wishes are to be pushed contemptuously on one side or their value for human life under-estimated. We are ready to trace out the fulfilments of them which they have created for themselves in the products of art and in the systems of religion and philosophy; but we cannot nevertheless overlook the fact that it would be illegitimate and highly inexpedient to allow these demands to be transferred to the sphere of knowledge. For this would be to lay open the paths which lead to psychosis, whether to individual or group psychosis, and would withdraw valuable amounts of energy from endeavours which are directed towards reality in order, so far as possible, to find satisfaction in it for wishes and needs.     (Freud 1933a: 159–60)

Unlike art and philosophy, religion is the "enemy" of science, because it is the enemy of both critical, autonomous thought *and* creative imagination (*ibid.*: 160). While art refashions fantasy and imagination into new kinds of reality expressing valid life truths that are recognizable to most human beings, religion collapses and vulgarizes these truths into simplistic concrete beliefs that require acceptance on the questionable basis of unthinking obedience and unquestioning trust. For Freud, these mental states belong most appropriately to the psychological stage of infancy.

It is now possible to have a clearer and more nuanced understanding of Freud's critique of religion as argued in *The Future of an Illusion*. As this chapter has argued, he has no interest in promoting atheism, he is not concerned to disprove the existence of God, and he does not view religion as totally valueless in the life of a human being. As was stated earlier, the question of atheism is as theoretically and conceptually meaningless for Freud as it was for Marx (1975b: 306), since the very notion requires a theistic premise in order to negate it. The object of Freud's "irreducibly social", anthropologically grounded (Preus 1987: 178) critique of religion is to propose a basis for an adequate knowledge of the world with a methodology that is appropriate to it. In this sense Freud uses psychoanalytic concepts to formulate a "naturalistic explanation" of religion (*ibid.*: 180). In postulating that the internalization of the paternal parent "contains the germ from which all religions have evolved" (*ibid.*: 188), Freud is arguing that while the beliefs flowing from this psychological process result in false propositions about external reality, they nonetheless contain a kernel of truth that has its origins *in that reality* (Blass 2004: 628). In this sense, religions are records not only of humanity's wishes and longings, they are also *reminiscences* that tell us something important about the nature and relational history of our own minds.

Freud's critique of religion contains a two-fold insight that argues that knowledge of the world involves knowledge of the minds that experience and perceive it. Psychoanalysis offers a theory of mind that is an important and necessary part of any naturalistic explanation of religion. Freud knew that like all experiential phenomena, science is a product of the minds that create it, and that minds are themselves part of the natural world. Knowledge of the mind is knowledge of the world, and psychoanalysis helps distinguish the permeable and shifting boundaries between them. The "task" of science, Freud writes:

> is fully covered if we limit it to showing how the world must appear to us in consequence of the particular character of our organization … the ultimate findings of science, precisely because of the way in which they are acquired, are determined not only by our organization but by the things which have affected that organization … *the problem of the nature of the world without regard to our percipient mental apparatus is an empty abstraction, devoid of practical interest.*
>
> (Freud 1927: 56, emphasis added)

We cannot know reality apart from what we bring to it. Concerning religion, this means that knowledge of the gods is knowledge of ourselves.

TWO

# "The mind is its own place, and in itself
# Can make a Heaven of Hell, a Hell of Heaven"

> The history of civilization is the history of the introversion of sacrifice
> – in other words, the history of renunciation.
>                                              (Horkheimer & Adorno 2002: 43)

Three years after *The Future of an Illusion*, Freud published what Peter Gay describes as his "most somber book" (1988: 543), *Civilization and its Discontents*. Freud's gloomy diagnosis of modern civilization had an almost prophetic quality; he sent the manuscript to the publisher a week before the New York stock market crash and the start of the Great Depression (Gay 1988: 544). With respect to Freud's ideas on religion, *Civilization and its Discontents* both extends the arguments of the earlier work and departs from it in some significant respects. In *The Future of an Illusion*, Freud offered a psychoanalytic explanation of "what the common man understands by his religion", combining beliefs in its promises of consolation and compensation as well as a picture of reality that privileges mythic narratives in place of empirical, evidence-based inquiry. In *Civilization and its Discontents*, Freud reiterates his concern with the ways in which religion prohibits critical independent thought and undermines moral freedom in its demands for "unconditional submission" to its teachings and authority (1930a: 85). Religion is not an antidote against misery, as it claims itself to be. As Freud argues in *The Future of an Illusion*, the best chance for humanity to improve its lot lies in knowledge about the "reality of the world" (1927: 55). Knowledge that is commensurate with the real conditions of life allows human beings to find ways of living that alleviate suffering and maximize the possibilities for the satisfaction of material needs. The concrete benefits that would ensue from a more realistic adjustment of our attitudes and approach to life would no longer require those inhibiting religious illusions that support the status quo and prevent people from taking charge of their own lives. Freud could not have been clearer that science, not religion, holds the key to human welfare.

*Civilization and its Discontents* is even more emphatic in its insistence that belief in the "enormously exalted father" that religious adherents call God is not only "patently infantile" (Freud 1930a: 74), it also impairs the individual's capacity for full psychological maturity. Freud repeats his contention that religion trades in palliative illusions and even "delusional remoulding[s] of reality" (*ibid.*: 81) so that the more egregious burdens and disappointments of life may be tolerated and their more painful effects blunted with promissory guarantees of heavenly compensations. As the antithesis of genuine knowledge and moral responsibility, the "religions of mankind", Freud concludes, "must be classed among the mass-delusions" (*ibid.*). These statements reiterate the main features of Freud's published critique of religion that go back at least to his 1907 essay comparing religious ritual and neurotic obsession. Thus it may be surprising to find that in the very first chapter of *Civilization and its Discontents*, Freud introduces a new focus in his thinking about religion not yet broached in his previous work. Before he returns to a discussion of the central themes laid out in *The Future of an Illusion*, Freud decides to address the psychological dynamics of subjective religious experience. A truly interesting aspect of this discussion is the way Freud undertakes his analysis of "the deepest sources of the religious feeling" (Freud 1930a: 74). In these opening pages of *Civilization and its Discontents*, Freud attempts to explain the more privately emotional dimension of religiosity with a more open intellectual curiosity than is found in his earlier work. Although Freud never explicitly says so, there is nothing in his psychoanalytic treatment of subjective religious feeling to suggest that in itself it necessarily negates epistemological or moral autonomy, as do religious beliefs ordered and restricted by doctrinal authority and ecclesiastical institutional power structures.

## The "oceanic feeling": origins in narcissism

Freud's discussion of religious feeling was prompted by an inquiry from his admired and respected friend, Romain Rolland, about the nature of "religious sentiments" (1930a: 64). The entire first chapter of *Civilization and its Discontents* is a response to Rolland's question as to why Freud failed to take the nature of religious feeling into account in his analysis of religion that Rolland considered to be "just" (in Parsons 1999: 36). Rolland was a French intellectual, writer, social critic and Nobel Prize winner who authored and sent to Freud biographies of the Indian mystics Ramakrishna and Vivekananda. Freud's admiration and affection for Rolland would have been part of the reason why Freud considered his friend's inquiry so seriously, but not the entire reason. Freud seems to be genuinely interested in the psychology underlying mystical experience despite his protestations that he has "nothing to suggest" that could provide a decisive explanation of this phenomenon (1930a: 65). Nonetheless,

Freud seems to find the topic psychoanalytically interesting. The entire first section of *Civilization and its Discontents* ruminates upon the nature of those subjective mental states that are most often described in terms of a "mystical" or "unitive" sense of relationship with the world. Rolland agrees with the main outlines of Freud's critique of religion as a set of doctrines and moral commands that require unquestioning obedience from believers. For Rolland there is a more valuable and authentic dimension to religion that involves spontaneous feeling leading to a direct experience or sense of contact with an eternity. This dimension is the antithesis of faith drained of life by religious orthodoxy and dogmatic teaching. Rolland not only invites Freud to address the subjective emotional experience of connection with an eternal reality, he also wants him to consider that the energy supporting or generating these emotional states is the "true source" of religion (Freud 1930a: 64). Rolland's description of mystical experience shares some similarities with Jesuit psychoanalyst William W. Meissner's more theologically oriented view that sees it as "a universal phenomenon" that reflects the "basic, innate capacity in the human psyche for ecstatic experience and altered states of consciousness" (2005: 533).

For Rolland, as well as some of his contemporaries in the field of the psychology of religion like William James ([1902] 2004), the central defining feature of subjective religiosity includes a sensation or a feeling of something limitless and unbounded – "oceanic", as it were (Freud 1930a: 64). From this perspective, religion is more properly considered as a state of mind reflecting an inner experience rooted in powerful emotion. Again, in contemporary psycho-theological terms, Rolland's oceanic feeling may be described as a "*unio mystica*" that is experienced as a "dissolution of the sense of self", where the elements of self-representation are "absorbed into the transcendent and sublimely loved" divine other (Meissner 1984: 153). For Freud, in so far as he can comprehend Rolland's description, this "purely subjective" feeling is "the source of religious energy" and the single criterion by which an individual may "rightly call oneself religious ... even if one rejects every belief and every illusion" (Freud 1930a: 64). Despite his admission that he never had such an experience himself, Freud makes a considerable effort to understand and at least partially explain it. Whatever the oceanic feeling is, Freud does not agree that sensations of an "indissoluble bond" with the universe have their own special "primary nature" that somehow operates separately from the intellect. For Freud, the sense of oneness with the world represents a "feeling-tone" that infuses an "intellectual perception" (*ibid.*: 65) that is more properly associated with secondary rather than primary forms of mentation. Although the oceanic experience originates in unconscious experiences and fantasies associated with infancy, the religious experience itself is "an *adult* phenomenon" (Werman 1986: 136). Freud's other important point is that sensations of mystical union are the *products* of religious experience, not its *source*.

Freud's disagreement with Rolland's premise that the oceanic feeling constitutes the "*fons et origio*" of the human need for religion does not deter him from trying to account for it psychoanalytically. As discussed in the previous chapter, *The Future of an Illusion* situates religious desire in terms of the child's early relationship with the father. The adult's relationship with God develops as an extension and reflection of an early sense of anxious dependency and helpless vulnerability made bearable by the sense that one has a personal connection with a father figure who provides safety and comfort in the face of the hardships of existence. While Freud reiterates these views concerning the unconscious motivations of religious belief, he goes on to consider the possibility that an even earlier, pre-Oedipal phase of psychological development might be postulated to account for a sense of oneness with the external world that is commonly reported in descriptions of mystical states. Freud's psychoanalytic interpretation of these mental states allows him to identify a kernel of existential truth derived from actual experience that lies at the psychological core of the oceanic feeling. He explains this phenomenon by returning to his theory of narcissism and its explanation of the earliest experiences of the child in relation to his parents, particularly the mother. Freud's inquiry into this aspect of the psychic source of the oceanic feeling leads him to consider at least briefly the possibility that even older dimensions of mind stand behind the feelings of helpless dependency that mobilize the individual's reliance upon a divine "exalted father". Freud is operating here on little more than a hunch that takes him to the limits of psychoanalytic explanation. Whatever lies beneath the need for a divine protector had to remain, at least for the moment, "wrapped in obscurity" (Freud 1930a: 72). As some later critics have pointed out, Freud's exploration of the oceanic feeling led him to catch a glimpse of the divine mother behind the father (Edmunson 2003: xxi).

According to Freud, then, the best available explanation he could offer for the oceanic feeling, partial as it is, lies in his theory of narcissism[1] and the development of the ego. Before turning to this discussion, there is another point that warrants consideration. One extremely important idea relevant to a fuller discussion of the oceanic feeling is Freud's insistence, maintained throughout his work, that all experiences of the individual remain preserved in some form within the mind. In one of his last major essays, he reiterates that:

> portions of the earlier organization [of mind] always persist alongside of the more recent one, and even in normal development the transformation is never complete and residues of earlier libidinal fixations may still be retained in the final configuration … What has once come to life clings tenaciously to its existence. One feels inclined to doubt sometimes whether the dragons of primaeval days are really extinct.
>
> (Freud 1937: 229)

In the first part of *Civilization and its Discontents,* Freud draws upon this view in emphasizing that the past remains "preserved in mental life", and that "only in the mind is such a preservation of all the earlier stages alongside of the final form possible" (1930a: 70–72). If we bear this premise firmly in mind, we are able to form a clear and coherent idea as to what Freud means when he accounts for the oceanic feeling as a part of a psychic process involving "the *restoration* of limitless narcissism" (*ibid.*: 72, emphasis added).

In two of Freud's most important metapsychological papers, "On Narcissism: An Introduction" (1914b), and the slightly later and but equally important "Libido Theory and Narcissism" (1917c), Freud outlines key aspects of the earliest stages of the development of the emerging ego. Freud speculates that there are "primary" and "secondary" narcissistic processes operating that facilitate the emerging ego's reaching out to the world by investing a portion of its energy into external objects from which it draws aspects back within itself. Prior to the onset of this fluid, dynamic psychic process, Freud, in one rendering of his theory, describes the earliest, most primitive state of being in terms of unformed and unorganized libidinal energies that gradually coalesce around the individual's physical sensations or impulses. This "original libidinal cathexis" (1914b: 75), or "auto-eroticism", for a time fixates on the subject's own body. At this stage, undifferentiated psychic energies "exist together", clustered within a still unformulated state that has yet to fully perceive and accept the external world as distinct from itself. In some way that Freud cannot fully describe, the ego begins to emerge beyond this state as it is motivated by internal needs, such as hunger, for something that will satisfy them. As rudimentary memory traces are established by virtue of associations between endlessly repeated experiences of internal, somatically based need impulses and their corresponding satisfactions coming from an external source, the infant gradually begins to perceive and eventually construct an expanded intersubjectively constituted sense of experience of self-in-other and other-in-self.

This outcome results from the child's growing awareness that the satisfaction of its needs is connected to and part of its earliest relationships with others who become part of the child's internal world. This is what Freud has in mind with the idea that a secondary form of narcissism becomes gradually "superimposed upon a primary narcissism" (1914b: 75). Self-love and love for the other become intermingled. Self-love is both made possible and enriched in the feelings of love the child experiences coming from an other, which in turn fosters the child's capacity to love the other as well. While it is true that under certain adverse conditions, secondary narcissism can "connote extreme forms of regression", such as expressed in psychosis and the impaired capacity to connect with others, it also becomes a "permanent structural feature" (Laplanche & Pontalis 1973: 337) of the mind that now includes representations of others within itself. Ego development occurs "by virtue of an identification with the

41

other" (*ibid*.: 256) so that even the primary narcissism of early infancy contains the traces of intersubjective experience by virtue of the internalization of others through relational encounters. In both papers on narcissism, and elsewhere in his writing, Freud (1940: 150–51) uses biological metaphors to describe the differentiating process of primary into secondary narcissism:

> Think of those simplest of living organisms [the amoebas] which consist of a little-differentiated globule of protoplasmic substance. They put out protrusions, known as pseudopodia, into which they cause the substance of their body to flow over. They are able, however, to withdraw the protrusions once more and form themselves again into a globule. We compare the putting-out of these protrusions, then, to the emission of libido on to objects while the main mass of libido can remain in the ego; and we suppose that in normal circumstances ego-libido can be transformed unhindered into object-libido and that this can once more be taken back into the ego. (Freud 1917c: 416)

By the time Freud revisits aspects of his theory of narcissism in his effort to account for the oceanic feeling, he has modified it in accordance with his later thinking on drives; the sexual and ego drives now exist together as part of Eros, which for Freud was a general term for life-energy. In his earlier drive theory Freud situated the sexual (reproductive) and ego (self-preservative) impulses in opposition to each other, which meant that the sexual drive belonged to (the gradually weakened idea of) auto-eroticism, while the ego drive sends its energies outward to connect with the external world, forging relationships with it, building culture, and bringing something of that world back into itself. In his later drive theory, Freud brings the sexual and self-preservative drives together under the aegis of Eros. The ego, motivated by inner need and encouraged by a responsive environment, undergoes a gradual developmental self-differentiating process that contains within itself representatives of the outside, such as the parental agency (not the individual parents themselves) and wider cultural authority. Having resituated the sexual and ego drives within the domain of Eros, Freud now writes:

> The antithesis between subjective and objective does not exist from the first. It only comes into being from the fact that thinking possesses the capacity to bring before the mind once more something that has once been perceived, by reproducing it as a presentation without the external object having still to be there. (Freud 1925a: 237)

The developing and differentiating ego, in its interactions with the world, takes elements of the world (as it experiences it to be) into itself where they are preserved in the memory traces of experience. In the earliest stages of life, however, the distinctions between self and other are extremely loose.

In drawing together some various aspects of Freud's ideas on narcissism from a selection of his texts, it now becomes apparent that the oceanic feeling represents a restoration in one's present of a much older experience of a primary narcissism originating in infantile helplessness, or maybe even further back than that, as Freud seems to suggest (1930a: 72; Laplanche & Pontalis 1973: 46). Most certainly the "infant at the breast", Freud writes, "does not as yet distinguish his ego from the external world as the source of the sensations flowing in upon him" (1930a: 66–7). The awareness of a self that is separate and distinct from an other unfolds within a gradual process of psychic differentiation, where a sense of internal and external boundaries may not always be as stable or permanently fixed as they might appear, as anyone who has fallen in love can attest; "originally the ego includes everything", Freud writes (*ibid*.: 66). Strong demarcations between one's subjective self and the objective world are only gradually established. The adult ego becomes a "shrunken residue of a much more inclusive – indeed, an all-embracing – feeling which corresponded to a more intimate bond between the ego and the world about it". Recalling Freud's contention that everything remains preserved in some form in the mind, it follows that for those "in whose mental life this primary ego-feeling has persisted to a greater or less degree, it would exist in them side by side with the narrower and more sharply demarcated ego feeling of maturity" (*ibid*.: 68).

Under certain life conditions, the "primary ego-feeling" that is common to all human beings at an early stage of development can become activated and made sense of in later life as intense mystical feelings of harmonious unity with the universe. Freud is quite prepared to accept that Rolland's oceanic feeling originates in a reminiscence involving actual experiences or sensations residing within the earliest stages of life that are later rekindled and understood as a mystical experience of a higher power. Again, Freud does not dispute the reality of such feelings. Instead, he attempts to interpret them as belonging to complex mental processes that can be explained in a psychoanalytic theory of the universal properties or tendencies of the human mind. Freud's psychoanalytic explanation of the oceanic feeling does not hesitate to acknowledge its emotional and psychological centre of experiential truth. As far as Freud is concerned, this is not a matter of dispute; what he does dispute is its religious interpretation. That people *have* such experiences in no way means that these are evidence or demonstrations of a special connection with or response to an existing supernatural reality. Freud remains firm in his arguments that religious experiences, no matter how subjectively vivid and intense they may be for any given individual or group, are products of the human mind that can be explained psychoanalytically. These products are articulated through manifold, historically diverse contexts of cultural specificity, such as mysticism, which in turn accord them meaning and coherence. From a Freudian perspective, religious interpretations of these psychological and emotional phenomena ironically conceal their deeper existential truth.

## Sacrifice, renunciation and the super-ego

The chapters following Freud's meditation on the oceanic feeling in *Civilization and its Discontents* are in some significant respects a much darker elaboration of the themes of *The Future of an Illusion*. In the later work, Freud concentrates more heavily on the internal psychological dialectic of the desire for happiness and the corresponding resistances against it that are precipitated by the increasingly harsh and prohibitive external pressures exerted by culture. As early as 1908, Freud pointed out the antagonism that exists between the demands of civilization and instinctual life, which he concluded contributes greatly to "modern nervous illness" (1908: 162). Freud was critical of the ways in which the primarily Christian-based moral systems of western European societies oppose sexuality as "a source of pleasure in its own right", advocating instead that it be replaced by an uncompromising, non-sexual and universal ethics of love of the neighbour. Freud derided such moral imperatives as both unrealistic and unreasonable (1930a: 108–12). As far as Freud was concerned, religious exhortations to love all humanity inhibit the capacity to love anyone. The imperative that demands love of a vague and empty abstraction, which is what the Christian category "neighbour" amounted to in his view, strongly undermines the capacity for a more focused, yet far more authentic love for a concrete other. Besides, Freud was not convinced that most neighbours are worth loving, and in fact are more likely to want what we materially possess rather than our love (*ibid.*: 111). In his view, the Christian command to love one's neighbour as oneself is based on misleading illusions about human nature that fail to consider seriously the reality of innate human aggression.

While there is some debate as to whether Freud believed that aggression is either a wholly independent, separate human disposition, or rather a derivative of the death drive that becomes aggression as it is deflected outwards by the counter-force of Eros,[2] it is somewhat subordinate to the more significant point in Freud's argument. While human suffering has multiple sources (*ibid.*: 77), only some of which are beyond his control, man is very definitely "a wolf to man" – *Homo homini lupus* (*ibid.*: 111). Furthermore, as Richard Bernstein observes, "Freud is far more radical and disturbing than Hobbes" in his view that the admixture of the life and death instincts constituting an "ineradicable ambivalence" within the psyche is resistant to both reason and control (2002: 139–40). Since ambivalence is innate, human beings cannot be held morally responsible for the existence of their more destructive impulses. In the face of these amoral impulses, it is the ego that strives to be moral (Freud 1923b: 54) in response to the pressures exerted by culture. The more that civilization demands the sacrifice of instinctual satisfaction through its increasingly intensified forms of repression and renunciation, the more aggressive human beings become; they simply cannot bear the sustained pain of deprivations suffered in the name of morality and that are sanctified by religion (Freud 1908: 187). Yet, at the same time, religion's severe prohibitions against the satisfaction of human needs also encourages a responsive longing for "palliative measures" that religion claims only it can offer (Freud 1930a: 75). Freud understood that as long as people invested their hopes for better times in the next world, they would not be able to set about changing this one.

As we have seen in *The Future of an Illusion,* Freud argues that belief in God has its psychological roots in an infantile identification with the father based on the internalization of the infant-father relationship. Freud reiterates this argument in *Civilization and its Discontents,* but in more extensive psychoanalytic detail. As the child develops, the psychological dynamics of identification and internalization of the father and the relationship with him become gradually transformed into the representatives of the multiple interconnecting webs of cultural authority that comprise the sources of instinctual deprivation. The libidinal or affectionate attachment of the child to the father, his desire for the father's protection and love, along with the child's aggression and rebellious impulses against the father's authority, infuse and shape the adult's ties to his culture, its leaders and its moral norms. The internalized paternal authority is the pillar of the individual conscience, which is believed to be God-given. The super-ego (*das Über-Ich*) is a "metamorphosis of the parental relationship" that comes to represent the regulating values of culture and their demands for obedience (Freud 1933b: 62). The super-ego is the psychical precipitate that is distilled from the infant's relationship with the father.

As the child develops and learns to tame his/her libidinal desires for both parents in conformity to the demands of culture as represented in the family and other social institutions, the contradictory feelings towards them gradually transform into more socially acceptable forms of filial affection and respect. This marks the dissolution of the Oedipus complex to some degree. The resolution of Oedipal conflicts are rarely fully or evenly resolved. This long psychic process involves both an introjection of the parental objects, as well as identifications with them, that provide the "sole condition under which the id can give up its objects" (Freud 1923b: 29). The "character of the ego" contains "the history of those object-choices", which includes the history of those parental relationships that are now desexualized (*ibid.*). The love for the parental objects is brought back within the ego so that object-love has become transformed into narcissistic love (secondary narcissism), where the elements of identifications with others come to constitute important parts of the self (*ibid.*: 30 n. 1).

These internal parental imagoes exert a general and permanent influence on the individual as they result in the establishment of an "ego-ideal" that pressures the ego to comply with the moral and social authority of culture. Freud emphasizes that it is the desexualized parental figures who reside at the heart of the ego-ideal,[3] which is heir to the Oedipus complex. Mixed gendered parental identifications become united with each other under the dominant image of the father. *"This modification of the ego retains its special position; it confronts the other contents of the ego as an ego-ideal or super-ego"* (*ibid.*: 34) that is paternal in character.

Freud's discussion of the super-ego or ego-ideal can be confusing since they appear at times as distinct psychic entities, while at other times Freud uses the terms interchangeably. However, the two terms eventually become indistinguishable as Freud's concept of the super-ego becomes more clearly and decisively delineated. The super-ego is laced with ambivalence: it holds the ego to strive towards the ideal of being like the father while simultaneously acting as a prohibiting agent that punishes and humiliates the ego when it either falls short of the standards represented by the ego-ideal and/or persists in its forbidden desires towards the parents. Freud describes the super-ego as "not simply a residue of the earliest object-choices of the id; it also represents an *energetic reaction-formation against those choices*" (1923b: 34, emphasis added). Another way of putting this may be expressed in the formulation that the earlier idea of an ego-ideal pressures the individual to emulate the father, while the super-ego forbids the ego from doing, or *even wishing* to do, everything that he does (*ibid.*: 34). Only the father, for example, may possess the mother sexually; only he may exercise absolute authority and command obedience within the family; and only he metes out harsh punishment for violations of his laws. The super-ego is organized along the lines of domination–submission and command–prohibition. When it runs into conflict with the ego, it will exact varying degrees of guilt and self-loathing. The psychic energies required to repress the individual's forbidden erotic longings for both the mother and father, and then later for anything defined by culture as off-limits, are "borrowed" from the father's strength and authority. Eventually the repressive dynamics of the super-ego expand to include culture, where they become absorbed within and reinforced by religion, education and the general authority of culture, all of which retain the paternal character (*ibid.*: 34–5). As a substitute for the desire for the father, the super-ego "contains the germ from which all religions have evolved" (*ibid.*: 37). Freud is clear that the highest moral achievements of human beings, along with the loftiest teachings of religion, have their origins in, and are maintained by, the super-ego. As culture demands increasingly unrealistic and painful renunciations and self-sacrifice, both the psychic fabric of the individual and the social cohesion of culture become dangerously threatened.

The super-ego is the internalized representation of the moral values and authority of masculinized culture: "The male sex", Freud writes, "seems to have taken the lead in all these moral acquisitions" (1923b: 37). Male authority "is the representative for us of every moral restriction, the advocate of a striving towards perfection – it is, in short, as much as we have been able to grasp psychologically of what is described as the higher side of human life". The super-ego comes into being through the influence not only of parents, but of educators and all forms of paternal authorities "analogous to them" (Freud 1933b: 67). Freud's description of the super-ego firmly establishes it as an inter-subjectively constituted psychic agency that arises from a series of expanding "critical influence[s]" that begin with the parents and end with "public opinion" (1914b: 96). As far as the influence on the developing child of the parents is concerned, Freud refines his argument by pointing out that what the child internalizes is not so much the parents *per se* as the parents' super-ego, about which he writes:

> the contents which fill it are the same and it becomes *the vehicle of tradition and of all the time-resisting judgements of value which have propagated themselves in this manner from generation to generation ... The past, the tradition of the race and of the people, lives on in the ideologies of the super-ego, and yields only slowly to the influences of the present and to new changes; and so long as it operates through the super-ego it plays a powerful part in human life.*
> (Freud 1933b: 67, emphasis added)

In this sense the super-ego plays a crucial role in the transmission of cultural moral values and social practices. This conclusion can be pushed even further to suggest that besides its role as the transmitter of cultural authority, values, beliefs and worldviews, the super-ego also – and at times aggressively – mimics and reinforces culture's insistence on sacrifice and renunciation of desire. From this perspective, Freud speculates that the super-ego derives from a far older, brutally aggressive external authority whose destructive power remains active in the mind even if it has long passed from the realm of material existence: "The aggressiveness of conscience keeps up the aggressiveness of the authority" (1930a: 128), so that the individual ego that is gripped with anxiety and guilt unconsciously participates in maintaining its own enslaved condition in an effort to appease a hostile and aggressive, punishing super-ego. The relationship between the authoritarian super-ego and the ego, or conscious self, mirrors and reproduces in an internal and distorted fashion an older "real relationship between the ego, as yet undivided, and an external object" (*ibid.*: 129). Religion plays a key role in supporting and preserving these internal psychodynamics of domination and submission by redirecting and reshaping the ego's terror of punishment and even possible annihilation at the hands of the super-ego into a fear of God. The internal psychological dynamics of human development are rewritten on a cosmic scale. One of Freud's most important and contested claims is that these internal Oedipal conflicts and fantasies have their origins in historically objective events. The dynamics of religious feelings and beliefs arise out of the internalized psychic remnants that are endlessly repeated echoes of ancient and lethal struggles between real sons and their real tyrannical fathers.

## The founding myth of the super-paternal super-ego: *Totem and Taboo*

*Totem and Taboo* (Freud 1913b) is a meditation on the phylogenetic origins of culture. The social anthropological premise underlying Freud's ingenious but controversial argument is that religion, morality and subsequent social and cultural institutions up to the present derive from an originary trauma of a "forgotten" murder, the psychic consequences of which humanity grapples with in each successive generation. Inspired by Darwin's idea of a "primal horde", Freud hypothesizes that pre-historic primitive peoples lived in groups, each dominated by a powerful and brutal patriarch who forbade his sons, the young men of the group, access to the women he guarded for the satisfaction of his own sexual needs. At some point the sons, whom the father drove out, returned to the horde to kill and devour the father, thereby ending his absolute rule, usurping his power and literally incorporating his strength into their own bodies. However, in addition to hating and fearing the primal father, they also loved and admired him. The ambivalent mixture of hatred, hostility, love and longing for the father accounts for the eventual guilt and remorse the sons felt because of their murderous act. At some later point (Freud provides no historical time line), the sons found a way to manage their contradictory feelings towards both the father and their own crime by reinstating the father in the form of a totem animal, a commemorative symbol of paternal power that they worshipped.

Stirred by filial feelings of guilt and revived affection towards the father that included an anxious awareness that a replacement of the tribal leader would be vulnerable to the same brutal fate, the brothers attempted to ensure both their own survival and social stability by instituting taboos against patricide and incestuous relations with the mother. As a result of these taboos, the rules of social cooperation and exogamous union came into being. These taboos inaugurate the laws of culture and the anchors of individual moral conscience in the psychic form of "the two repressed wishes of the Oedipus complex" (Freud 1913b: 143). The originary patricide resounds and echoes in the Oedipal fantasies of the sons of countless subsequent generations who continue to re-enact it through the inevitable internal dialectic of love and admiration, and hatred and envy, towards their fathers. Eventually the brothers recognized that repeated cycles of authoritarian rule followed by bloody rebellion and social chaos would have to give way to a new and different form of social organization if they and their communities were to survive. There are political implications in Freud's anthropological scenario as well. The dawning awareness that "no one of them must be treated by another as their father was treated by them all jointly" (*ibid.*: 146) is the fraternal pact marking a rudimentary but decisive shift from despotic authoritarian rule to a democratic organization of society. For Freud, this move represents "the founding act of civilization" (Whitebook 1995: 96).

Eventually the prohibitions against patricide, and then by rational association, fratricide, transformed into the more encompassing moral imperative forbidding murder altogether. Thus, by first renouncing the tribal rule of brutal patriarchal leaders through murder and social rebellion, and then by justifying and atoning for these actions, the sons found a way to regulate themselves and their new social group by memorializing the dead father in the form of a sacred totem animal they revered, celebrated and occasionally ate. As the memory of the primal crime faded into the mists of prehistory, the totem animal gradually morphed into gods and then culminated in the one God of the later monotheistic world religions. This process had particularly momentous implications for the emergence of religion and morality through which the basest human desires and passions became regulated and transformed into the highest ideals of culture. Throughout his career, Freud maintained that "the killing of the father [is] the nucleus of totemism and the starting point in the formation of religion" (1925b: 67). The taboos against murder and incest constitute the "nature and origin of *conscience*" (Freud 1913b: 67). Culture and social order are rendered possible only on the basis of endlessly repeated renunciations of desire.

Although Freud drew heavily on the work of selected anthropologists of his day, including James Frazer, Charles Darwin and William Robertson Smith, his assertion that there were in fact primal hordes where rebellious sons *actually* murdered their fathers was dismissed almost immediately as nothing more than a *Just So* story. While the material facts of Freud's account seem to have little basis in solid ethnographic or historical evidence, there is nonetheless something compelling about his anthropological theory that may well capture a psychological truth that glimmers through. Alfred L. Kroeber concurs with this view as he remarks in his review of *Totem and Taboo* that a *Just So* story may well contain "a profound psychological truth" (1971: 45). Levi-Strauss shows appreciation for the psychological value of Freud's account in his astute observation that "like all myths, it doesn't tell us how things really happened. It tells us how men need to imagine things happened so as to try to overcome contradictions" (in Bernstein 2002: 141). While a number of Freud's *specific* assertions about the historical facts of the primal parricide and its role in the origins of totemism remain the subject of some debate to this day, it would not do justice to the more deeply relevant psychological insights advanced in *Totem and Taboo* to evaluate each and every one of its assertions in strict historically factual terms. Evaluations of *Totem and Taboo* that are based strictly on empirical investigation overlook the key point of Freud's argument.

Freud was well aware of the shaky material premises of his theory of the origins of culture and the negative responses it provoked. However, as Strachey rightly points out in his editor's introduction to the text, Freud was quite consciously fashioning an "endopsychic myth" ([1961] 2001: x) whose main purpose was to advance the claims of psychoanalytic theory rather than those of objective historical investigation. The psychodramatic narrative of the primal horde illuminates the "dim inner perception of one's own psychical apparatus" that "stimulates illusions of thought, which are naturally projected outwards and characteristically into the future and the world beyond. Immortality, retribution, life after death, are all reflections of our inner psyche … psycho-mythology", Freud writes (in Strachey [1961] 2001: x). The "psycho-mythology" of the primal horde is the narrative vehicle whose purpose is to illuminate the psychic truth that lies at the heart of religion and culture and the minds that produce them. Freud understands that as a theory *and* clinical practice, psychoanalysis inevitably privileges psychic truth over empirical fact in its efforts to comprehend how the human mind fashions reality. In order to study and interpret the range of neuroses Freud encountered in clinical work, he had to pay close attention to the patient's narrative accounts, however distorted they may have appeared, in order to unearth the psychological truths contained within them. "[I]n the world of the neuroses", Freud says, "it is psychical reality which is the decisive kind" (1917b: 368). But the strange distortions and elaborate fantasies generated within the minds of neurotics are not utterly divorced from real past-life events. Freud repeatedly insisted that there is a kernel of truth in every psychosis, no matter how florid. We will have occasion to see the importance of this idea even more in later chapters.

From the perspective of psychic truth, it is easier to understand Freud's speculations upon the phylogenetic origins of religion, morality and culture that are concealed within the inner world of unconscious fantasies and conflicts. His approach in *Totem and Taboo* is similar to that of the analyst who struggles to comprehend the strange narratives and disturbing world views of traumatized, dissociated patients. Both the analyst engaging in clinical work, and Freud engaging in theoretical work derived from his own clinical experience, know that *something* happened in the life of the patient to leave a damaging mark on the mind. Neither the clinician nor Freud needs the support of irrefutable forensic evidence to know that human beings are vulnerable to all manner of traumatic impacts arising from events that may or may not concretely have occurred. What the initiating trauma really was may never be known, particularly if it occurred in early life, because the mental structures of mind that support explicit memory have not yet been developed. Freud seems to be thinking along these lines in his comparison of neurotics with prehistoric, or primitive, human beings. At the same time, the mind will find ways to organize and make sense of traumatic experiences that are inaccessible to conscious recollection by providing those inchoate chaotic impressions with narrative structures derived from existing cultural repertoires. Freud almost certainly has this in mind when he writes:

> The lack of precision in what I have written in the text above, its abbreviation of the time factor and its compression of the whole subject-matter, may be attributed to the reserve necessitated by the nature of the topic. It would be as foolish to aim at exactitude in such questions as it would be unfair to insist upon certainty. (Freud 1913b: 142–3 n. 1)

Despite such statements, Freud nonetheless ends *Totem and Taboo* with the declaration that "in the beginning was the Deed" (*Im Anfang war die Tat*) (*ibid.*: 161). The matter does not end here, however. Is "the Deed" a psychological or empirical event, or a combination of both? The answer to this question lies in a more complex understanding of what Freud meant by "the Deed".

As we have seen, *Totem and Taboo* in some respects reprises and expands the argument advanced in 1907 that postulates analogies between religion and neuroses. Although he cautions that the analogies between neuroses and religion must be held lightly, he does insist that there are important connections between the inner worlds of neurotics and ancient, primitive peoples. Like the latter, neurotics are governed by "the principle of the 'omnipotence of thoughts'" (Freud 1913b: 85) in believing that transgressive desires and thoughts are the psychic and moral equivalent of deeds. Freud returns to this idea in *Civilization and its Discontents* in his discussion of the origins of the sense of guilt. Again, based upon his clinical work with patients, Freud understood that guilt does not require the commission of actual deeds in order to exist. "[E]ven when a person has not actually *done* the bad thing but has only recognized in himself an *intention* to do it, he may regard himself as guilty; and the question then arises of why the intention is regarded as equal to the deed" (Freud 1930a: 124). To think, fantasize and/or feel a transgressive impulse is psychically equivalent to acting on it. The truth of neurotic guilt lies in the actuality of having unacceptable unconscious wishes, and in this sense the guilt is justified. Thus murderous Oedipal hostility towards the father is *felt* as an actual parricidal crime even though it is only imaginary. "An obsessional neurotic may be weighed down by a sense of guilt that would be appropriate in a mass-murderer, while in fact, from his childhood onwards, he has behaved to his fellow-men as the most considerate and scrupulous member of society" (Freud 1913b: 87).

The equivalence of thought and deed is not new; it is, for example, a central precept of both Christianity and Western legal traditions that regard intention as an integral part of assessing moral responsibility for actions. It is thus hardly surprising that human beings are vulnerable to intense feelings of guilt no matter how irreproachable their actions may in fact be. Even if no transgressions have actually been committed, clinical experience would have taught Freud that bad thoughts inevitably generate expectations and fear of punishment in fantasies, and are inextricably bound up with feelings of guilt. This partly explains why the guilt-ridden obsessional neurotic attempts to protect himself from the evil within by engaging in elaborate "magical" obsessive rituals in much the same way Freud thought primitive peoples did in relying on magic to ward off evil spirits. Since evil spirits and demons are the externalized instantiations of unconscious reprehensible and forbidden wishes (Freud 1923a: 72), the efforts to regulate and contain demonic power through ritual action simultaneously provide a means of organizing, and limiting, the disruptive force of frightening internal affects. With these ideas in mind, Freud advances his (now outmoded) evolutionary view of human religious development as proceeding through the progressive stages of animism (belief in spirits), to religion (belief in a god, or gods), and finally, to the abandonment of religion in favour of science and its repudiation of belief and reliance on evidence and reason. Freud writes, "At the animistic stage men ascribe omnipotence to *themselves*. At the religious stage they transfer it to the gods but do not seriously abandon it themselves, for they reserve the power of influencing the gods in a variety of ways according to their wishes" (Freud 1913b: 88). With the achievement of the scientific attitude towards the world, Freud implies that the tight psychic connections between thought and deed are broken when he concludes, "The scientific view of the universe no longer affords any room for human omnipotence; men have acknowledged their smallness and submitted resignedly to death and to the other necessities of nature" (*ibid.*). In other words, human beings have become educated to reality.

Guilt, remorse, fear, helplessness and shame motivate individuals to create the gods in the hopes of alleviating the suffering caused by internal and external conditions. Freud contended that the admixture of love and hatred towards the primal father (including individual fathers) mediates and extends the feelings towards the divine father that persist throughout all the stages of religion's development because ambivalence is a feature of the mind itself, "present to a greater or less amount in the innate disposition of everyone" (*ibid.*: 60). It can never be completely overcome, and not even religion can entirely conceal this psychological truth from its adherents. While the occasional sacrifice of the totem animal for the communal sacred meal commemorates and celebrates the divine father, it *also* denotes the triumph of the sons over him. The "sacramental" killing and ingesting of the sacred totem animal both consolidates the social bonds within the community and reinforces the clansmen's "likeness to the god" (*ibid.*: 137–8). In Freud's view, this early ritual action of ingesting divine power persists through countless generations, resurfacing in an histori-cally later version of the Christian Eucharist, which preserves and recapitulates the central features of the totem meal (*ibid.*: 154).

As the totem animal symbolizes the believers' ambivalence towards the divine father in its dual meaning as both "substitute" for and triumph over him, so Jesus represents another culturally constructed narrative detailing the victorious installation of a "son-religion" over the "father-religion". The Easter story of Christianity is an "undisguised" acknowledgment of the primal murder that finds "the fullest atonement" for the guilty deed in the sacrifice of the son. A fresh victory over the father lies hidden within the willing sacrificial act and "the inexorable law of ambivalence" reasserts itself. "The very deed in which the son offered the greatest possible atonement to the father brought him at the same time to the attainment of his wishes *against* the father. He himself became God beside, or more correctly in place of, the father. *A son-religion displaced the father-religion*", Freud writes (Freud 1913b: 154, emphasis added). In a stroke of theoretical brilliance, Freud penetrates the ambivalence at the heart of the love-based ethics of Christianity in further illustration of his argument that religious desire encompasses both a loving longing and murderous hatred for the father. This psychological truth for Freud constitutes the "*root of every form of religion*" (*ibid.*: 148, emphasis added). A Freudian psychoanalytic theory of religion concludes that "religion, morals, society and art converge in the Oedipus complex" (*ibid.*: 156). We are now in a better position to understand what Freud means by a "Deed" that is re-enacted between fathers and sons in every generation. That it is psychological does not, from a psychoanalytic perspective, diminish its truth.

## Religion and violence

Although Freud's "fascinating construct" (Burkert 1983: 74) as presented in *Totem and Taboo* is nothing more, but also nothing less, than a "psycho-mythology", some of Freud's main ideas are given significant if modified support in later historical studies of religion that have some psychoanalytic awareness and sensitivity. In his study of ancient Greek sacrificial ritual and myth, for example, classicist and historian of religion Walter Burkert situates the origins of religion in the hunting and sacrificial rituals associated with kill-ing animals. "In hunting societies accessible to ethnological study", he writes, "hunters are said to have expressed clear feelings of guilt with regard to the slaughtered animal" (Burkert 1983: 16). Burkert claims that hunting was a com-munal activity, requiring the cooperation of "a new type of male community", or *Männerbund*; that is, "biologically analogous to a pack of wolves" engaged in a repetitive cycle of killing, eating and moving constantly between their families and their band (*ibid.*: 18). Hunting, killing and devouring became organized around ritual ceremonies that allowed the hunters to psychologically manage and find meaning in the traumatic "imprinting" that the repeated witnessing of the suffering and death of other living creatures would most certainly have had on their minds. Their prey were regarded in quasi-human terms and "treated accordingly":

> Hunting concentrated on the great mammals, which conspicuously resembled men in their body structure and movements, their eyes and their "faces", their breath and voices, in fleeing and fear, in attacking and in rage ... One could, perhaps, most clearly grasp the animal's resemblance to man when it died.          (Burkert 1983: 20)

Given the masculine attributes associated with big animals that were not immediately killed but captured and kept alive for periods of time by the group, it is plausible that such animals became associated with "a kind of father, a father-symbol, a father-substitute. Conscious killing is a kind of patricide" (*ibid.*: 75). The repeated killing of animals and the feelings associated with it became part of a "formative experience" (*ibid.*: 21) that "comprises by far the largest part of human history" (*ibid.*: 17) thereby contributing to the shape of the human mind and giving form to its psycho-mythologies. "With remarkable consistency", says Burkert, "myths tell of the origins of man in a fall, a crime that is often a bloody act of violence" (*ibid.*: 21–2), and in many respects, *Totem and Taboo* is precisely such a myth. Freud would have no trouble agreeing with Burkert's hypothesis that the repeated shock of witnessing the life flowing out of the bleeding animal would have aroused powerful feelings of anxiety, guilt and remorse. The psychological intensity of such feelings, which would likely include a terrifying fear of retribution from the animal's spirit, would have to be contained and regulated in ritual action to ensure that violence and aggression did not spin out of control and threaten the community. Such ritual acts would also provide a degree of emotional reassurance that life not only triumphs over death, but is also preserved and sustained by death in the devouring of the animal. On the level of experience, killing and death are closely intertwined with the regeneration and sustaining of life. "The power to kill and respect for life illuminate each other", Burkert writes (1983: 21).

Robert Paul (2010), who describes himself as belonging to the "handful of anthropologists and psychoanalysts" who continue to regard *Totem and Taboo* as worthy of intellectual respect, advances similar arguments in explicit support of Freud. While Paul rightly rejects the more outdated and antiquated elements of Freud's theory, he is able to appreciate and demonstrate its fundamental compatibilities with contemporary anthropological and evolutionary theory. Paul argues not only that *Totem and Taboo* "contains an important truth about human social organization" (Paul 2010: 231) that must be reconsidered, but goes even further in validating Freud's most controversial claim that not only did a primal crime take place within a horde-like context, but that this claim can be interpreted as lying within the accepted bounds of "mainstream evolutionary thinking" (*ibid.*: 232). Drawing heavily upon the anthropological studies of Bruce Knauft (1991), Christopher Boehm (1999) and Bernard Chapais (2008), which he cites in some detail, Paul reframes the essential points of the Freudian phylogenetic account of the prehistoric primal horde as a "multimale, multi-female system in which mating success, feeding opportunities, and social power were determined by a dominance hierarchy headed by a senior alpha male" (2010: 233). Eventually this system of "dominance hierarchy" was eliminated, giving way to a more egalitarian social system that proved more effective in facilitating the cooperative forms of social organization necessary for the survival of the group.

Relying on Knauft's idea of a "U-shaped" trajectory in human evolution, Paul argues that following the "rebellion" against the authoritarian leader, there might well have been a "protracted period of relative egalitarianism among our hunting-and-gathering first human ancestors", which in turn would have given way in a later period of established settlements to a renewed trend towards "hierarchy and despotism" (*ibid.*: 234). Over a time span of possibly thousands of years and involving countless repetitions, the despotic leader would be overthrown and replaced by more egalitarian, cooperative social organizations because they are more conducive to human survival. The repeated and cumulative experiences of cycles of domination and overthrow with their inevitable replacement by egalitarian social organizations would become a "fixed action pattern" within the evolutionary development of the human species. Paul's explanation as to how this happens is worth quoting at length:

> The only answer that can be given that is consistent with contemporary biological thinking is that it happens through the interaction of random mutation and external selection pressures operating differentially among individuals in a population ... Freud's theory is rescued for contemporary science by his insistence that the primal crime was not a unique event but happened countless times in countless social groups over eons of evolutionary time. Such a context constitutes precisely the condition under which a trait such as the supposed mental sequelae of the primal crime can be propagated by natural selection, rather than by the (impossible) memory of a single traumatic event ... If having a memory of the rebellion against dominance hierarchy served

individual fitness – as it would have if it enhanced social cooperation – then it would have been selected for regardless of whether the event itself ever happened. In this case, I make the stronger argument that the psychological dispositions supporting dominance hierarchy and its overthrow were not based on fanciful memories, however, but rather, on long-lasting evolved psychological propensities that once supported the social life of our ancestors.                    (Paul 2010: 239)

Paul insists that if his account is closer to Freud's intent, which he thinks it is, then the repeated charge against Freud – that a Lamarckian theory of inherited characteristics informs the basis of Freud's arguments in *Totem and Taboo* – is misleading. Freud combined his extensive knowledge of the anthropology of his time with the clinical experience he acquired listening to the repeated stories of his patients' Oedipal fantasies. He concluded that these had a real basis in human prehistory, if not in an individual life history, in each case. If we combine his anthropological theory of the primal horde with his psychoanalytic theory of individual Oedipal fantasies and their conflicts along lines suggested by Paul, we see that Freud is providing an organizing narrative coherence to explain the ways repeated trauma impacts and resonates within the psyche. At the same time, the unconscious ambivalent feelings towards parents that Freud attributed to all human beings generate their own traumatic impact in the form of anxiety and guilt. As a clinician, Freud knew that neurosis is bound up with varying degrees of unresolved trauma that continue to cast dark, corrosive shadows across the trajectory of psychological development. The pattern of consistent similarities he noted in his patients' Oedipal fantasies led Freud to believe that they must be derived from a common origin somewhere in the lived human experience of prehistory. However, he could not satisfactorily account for their transmission, given the level of the anthropological and evolutionary theories of his time. Paul, on the other hand, is able to marshal his considerable knowledge of the subsequent advances of contemporary anthropology and evolutionary theory to provide *Totem and Taboo* with a reconstituted explanatory power that is close to capturing Freud's general intent without endorsing its outdated elements.

## Whither the Oedipus complex?

But what of the Oedipus complex? How can contemporary psychoanalysis preserve and refashion this central pillar of Freudian theory without becoming sidetracked by the controversies within anthropological and evolutionary explanations of human social origins? Questions disputing the factual truth of Freud's primal horde notwithstanding, a significant number of psychoanalytically informed theorists and clinicians still recognize that there is a basic reality to the phenomena described as Oedipal family dynamics that constitutes a universal feature within widely varying and culturally diverse expressions of human experience.[4] Part of this idea is based on the Freudian assumption that fantasies are not simply the "utterly free creations of different individuals"; rather, they share a stereotypical quality which suggests that they "exist prior to and [are] independent of the individual psyche" (Paul 1987: 90). The "public realm" of mythic narratives and wide-ranging symbolic forms are the culturally contextualized direct expressions of the "core structural features of the psyche in general" (*ibid*.: 91). For Freud, the Oedipus complex is one of the most important examples attesting to the presence of typical universal fantasies, which, given its appearance in the early stages of life, means that it must therefore have a phylogenetic basis (*ibid*.: 90). The Oedipus complex tells the story of conflicted father-son experience that all men share. This probably accounts for the relevance of the Sophoclean tragedy, whose audiences since ancient Greece continue to recognize elemental features of their own experiences within the play. Recognition of this universally shared experience allows psychoanalyst Hans Loewald, in his reformulation of Freud's Oedipal theory, to argue that healthy psychological development necessarily and inevitably involves an "active urge for emancipation" from parental authority (2000: 389). In order to become an autonomous adult, it is a "developmental necessity" (*ibid*.: 390) that the individual both sever and transform the emotional ties of infancy and childhood to his or her parents. In other words, the parents must "die" for the psychologically mature individual to be born.

Paul Ricoeur makes a similar point in his observation that *Totem and Taboo* is not a work of ethnology or history as such. Rather, it is a text of *psychoanalytic interpretation* wherein "every history" is subordinate to the "history of desire in its great debate with authority" (Ricoeur 1970: 179). The process of "emancipating individuation" (Loewald 2000: 393) that is integral to psychological maturation involves the waning of parental importance and the repudiation of parental authority. Inevitably, as Loewald argues, the individual's transformed relationship with his parents generates feelings of guilt, remorse and, if all goes well enough, a need to atone for (what amounts to) the "crime" of psychic parricide. As the maturing child overcomes infantile dependency and eventually resolves the guilt that derives from emotional ambivalence, he learns to assume ethical responsibility for those needs, impulses and desires that "we appear to have been born with or that seem to have taken shape in interaction with parents during infancy" (*ibid*.: 392). The psychologically mature individual, having resolved his Oedipal conflicts and ambivalent desires in a more balanced, integrated psyche, has in effect achieved a reconciled relationship with his own differentiated mind, which further allows him to form reconciled relationships with a variety of others in the external world. Remorse, guilt and atonement are for Loewald crucial motivational elements in the development of the self. The mental capacity for atonement for the parricidal "crime" involves a two-fold process of reconciliation with one's own internal conflicts and one's parents. "The self", writes Loewald, "in its autonomy, is an atonement structure, a structure of reconciliation, and as such a supreme achievement" (*ibid.*: 394). Loewald resituates and reconfigures the Freudian originary crime within a strictly psychic developmental maturation process that culminates in the transformation of ambivalent desire into reconciling love. Eventually, this reconciling love becomes the basis of the autonomous ethical life. For Loewald, there is no need to speculate about concrete acts of parricide. For him, the truth of the primal horde is a psychic truth the validity and justification of which neither requires nor depends upon narrowly defined empirical historical data.

The effects of the primal parricide upon which the foundations of culture are erected "have left ineradicable traces in the history of humanity", Freud writes (1913b: 155). For Freud the traumatic impact of a pre-historic patricide has somehow entered the "collective mind" of humanity, where it continues to resonate and reproduce itself within individual minds. "I have taken as the basis of my whole position the existence of a collective mind, in which mental processes occur *just as they do* in the mind of an individual", he explains (*ibid.*: 157, emphasis added). For Freud, the anxiety and guilt associated with the original patricide was so devastating that it continues to operate within the repeated Oedipal dynamics of individual psycho-sexual development, even in contexts where no individual father exists (*ibid.*: 158). Freud's social-psychological anthropology in part requires the postulation of a collective mind that transmits generational trauma along with feelings typically associated with it. In answer to his own question concerning "the ways and means employed by one generation in order to hand on its mental states to the next one", Freud offers a theory of "the inheritance of psychical dispositions" (*ibid.*: 158) that, as Paul argues, may be cautiously considered as potentially reconcilable in some important respects with contemporary biological and evolutionary theory. Nonetheless, this aspect of Freud represents one of the most deeply disputed themes in his entire psychoanalytic theory. To the end of his life, Freud argued for the transmission of psychic dispositions or traits that accounted for what he saw as the universal pervasiveness and persistence of powerful Oedipal wishes that structured both psychological and cultural development. For Freud, ontogeny (individual development) recapitulates phylogeny (development of the species). The traumatic impact of a long-forgotten but actually experienced event, repeated countless times over thousands of years, left its indelible mark on the individual psyche, which for Freud goes a long way to explain the tenacious and ubiquitous nature of religion. The relationship between phylogeny and ontogeny, and the mysterious ways in which psychic dispositions are transmitted through inheritance, is perhaps nowhere brought more sharply into focus than in his highly controversial study of the man Moses and the monotheistic religion he founded, to which we must now turn.

# THREE

# Crime, punishment and the return of the repressed: the triumph of the intellectual and the moral mind

> Thus, blood and violence lurk fascinatingly at the very heart of religion.
>
> (Burkert 1983: 2)

*Der Mann Moses und die Monotheistische Religion* (*The Man Moses and the Monotheistic Religion*), known under the title *Moses and Monotheism* in the standard English edition, is perhaps Freud's most "curious" text (Gay 1988: 604) and "most audacious cultural speculation" (Santner 2001: 26). The man Moses, the story of his relationship with the Jews and his legacy of the monotheistic religion that eventually became Judaism "pursued" Freud throughout his entire life, as he wrote in a letter to Lou Andreas Salomé (in Bernstein 1998: 118). The first part of the German title, *Der Mann Moses* (*The Man Moses*), alone suggests that Freud was fascinated with the *man* Moses for much of his life. A number of Freud's commentators have argued that he strongly identified with Moses, in whom he found a parallel between his own gift of psychoanalysis and Moses's gift of monotheism to a world incapable of comprehending the moral and intellectual rigour of either system of thought (Paul 1994: 835). Some twenty years prior to *Moses and Monotheism*, Freud devoted a highly imaginative yet closely argued paper to an intricate and finely detailed study of Moses's character that was inspired by Michelangelo's masterful sculpture, which he visited every time he was in Rome. "No piece of statuary has ever made a stronger impression on me than this", he writes in "The Moses of Michelangelo" (1914c: 213). A re-reading of "The Moses of Michelangelo" after *Moses and Monotheism* shows that the latter is a more extensive and conceptually expansive continuation of the former. For this reason, I will leave my discussion of "The Moses of Michelangelo" to the end of the chapter. Like his meditation on Michelangelo's statue of Moses, Freud's *Moses and Monotheism* also advances a highly speculative but compelling theory that draws upon his considerable knowledge of archaeology, anthropology, myth and, of course, psychoanalysis. *Moses and Monotheism* combines reason with imagination in a brilliant if deeply flawed hermeneutic that selectively but plausibly draws upon a number of the scholarly disciplines of Freud's day, which is partly why the book commands serious attention. Like *Totem and Taboo*, *Moses and Monotheism* cannot be seriously considered as a work based on objective historical events. Even Freud described his "Moses book" as a "historical novel" (Bernstein 1998: 117; Strachey 2001: 3) and worried that it was not well substantiated. At the same time, he held out the hope that, in similar fashion to his methodology in *Totem and Taboo*, he might unearth the real events behind the Exodus story.

Throughout *Moses and Monotheism*, Freud again appears to "oscillate" between what he insists is a factual basis for the main points of his analysis of the story and what may more properly be described as a psycho-mythological account. It seems that Freud could not finally decide whether his Moses was a figure of history or a figure of memory (Assmann 1997: 148; Paul 1996: 224 n. 8). Despite his great fascination with the story of Moses, Freud was only too well aware that its "historical foundations ... are not solid enough to serve as a basis" for his conclusions about it (Bernstein 1998: 118). There were very probably a number of other factors accounting for Freud's uneasiness with this work, some to do with the problematic nature of the argument itself and others with the social and political circumstances at the time he was writing the Moses book. For one thing, Freud was anxious about how publication of the text would be received in the predominantly Roman Catholic context of 1930s Vienna, where anti-Semitism was becoming increasingly violent as the Nazi menace loomed on the horizon. In the early to mid-thirties, as he was working on his Moses book, Freud was still living in Vienna. He did not emigrate to England until 1938. Given his view at the time that the Catholic Church was the only oppositional force to the steadily encroaching Nazi threat, he understandably feared offending the Catholic hierarchy with what he was certain would be a highly controversial, if not outright offensive, account of the origins of monotheism. In addition to these qualms, Freud was even more reluctant to do anything that would risk the imposition of a ban on psychoanalysis (Freud 1939: 55).

Beyond these very real political considerations concerning the preservation of psychoanalysis that included the welfare and safety of his analytic colleagues, Freud remained insecure about the credibility of the major underlying premises upon which his entire argument was erected, namely that monotheism was an Egyptian invention; that Moses was an Egyptian who led the Jews out of bondage and rescued his religion by imposing it on them; and that he was murdered by the Jews at some point during their desert wanderings. Freud knew that in attributing historical fact to these particular claims, his "last creative effort" could be dismissed as little more than an "imposing statue" constructed "upon feet of clay" (Bernstein 1998: 23). He was also very well aware that as a Jew declaring that Moses was an Egyptian, an idea that had been circulating in scholarly circles because of the Egyptian etymology of the name (Assmann 1997; Carroll 1987; Gay 1998: 606), he also risked alienating the Jewish community and exposing them to further dangers. This risk, he knew, could not be undertaken lightly, especially in the context of intensifying anti-Semitic persecution, and a number of Jewish scholars pleaded with him to withhold publication of the book. However, after Freud fled Vienna and the Nazis in 1938, these considerations eventually were overtaken by issues of far greater importance to him and that constituted the very heart of his passionate interest: the nature of Jewish identity, its "particular character" (Bernstein 1998: 117) and its ability to survive centuries of murderous persecutions. In Freud's view, an understanding of the moral capacity and intellectual achievement of the Egyptian Moses was key to answering these questions. Without Moses, the *Egyptian* monotheist, there would be no *Jewish* people. This was a scandalous and unacceptable thesis to many of his fellow Jews, and Freud knew it.

The first site of controversy concerning *Moses and Monotheism* was within Freud himself; he remained ambivalent about this work (1939: 58) even after he released its third and final section for publication in 1938. However, as is the case with respect to all his other writings on religion, *Moses and Monotheism* is first and foremost a psychoanalytic hermeneutic. The book provides further evidence of Freud's continued conviction that the key to explaining religion lies in the study of neurosis and the Oedipal conflicts that are themselves psychic derivatives of the unconscious memory traces of a primal parricide. In this sense, religion is again "a form of reminiscence" for Freud (Rose 2004: xxi). *Moses and Monotheism* takes some of the main ideas broached in the earlier *Totem and Taboo* in new directions. Freud's Moses book, again in a fashion consistent with each of his writings on religion, introduces something different and distinct not raised before, namely an analysis of Jewish identity and the psychodynamics involved in its religious and ethical tradition that explain its survival. But Freud's treatment of these issues is entangled in thorny and unresolved questions surrounding the transmission of cultural identity and religious tradition. How does the founding event of civilization, the primal parricide, remain preserved in the unconscious memory of a people over countless generations until it is triggered into consciousness by a later crisis or set of traumatic events? Freud was interested in illuminating what he believed was an unconscious phylogenetic template of hidden memories that shapes and informs the cultural and religious beliefs and practices of a people through its psychological *transmission* across centuries. What Freud could not account for satisfactorily was *how*, by what means, this transmission occurred. Another set of problems of a more historical and political nature related to his contention that an *Egyptian created the Jews* out of the people *he* chose to carry on the monotheistic legacy of the *Egyptian* Pharaoh Akhenaten (fourteenth century BCE). Understandably, these claims upset many of Freud's Jewish contemporaries, and they continue to trouble many of his later critics (Bernstein 1998: 87;

Yerushalmi 1991). Marthe Robert concludes that in making these assertions, Freud declared "a whole people illegitimate" (1976: 151). Her view perhaps best sums up the many negative responses to *Moses and Monotheism*.

Statements about Moses's ethnic identity were not the only elements of "clay" mixed in the base of Freud's theoretical structure. Freud appears to be most vulnerable at those points where his argument comes up against the (not entirely unjustified) accusation that he relied on the discredited evolutionary theory of the French biologist Jean-Baptiste Lamarck (1744–1829) postulating the biological inheritance of acquired characteristics or psychological traits. Critics understandably argue that Freud to some extent relied on Lamarck's theory as the basis of his own explanation for the transmission of memory traces within the mind of a people. Freud was aware that Lamarckian theory was unacceptable to the biological and evolutionary science of his day (Freud 1939: 100; Gay 1988; Jones 1957). The question as to whether or not Lamarckian ideas were absolutely essential and decisive in shaping Freud's thinking about the transmission of Jewish identity cannot be pursued here, although I will briefly touch upon some of the general features of this controversy for the sake of coherent explanation.

Evaluating the merits and demerits of Lamarckian theory itself is beyond the scope of this study, and not particularly pertinent to it in any case.[1] This is especially true if *Moses and Monotheism* is read first and foremost as a *psychoanalytic* text, as I contend it should. The originality and power of Freud's arguments for the study of religion lie precisely in his creative use of psychoanalysis and its interpretive insights into important aspects of how religion is generated by human minds. If *Moses and Monotheism* is read primarily as an interpretive work of psychoanalysis, a number of the problematic aspects of historical objectivity and Freud's understanding of evolution, while still important, move to the margins. For the moment, this is where they more properly belong. Although Freud borrows heavily on history, archaeology, anthropology and biblical exegesis in order to construct his argument, his study cannot be confined to any one of these disciplines. That Freud was mistaken in a number of his historical claims is almost certainly true. However, an over-emphasis on these points obscures the relevance of Freud's more important and lasting insights concerning the meaning of tradition and Jewish identity (Bernstein 1998; Paul 1991, 1996). These were the issues that occupied Freud's interest and remained among his most pressing concerns.

## Mind and matter

The single most significant aspect of Freud's Moses book involves the way in which he uses psychoanalytic concepts to conceptualize the persistence and dynamics of Jewish identity and religious tradition. This inquiry stands as one of his most interesting contributions to the study of religion. It also serves to develop further his larger explanatory approach, which is consistent with his general psychoanalytic theoretical framework. Disputes over the biographical Moses make it too easy to lose sight of this more important aspect of his critical theory of religion. Complicating the issue of the ethnic identity of Moses is the fact that there has never been any compelling historical evidence to prove that he even existed, as Freud himself acknowledged (1939: 7). And although the question of Freud's "Lamarckism" (Yerushalmi 1991) may be far more complex and difficult to establish authoritatively than many of his critics are willing to recognize (Bernstein 1998; Derrida 1995), it must also be admitted that Freud himself muddied the waters on this point. For example, he writes that the thesis he advances in *Moses and Monotheism* could not "do without this factor [the inheritance of acquired characteristics] in biological evolution" (1939: 100). Despite statements like this, it is still not sufficiently clear that Freud in the end relied upon a "strong" concept of the inheritance of acquired characteristics that are biologically passed on (Bernstein 1998: 51–2) in order to make his arguments favouring the transmission of culturally acquired *memory-traces* and psychological dispositions or "aptitudes" (Freud 1939: 111). Freud may have been operating with a weaker "psycho-Lamarckism" where "decisive experiences in the history of a people shape the psychological character of future generations" (Bernstein 1998: 52). At the same time, Freud was also aware that the transmission of cultural traditions could not be considered without taking into account the biological basis of the mind.

The first two decades of Freud's career as a neuroscientist would certainly have inclined him towards the view that psyche and soma are inextricably linked, and that mind is a property of brain, since without the brain there is no mind. This view does not, however, necessarily translate into the strong thesis that mind and brain are identical, or that brain function strictly determines the *contents* of the mind. All that can be reasonably said so far is that the workings of the mind are *supported* by brain, given that the brain is the precondition of their existence. As a neuroscientist, Freud would certainly have understood this. What Freud *may* have been suggesting with his appeal to "biological science" can be understood along the lines of his awareness of the indisputable fact that memory, along with all psychological functioning, is neurobiological in nature. What Freud did not know about the precise nature of the mind–brain relation, namely how the brain gives rise to mind (Kandel 1998: 460), eludes cognitive neuroscientists to this day. More recently, that particular formulation has given rise to the more integrated notion of "BrainMind" and "MindBrain" found in affective neuroscientific theories (Panksepp & Biven 2012). Although neuroscientific knowledge has developed enormously since Freud's time, it still cannot completely account for the full nature of consciousness, and neither, of course, could Freud. As a psychoanalyst who was educated and trained in neuroscientific research, Freud nonetheless always acknowledged the obvious fact that psychology must be understood as rooted in neurobiology, but not totally determined by it. However, he did not know how to conceptualize their relationship and the ways in which brains are involved in facilitating the transmission of affects, ideas and beliefs. It is interesting to note as an aside that, more currently, evolutionary theorist Richard Dawkins has broached a "mimetic theory of religion" (2006: 199) based upon the concept of "memes", which are "units of cultural transmission" that replicate and propagate themselves "by leaping from brain to brain via a process which, in the broad sense, can be called imitation" (1989: 192). It might well be worth wondering if Freud's struggles in thinking about cultural transmission might be helpfully reframed and developed from the perspective of meme theory (Paul 1996: 186–9), but this path of inquiry, too, must be left to another study.

Freud's limited appeal to biology is based upon his conviction that biology must *somehow* be involved in the transmission of phylogenetically based memory-traces, even if the neurobiological sciences of his day could not exactly say how. Freud's evolutionist ideas were also deeply influenced by Darwin, to whom he makes several references in *Moses and Monotheism*. Darwin's evolutionary model was not at first considered antagonistically with respect to Lamarck (Grubrich-Simitis 1987: 100). On the question of Freud's use of Lamarckism, it is important to consider the persuasively argued observations of Bernstein and Paul that nowhere in his published work, including the cultural texts, does Freud ever directly cite, or even appeal to, the Lamarckian theory of inherited acquired characteristics (Bernstein 1998 46ff; Paul 1991: 282; 1996 172). Those critics who emphasize that Freud's arguments in *Moses and Monotheism* hinge decisively on a strong Lamarckian thesis obscure the power and potential depth of meaning in all his cultural works (Paul 1996: 1). There are exceptions, of course. Jacqueline Rose, who also views Freud as Lamarckian, at the same time recognizes that the central point of *Moses and Monotheism* is to:

> understand, even respect, the unconscious transmission of mass or group. To understand why people, from generation to generation – with no solid ground and in the teeth of the most historically unsympathetic conditions – *hold on* … Individual and collective join at the seam of historical identities transmitted over time. (Rose 2004: xxxiii–xxxiv)

Rather than ignoring the tensions within the text between Freud's psychoanalytic theory of Jewish identity and its religious–ethical tradition by dismissing them on account of what many consider to be a discredited theory, the arguments advanced here attempt to maintain those tensions so that the value and deeper relevance of Freud's thesis for the psychoanalytic study of religion may come through.

## The drama of the primal horde repeated

It is important to bear in mind that while Freud draws upon a wide range of selected themes within a variety of scholarly disciplines, he deliberately inter-prets them in the service of his own interests. At one point, Freud justifies his arguments in *Moses and Monotheism* with the outright declaration that "I am not an ethnologist, but a psychoanalyst. I had a right to take out of ethnologi-cal literature what I might need for the work of analysis" (Freud 1939: 131). Freud does not hesitate to selectively harness his considerable knowledge of humanities and social science scholarship in the service of his psychoanalytic interpretation of culture. The results of his academic cherry-picking are not always salutary. For example, he took only the idea of the murder of Moses from the theological scholar Ernst Sellin, who argued that traces of the crime could be detected in the prophet Hosea; beyond that, Freud used nothing else of his work (Paul 1994: 826). Although Freud openly acknowledges that he is in "no position to judge whether Sellin has interpreted the passages from the Prophets correctly" (1939: 37), he is nonetheless willing to use Sellin's idea as a creative point of departure for his own bold hypothesis. Sellin's value for Freud lies only in how it can advance his psychoanalytic approach. Freud is not con-cerned to assess the scholarly value of Sellin's hypothesis; nor is he competent to do so. The possibilities inherent within psychoanalysis to explain religion trump the scholarly concerns of other disciplines and allow Freud a significant degree of creative intellectual autonomy. "But apart from this we shall venture to maintain independence of the authorities and to 'proceed along our own track'", he maintains (Freud 1939: 37).

The basic narrative of *Moses and Monotheism* is simple enough and, in key respects, repeats the narrative of the primal horde in *Totem and Taboo*. The hypothesis that Moses was murdered by his chosen people is nonetheless cru-cial to Freud's entire reconstruction of the story of Moses, the Exodus and the persistence of monotheism. Upon the death of the Pharaoh Akhenaten, the monotheistic religion he established was rooted out by the priests of Amun, whose gods and clerical power he displaced in favour of the exclusive worship of his god of the light of the sun, Aten. Not only was the religion suppressed, but all memory and physical traces of it, including Akhenaten's very existence, were all but wiped out in the restoration of the old polytheism. Moses, in his desire to preserve the monotheism to which he remained faithful, took a band of socially marginal Semitic labourers and pastoralists out of Egypt and forced his religion upon them. Moses replaced the concrete religiosity associated with their polytheistic pantheon with the demand to worship one god only, an invisible deity representing the abstract ideals of justice and truth (Ma'at) idealized by Akhenaten. Moses also introduced circumcision, an Egyptian custom, as another means of forging and "consecrating" the people's new identity and establishing them as "a superior substitute for the Egyptians he had left behind", thereby making them "at least the equals of the Egyptians" and by keeping them apart "from all foreigners", just as the Egyptians had done before them (Freud 1939: 30).

At some point during their long wanderings in the desert, these substitute Egyptians found the severity of the moral commands and the harsh renunciation of instinct Moses forced upon them unbearable, with the result that they rebelled and murdered him. Eventually, they encountered residing in the area of Midian other Semitic tribes, whose volcano god, Yahweh, they adopted. The exiles from Egypt and their descendants fused with these Midianite tribes. Freud thought that the memory of the murdered Egyptian Moses and the religion he gave them had somehow remained preserved within their collective unconscious. Freud's account of the many vicissitudes experienced by these wanderers is highly imaginative and its logic too intricately detailed to completely reproduce here. One important part of his narrative has these exiles from Egypt encountering and adopting a "second Moses", in the form of a Midianite leader, and merging with his people. Freud concludes that within the newly merged tribes of the Egyptian remnant and the Midianite Yahweh adherents, the former constituted an "influential minority [who were] culturally superior to the rest" (1939: 39). The latent repressed memory of the original Mosaic religion and the murder of Moses ultimately revived, bringing with it renewed painful feelings of guilt and remorse. Very much along the lines of the distortions and displacements involved in dreaming, so, too, this human remnant fused its own memory fragments of the exodus from Egypt under the leadership of the first Moses and their former monotheistic beliefs with those of the new Yahweh religion (*ibid.*: 40–53) and the new leader, the Midianite Moses. However, Freud thinks that behind their conscious devotion to Yahweh lay deeper unconscious memories of and loyalty to the original Egyptian god and the first Moses, which gradually resurfaced. These revived memories, the "return of the repressed", altered and distorted as they inevitably would have been, effected a transformation within the Yahweh religion, whose form was gradually "changed back into conformity, or even perhaps identity, with the original religion of Moses" (*ibid.*: 47).

Freud is clear that the Yahweh religion was inferior to the original Mosaic religion, given its violence and narrow-mindedness. The new religion was likely not even genuinely monotheistic in so far as Yahweh demanded merely the simple and primitive narcissistic gratification of being worshipped as the most powerful among many gods whose existence was not in question. The "highly spiritualized notion of god" as a single deity (*ibid.*: 50), the disdain for sacrifice, magic and ceremonial in favour of the ideals of justice and truth (Ma'at) that were bequeathed from Akhenaten and the first Moses persisted in the unconscious memory of the descendants of the Exodus. These memory traces were preserved, emerging gradually and taking shape in the form of a tradition that grew stronger over the centuries, allowing "the people of Israel to survive all the blows of fate and that kept them alive" (*ibid.*). Freud hypothesizes that it was most likely the prophets, an "unending succession of men who were not linked to Moses in their origin but were enthralled by the great and mighty tradition which had grown up little by little in obscurity", who kept the memory of Moses and his teaching alive in their tireless preaching of the:

> old Mosaic doctrine – that the deity disdained sacrifice and ceremonial and asked only for faith and a life in truth and justice (Ma'at). The efforts of the Prophets had a lasting success; the doctrines with which they re-established the old faith became the permanent content of the Jewish religion. It is honour enough to the Jewish people that they could preserve such a tradition and produce men who gave it a voice – even though the initiative to it came from outside, from a great foreigner.
>
> (Freud 1939: 51)

The teachings of the prophets and their loyalty to the first Moses were not sufficient, however, to keep the monotheistic spirit from the Amarna period of Akhenaten alive. Conventional communicative means would have been insufficient to support the survival and transmission of a religious tradition over centuries marked by the repeated upheavals and cultural displacements that must have been experienced by the descendants of the Egyptian remnant. As far as Freud is concerned, oral transmission alone cannot explain the survival of the Mosaic tradition over the long centuries separating the Exodus, the murder of Moses and the long years of desert wandering that constitute the chasms of time and space between the original monotheism and its later revival. Freud writes:

> The priestly narrative seeks to establish continuity between its contemporary period and the remote Mosaic past; it seeks to disavow precisely what we have described as the most striking fact about Jewish religious history, namely that there is a yawning gap between the law-giving of Moses and the later Jewish religion. (Freud 1939: 65)

Against the traditional priestly account, Freud argues that Judaism only became "permanently established" after a centuries-long historical interval, a "delayed effect" in need of explanation (*ibid.*: 66). In the place of history that is unable to provide a plausible explanation for this phenomenon, Freud attempts both to fill in the gap between the Exodus and the Midianite period, and to explain the survival of Jewish monotheism. To do this, he searches for clues outside the biblical narrative by asking the question, "where do we meet with a similar phenomenon?" (*ibid*.: 66). For him, the answer is clear: psychoanalysis.

## Trauma as history and the history of a trauma

As has been argued earlier, a central explanatory thread that connects all Freud's works on religion is his analogy between the development of the internal psychic world of individuals and the unfolding of culture, expressed in the well-known Freudian formulation that ontogeny (individual development) recapitulates phylogeny (development of the species). Although Freud is well aware of the limitations within the analogy linking the individual and society, he maintains it nonetheless with some interesting results that bear consideration here. The Oedipal fantasies of bisexual desire, crime and punishment encode within individual psychosexual development the experiences of the ancient parricides of prehistory, the factual reality of which Freud appears at times to insist upon, as evidenced by his bold declaration at the conclusion of *Totem and Taboo*: "In the beginning was the Deed!" While it would be foolhardy to accept this *literal* reading of prehistory in *exactly the way* Freud described it, there is an interesting and important line of contemporary scholarly argument that attempts to penetrate more deeply into the truth it determines to lie within the heart of Freud's argument. This line of inquiry, advanced by scholars such as Jan Assmann, Robert Paul and Richard Bernstein, maintains that the notion of a concrete reality involving a parricidal crime carried out in history is not essential to a theoretical justification of the central points within Freud's theory of religion. With the exception of Assmann, (who doesn't devote much attention to it), Paul and Bernstein also question the validity of the charge of Lamarckism levelled against Freud by so many of his critics. What these authors find of value in Freud's psychoanalytic theory of religion is the ways in which he illuminates the inner dynamics of the religious mind and their *implications* for the study of culture. Bernstein and Paul would agree, I think, with Assmann's statement that, since Freud, "no theory of culture can afford not to take these concepts into consideration" (1997: 215).

Assmann, Bernstein and Paul share a particular interest in Freud's thesis concerning the transmission of the religious tradition and the preservation of the religious identity of the Jews through centuries of violent persecutions that continually endangered their survival. These authors are aware that there is something in the nature of emotional trauma that leaves a psychic imprint on the human mind where the event(s) and/or its impact is repeated in unconscious fantasies and manifest symptoms, whether or not the trauma itself is accessible to memory. Any clinician who has worked with trauma victims knows this to be the case, and Freud knew it, too. What is in part distinctive about Freud's studies on religion and culture is how he uses his clinical experience as a lens to more sharply focus his theories on the repressed origins of society. The psycho-analytic formula "trauma–defence–latency–neurosis–return of the repressed" that charts the course of an individual neurosis is applied analogously to the cultural trajectory that begins with a father-murder, the memory of which is buried within the unconscious until some social crisis provokes it into [re] enactment in highly distorted or mutated expressions and symbolic forms.

Assmann interprets the Moses narrative in terms of a conceptual distinc-tion between "mnemohistory" and history – that is, between those events that are only remembered (legend, myth), and those belonging to the historical record (archaeology, recorded events). Despite the fact that there is no evidence whatsoever that Moses ever existed *within history*, Moses nonetheless persists as an extremely important "figure of memory". Curiously, the Egyptian Pharaoh Akhenaten, the founder of monotheism, is a figure of history whose existence has been established through the archaeological record rather than through memory (Assmann 1997: 2, 23). After the Egyptian ruler's death, the Aten religion was abolished, along with the monuments and other public material representations of its existence and its founder's reign, all stricken from the ancient historical record. The name of Akhenaten was relegated to oblivion, his existence only discovered in the archaeological investigations of the nineteenth century, prior to which there was "virtually no memory" (*ibid.*: 23) of him at all. With Moses, however, the opposite is true: while there is a long religious tradi-tion revering him as the liberator of the Jews and the creator of Judaic religious law, there are "no traces" confirming his material historical existence (*ibid.*).

In an argument clearly influenced by a psychoanalytic perspective, Assmann describes the entire Amarna period of Akhenaten as emotionally traumatic for the Egyptian people, who were forced to accept that their former religion and the way of life it organized and sustained were false and that their gods were nothing more than valueless idols that must be destroyed and repudiated in favour of a single, heliocentric deity, Aten. Assmann describes this experi-ence of cultural destruction as leaving unbearable traumatic memories that could only be tolerated through a process of social and psychological "encryp-tion" and "dislocation" that was eventually fixed upon the Jews (1997: 5). The traumatic experiences associated with Akhenaten's religious revolution and the eventual restoration of the old gods were marked not only by violence and destruction, but also by a deadly plague that swept the land sometime shortly thereafter (*ibid.*: 25). Assmann argues that this series of violent events unleashed by the monotheistic revolution, followed by the onset of a deadly plague, left an imprint of what must have been accumulated traumatic shock that penetrated deep within the consciousness of the people, lingering there long after the generations who lived through it were gone. This portrayal parallels clinical experience since it is invariably the case that the psychic impact of the *effects* of severe trauma is *never* abolished. Rather, these effects take shelter within dissociated, split off or repressed parts of the mind that become saturated with their toxic psychic residue.

Depending on the nature of the trauma and the individual involved, its effects are also encrypted in the body, which keeps a kind of mnemonic score that is beyond and beneath the capacity for memory. This psychoanalytic understanding of the impact of trauma upon individuals further parallels Assmann's suggestion that the experiences of the entire Amarna period continued to survive in the permanent *affective impressions* that colonized and shaped the changing contents of subsequent new experiences long after the original trauma was "forgotten". The Jew, or, rather, the image of the Jew, eventually stood in for the no-longer remembered Akhenaten and the destructive disruptions associated with his reign. The abstraction "Jew" became emblematic of the "religious enemy par excellence – as atheist, iconoclast, sacrilegious criminal". In this way Jewish individuals are subsumed within an antagonistic image of "the Jew" as the distilled representation of displaced, fantasized traumatic experiences and distorted memories in the form of "the return of the suppressed memory of Akhenaten" (Assmann 1997: 43). Here Assmann echoes and reframes Freud's insight that religions "owe their compulsive power to the *return of the repressed*; they are reawakened memories of very ancient, forgotten, highly emotional episodes of human history ... the strength of religion lies not in its *material*, but in its *historical* truth" (in Bernstein 1998: 118).

## Memory and the varieties of "truthful" experience

Freud's important distinction between "material" and "historical" truth fits well with Assmann's distinction between recorded history and mnemohistory. Assmann's idea helps to illustrate that the Moses of Freud's study is indeed the man of memory, not history. There are occasions in the text where it would appear that Freud might be in agreement with Assmann. If this is the case, why then does Freud also insist that Moses was a figure of history and the victim of an actual murder that stands in a long line of similar patricidal murders that have been repeated countless times over thousands of years (1939: 81)? Is the reader to take Freud's statement, "I have no hesitation in declaring that men have always known (in this special way) that they once possessed a primal father and killed him" (*ibid.*: 101) at face value, as a statement of concrete fact and nothing more? Freud's parenthetical "in this special way" may suggest the possibility that multiple meanings are contained within this statement of apparent fact. Considered in the light of Assmann's contrasting ideas of history and mnemohistory, Freud's distinction between "material" and "historical" truth offers interesting ways of reframing his vacillating statements related to the actual murder of a historical Moses. A reframing of Freud's argument from Assmann's perspective might help the reader work through Freud's own apparent hesitations in situating his Moses narrative within the realm of objective or "material" fact. Freud generates further confusion as he insists that these "facts" are not the most important parts of his theory after all. As if this were not puzzling enough, in the last section of *Moses and Monotheism*, Freud is unequivocally clear that the "historical" truth of the story is different from, more important and "truthful" than, its "material" or objectively factual truth. For Freud, "historical" in this context does not necessarily mean factual truth, while his term "material" truth does.

What then constitutes the "historical" truth of the Moses story for Freud? Here, Assmann can again offer assistance. As a figure of biblical narrative and thus of mnemohistory, Moses has defining importance for the "one who remembers" (Assmann 1997: 148), namely Freud and the Jews. The focus of mnemohistory is on the past "as it is remembered" and concentrates on those relevant elements embedded within a people's collective memory. Mnemohistory explores the ways in which the memories of the past shape identity by "haunting" the experience of the lived present (*ibid*.: 9). For the historian of memory, the truth of memory is not located in "factuality" but in "actuality". This means that truth lies in the *impact* of past events on the present, events that exist only within memory and for which there is little or no basis of conventionally recorded empirical evidence. In a statement that deeply resonates with Freud, Assmann describes the "truth" of mnemohistory as residing in "the identity that it shapes" (*ibid*.: 14). In a fashion that has important parallels with clinical analytic practice, mnemohistory analyses the mythical dimensions of a tradition's narrative self-rendering in order to discover its "hidden agenda" (*ibid*.: 9–10). From this perspective, myth does not connote an inferior or false form of the expression of a set of truths. Rather, mnemohistory records, as it were, the very real impact or set of psychic impressions of events, whether or not they can be said to have actually occurred in the external world. What this approach suggests is the assumption that *something* happened to cause traumatic impact. This is what is important in mnemohistory, and what really counts far more than establishing beyond a shadow of a doubt the concrete facts of any specific case. Similarly, in clinical practice with traumatized patients, the analyst does not need to know what happened to know that something, or a series of somethings, occurred that caused serious harm. This would be what the idea of "historical" truth means in the clinical situation, something Freud would have encountered repeatedly in working with patients. In *Moses and Monotheism*, Freud is working with both the paradigms of psychoanalysis and (psycho) history, where he attempts to "unearth a truth that was never remembered, but instead repressed and which only [Freud] is able to bring forth as a shocking opposite of everything consciously remembered and transmitted" (Assmann 1997: 145).

From this perspective, it is possible to see how the "historical" as opposed to the "material" truth of religion may be interpreted to correspond with the psychoanalytic or *historical* truth expressed in the individual Oedipal fantasy. The Greek tragedy presents in literary and mythic form an organization or configuration of psychological processes and conflicts that Sophocles' audience could easily recognize as their own: that transgressions of culturally established moral rules initiated by forbidden desires result in loss, isolation, punishment, shame, guilt and remorse. Paul describes the "historical truth" encoded in the memory traces of the symbol of the Oedipal murder and its disruptive affects in a way that lifts it out of the specifics of cultural particularism so that its relevance to a more universal aspect of human experience can emerge. Paul's argument bypasses the controversies surrounding the concept of cultural inheritance and is worth quoting at length. He writes:

> My answer to this question [of inherited memory] is that it arises from the intersection of two phenomena. One is the unconscious guilt that individuals feel, regardless of cultural setting, for fantasies of a broadly Oedipal nature: fantasies involving some interplay of feelings of passionate attachment, jealousy, sexual excitement, murderous rage, and dread of punishment. The other is immersion in a sociocultural system organized around a shared and valorized myth that by its particular symbolism is able to arouse, address, and organize in a culture- and ego-syntonic way the individual's own powerful but inchoate fantasies, molding them into a personality suited to abide by the rules and conventions governing the social system.　　　　　(Paul 1996: 171)

Thus, the psychic dispositions and conflicts experienced by human beings over the course of their psychological development can be understood as memory traces or archaic inheritance (*archaische Erbschaft*) not of specific characteristics but rather of universal mental processes and states of mind. These universal mental states comprise a diverse range of psychic and personality organizations whose specific expressions are shaped, mediated and generally filled in according to specific familial and general relational dynamics and cultural contexts. The "memory traces" of human experience that are shaped and reshaped over the changing course of cultural evolution are indeed passed down or transmitted from generation to generation in so far as *they represent the general psychological dynamics of sustained and continuous interactions between the internal worlds of all human beings and their specific environments.* Although

Freud's language is outmoded, it might be said that in the sense just described, "archaic inheritance" is constituted by the phylogenetic elements pertaining to innate *dispositions*, which are nothing more than human capacities or tendencies that take shape along particular developmental lines in response to specific, contextual external stimuli. As Bernstein puts it, Freud's argument amounts to the insight that "[e]ach of us is born with a set of dispositions that shape our individual contingent psychic lives and development" (1998: 53).

Freud was well aware that human social and cultural existence necessarily demands engagement in a constant process of negotiation between private desire and public obligation, a continuing dialectic of renunciation or modification of forbidden needs in response to cultural prohibitions that begin with the infant's earliest experiences within the family. That these infinitely multiple repetitions of the negotiation of desire and renunciation that structure the relations between self and other are rarely smooth or without conflict explains the genesis of neurosis. This, in turn, can provide a model for understanding the complex dynamics of religion. We may recall here Loewald's reframing of Freud's theory of the universal meaning of the Oedipal experience with all its contradictory dynamics of love and longing, and hatred and repudiation that inform and shape individual psychosexual development. Along with Freud, Loewald also recognizes that in order to achieve the autonomy and freedom of mature self-development, the internalized *parental agency* has to die in everyone. As a normal part of the maturation process, whose goal is an autonomously based ethical life that is a hallmark of mental health, the individual has little choice but to "kill" the internal parental/paternal authority that demands obedience to heteronomous norms. This requirement of healthy psychological development towards adulthood inevitably brings guilt and remorse along with it, which, in optimal circumstances, motivate an eventual loving reconciliation between the grown child and his parents.

The Oedipal love of childish fantasy eventually transforms into adult filial love of parents as real human beings who, although related, are also distinct and different from oneself. Unthinking obedience to external rules of conduct that are a necessary part of childhood is gradually replaced by autonomous ethical capacity, where the mature individual embraces abstract moral norms and ethical action, thus making his own the moral heritage handed down from his fathers. Moral values organized around truth and justice and the ethical life it entails are valued for their own sake. Loewald is able to retain the depth and relevance of Freud's Oedipal theory without resorting to the thesis that a *concrete* parricide occupies its core since it isn't necessary to the theory's own "historical" truth. Feelings of transgression, a sense that one has committed "crimes" of various sorts that threaten punishment and generate guilt, are ubiquitous features in the development of an individual life. Unfortunately, this process too often includes a degree of painful trauma along the way. The extent of the psychic damage inflicted by trauma depends in part upon the individual's familial and social environment and psychic constitutional dispositions. From all this knowledge derived during his years of clinical experience, Freud was able to formulate some of his most important psychoanalytic insights, which he applied to the study of culture, morality and religion. He demonstrated that the dynamics of the transmission of religious tradition are connected with the dynamics of trauma; thus, the psychoanalytic understanding of the inner world of individuals leads to the discovery of not only their own "historical" truth, but that of culture. In his 1935 postscript to "An Autobiographical Study", published ten years earlier, Freud describes his investigations of the origins of religion and morality this way:

> I perceived ever more clearly that the events of human history, the inter-actions between human nature, cultural development and the precipi-tates of primeval experiences (the most prominent example of which is religion) are no more than a reflection of the dynamic conflicts between the ego, the id and the super-ego, which psycho-analysis studies in the individual – are the very same processes repeated upon a wider stage.
>
> (Freud 1935: 72)

## Spirit and the light of the mind

We are now in a better position to examine and interpret what Freud means by "historical" truth and the theoretical implications of this concept with respect to his treatment of Moses. For Freud, the monotheism of the Egyptian Akhenaten represents a developmental achievement of inestimable impor-tance; it signifies a higher level of sophisticated mental functioning inaugu-rating new capacities for ethics and scientific reason. Freud notes that the reconceptualization of divine power from its more primitive expressions in "barbarous polytheism" (1939: 91) to a focus on the natural world symbol-ized by the sun light of the god Aten signifies an important step in human mental progress towards spirituality or intellectuality[2] (*Der Fortschritt in der Geistigkeit*). Freud writes:

> With magnificent inflexibility [Akhenaten] resisted every temptation to magical thought, and he rejected the illusion, so dear to Egyptians in particular, of a life after death. In an astonishing presentiment of later scientific discovery he recognized in the *energy of solar radiation* the source of all life on earth and worshipped it as the symbol of the power of his god. He boasted of his joy in the creation and of his life in Ma'at (truth and justice). (*Ibid.*: 59, emphasis added)

Here Akhenaten is the ancient precursor of both the modern scientific mentality and the intellectual values of truth and moral justice so valued by Freud. Akhenaten's divinization of the sun symbolically prefigures the movement towards the establishment of the light of reason over the darkness of superstition that was a central theme of Enlightenment thought centuries later. A Freudian perspective easily allows for the interpretation that Akhenaten was a precursor of the psychoanalytic method in so far as it also seeks to illuminate the darkness of the mind with the intellectual light of its theories and techniques. It is not difficult to appreciate how a figure such as Akhenaten would have appealed to Freud, who was himself an *"Aufklärer* (committed to the Enlightenment ideals of universal science and rational critique)", as Bernstein points out (1998: 86). Although Akhenaten's monotheistic gift to humanity was short-lived in his own time, it was not completely destroyed; it survived through Moses and his creation, the Jewish people, and the apotheosis of the light of the mind they eventually ushered into existence.

Freud was an *Aufklärer*, but he was also a Jew. Both these aspects of his self-identity were equally important for him and without contradiction. In the 1930 preface to the Hebrew translation of *Totem and Taboo*, Freud acknowledges that although he is "completely estranged from the religion of his fathers – *as well as from every other religion*" (Freud 1930b: xv, emphasis added), he feels himself as a Jew "in his essential nature". Although Freud did not embrace but in fact repudiated the beliefs and ritual practices of Judaism (and all religions), he did nonetheless claim for himself what he called the "very essence" of Jewishness. In the very last line of this short text, Freud hints that this "essence" may have something to do with "unprejudiced science" (*ibid.*). The question bears asking: how, in the light of everything Freud has said about the inimical relationship between the religious and scientific attitudes to reality, Judaism (considered as religion) could possibly be compatible with any form of scientific ethos? The answer to this puzzling question lies in a deeper understanding of Freud's idea of "Jewish essence" within his interpretation of the Akhenatian/Mosaic legacy. The memory traces of this legacy resurface in the consciousness of the Jews hundreds of years after the Exodus, with the result that the Midianite Yahweh becomes reshaped and absorbed within the image of the original Mosaic father. The traumatic imprint of that "shameful sequence of events" culminating in the murder of Moses, that "outstanding father-figure" (Freud 1939: 89), the abandonment of his religion and the adoption of the *"Baalim"* (local gods) of foreigners, had a powerful effect on the "inner life" of the entire Jewish people, encrypting the Exodus experience within their unconscious (1939: 69–70) minds.

Bearing in mind that for Freud, the "other" always resides within the mind so that individual psychology is at the same time *always* a social psychology, his arguments that phylogenetic memory traces are a feature of ontogenetic development *by analogy* make sense, whether we agree with them or not. It is a cornerstone of psychoanalysis that individual minds are necessarily socially constituted by virtue of the fact that they develop within familial, social and cultural environments. It is also apparent throughout Freud's work in such key formulations as his theory of the Oedipus complex and the construction of the superego. For Freud, it is an incontrovertible fact that human psychology is profoundly relational. The perspective provided by "group psychology" motivates Freud to "look about for analogies, for facts that are at least of a similar nature" (1939: 70), and this he finds in positioning the psychoanalysis of individuals with respect to cultures and religious traditions. As the developing human being must learn to renounce forbidden desire, transform and relocate his instinctual impulses into the pursuit of the higher goals of culture and morality, so must the authoritarian and murderous dynamics of the primitive tribe transform themselves into more egalitarian societies organized in terms of cooperative altruistic values if they are to survive. The long history of countless primal hordes and their murdered patriarchs stands behind Moses and his murder. At the same time, this violent history is *also* the history of the painstaking progress of the gradual repudiation of submission to the imperatives of brute drives and destructive impulses. It is also the history of the renunciation of magic and superstition as the basis of science and ethical life, and their eventual replacement by reasoned thought, evidence-based knowledge, autonomous moral values and universal laws regulating human conduct. In Freud's view, the Jews are the agents of this historical human progress (*Der Fortschritt in der Geistigkeit*). The Jews managed to preserve and transmit the legacy of Akhenaten that was transmitted to them by Moses, culminating in the teaching of the prophets and the entire subsequent edifice of Jewish ethics.

In keeping with the Mosaic ban on magic and ceremonial, it follows that the god of Jewish monotheism may not be named or seen or represented in concrete images. For Freud, God is an invisible, abstract entity of law and justice. He also represents the triumph of the patriarchal principle of spirit and intellect, and language and symbol, over the inarticulate and sensuous maternal principle. The belief in an unseen god presupposes the developmental achievement of mind over body, and reason over disordered passion, that is made possible through the renunciation of instinct and desire with all the "necessary psychological consequences" this process entails (Freud 1939: 113). The "turning from the mother to the father points ... to a victory of intellectuality over sensuality ... since maternity is proved by the evidence of the senses while paternity is a hypothesis ... Taking sides in this way with a thought-process in preference to a sense perception has proved to be a momentous step" (*ibid.*: 114) in the direction of civilization. With this, the Jews rediscover and redivinize the ideals of truth and justice whose repressed source is the Akhenatian/Mosaic gift of Ma'at. Freud undoes that repression with the explanatory force of psychoanalysis that he has dedicated to unearthing the "historical" truth of religion since his 1907 paper. Freud's consistently Feuerbachian approach (Bernstein 1998: 66) demystifies the invisible monotheistic Jewish god and relocates him within the internal dynamics of the human mind. Monotheism is the creation of the Egyptian Akhenaten; the Jews are the creation of his loyal servant, Moses; the Jewish god represents the restoration of Moses's leadership and the worship of Aten. This is what Freud means when he describes this process as the return of the repressed.

The historical truth of the Jews, then, lies in their own struggle against desire, impulse and unbridled efforts for drive satisfaction in order to achieve a higher, more creative and cooperative level of existence, one defined by morality and law that structures and mediates all the social relationships and institutions of civilization. As far as Freud is concerned, this is their gift to humanity. The "rejection of magic and mysticism", the "invitation to advances in intellectual-ity" and the "encouragement of sublimations" (1939: 85–6) are contained in the "permanent imprint" of the monotheistic legacy of Egypt on the Jewish character. The belief in a non-visible god establishes Jewish monotheism as a "religion of drive renunciation", which is the necessary precondition for ethical life (*ibid.*: 118). Over time, the Jews took pride in their capacity for intellectual-ity and the cultural benefits associated with it. As the Jews progressed in their advances towards the achievement of intellectuality or spirituality (*Geistigkeit*), they gained an increasing self-respect that, in turn, provided them with fresh motivations for further intellectual work and renunciation of drives (*ibid.*: 123). Moreover, the memory traces associated with a sense of being specially chosen by the paternal Moses transformed into the narcissistically gratifying consciousness of being chosen by the father-god, and being in possession of the moral truth associated with adherence to his sacred law, another factor contrib-uting to the survival of Jewish identity and religious tradition. In a restatement of the central thesis of *Totem and Taboo*, Freud asserts that this process revives and re-enacts a far older experience located in the earliest days of the human family, long vanished from consciousness (*ibid.*: 129) but preserved within unconscious memory traces transmitted through psychical deposits, the full impact of which took centuries. In this way, Freud can conclude that "the idea of a single great god" is a "completely justified memory" (*ibid.*: 130), no matter how distorted, containing the "historical" truth of the Jewish people.

Freud finds further confirmation of his theory with the appearance of Christianity, the "son religion" that comes closest to bringing the ancient par-ricide to conscious awareness. The inherited sense of guilt associated with the primal parricide was not restricted to the Jews alone, but "caught hold of all the Mediterranean peoples as a dull *malaise*, a premonition of calamity for which no one could suggest a reason", Freud claims (1939: 135). It took a Roman Jew, Paul, to continue the primal history and articulate its memory in the distorted form of an "original sin" behind which stands the original forgotten act of parricide that contaminates all humanity. Freud's psychoanalytic description of Paul portrays him as an individual of "innately religious disposition" in whose mind "dark traces of the past lurked", poised to break through to consciousness (*ibid.*: 86–7). As noted in the previous chapter, the crucifixion of Jesus provided the blood sacrifice required for the price of atonement for the earlier crime, thereby ensuring the victory of Christianity, the "son religion", that proceeds out of the older "father religion" of Judaism. The resurrection both reveals and conceals that Jesus was "the resurrected Moses" behind whom, of course, stands the primal father, now transfigured as the son who replaces him (*ibid.*: 90). "It is plausible to conjecture that remorse for the murder of Moses provided the stimulus for the wishful phantasy of the Messiah, who was to return and lead his people to redemption and the promised world-domination", Freud writes (*ibid.*: 89). For Freud, this is the "historical truth" of Christianity.

The challenge to Judaism mounted by Jesus represents and conceals a further re-enactment of the rebellious brothers of the primal horde. The death of Jesus holds the promise of expiation and atonement for that ancient crime. While the Jews continue to "disavow the father's murder" (*ibid.*: 90), the Apostle Paul takes a different approach in admitting to the reality of original sin that, in Freud's view, covers over the "unnameable crime" for which Jesus appeared to guiltlessly atone. In this way, Paul partially liberates unconscious inherited memory by transforming the story of the crucifixion into a message of hope and salvation founded upon blood sacrifice. With Paul, the "blissful sense of being chosen was replaced by the liberating sense of redemption" (*ibid.*: 135), and in this way Christianity is able to offer some measure of absolution and relief from the burden of guilt borne by humanity over countless generations. Yet the price of retrieval of this piece of distorted memory is paid for with regression to an older polytheistic religiosity within Christianity. The story of the primal parricide and the cannibalism associated with it breaks through in the Christian ritual of the Eucharist, which both commemorates the killing of Jesus while recalling the totem meal through Jesus's invitation that his followers eat his flesh and drink his blood (Paul 1996: 201). "He who eats my flesh and drinks my blood abides in me, and I in him", Jesus proclaims in the Gospel of John (*ibid.*). The symbolic act of ingestion of the god, thereby absorbing some of his power, is enshrined in Christianity's central ritual of the Eucharist, which itself signifies the presence of another trace of the return of the repressed. Freud was certainly aware of this Christian ritual and its central role in the liturgy. With this knowledge of the Eucharist, Freud was able to conclude that over time, Christianity "took up components from many other sources, renounced a number of characteristics of pure monotheism and adapted itself in many details to the rituals of the other Mediterranean peoples. It was as though Egypt was taking vengeance once more on the heirs of Akhenaten" (Freud 1939: 136).

## Moses, the man

Freud's fascination with Moses existed long before the publication of *Moses and Monotheism*. The powerful attraction of Moses and the degree to which he captured Freud's imagination is vividly apparent in his only essay on aesthetics, "The Moses of Michelangelo" (1914c). This remarkable essay attests to how deeply Freud was moved by the beauty and power of Michelangelo's sculpture, which he first saw in the church of San Pietro in Vincoli, Rome, in 1901. On every subsequent visit to this city that he loved, Freud would visit the statue; in his mind, Rome and the Moses statue were inseparably linked (Blum 1991: 516). The essay on Michelangelo's Moses is a thorough and detailed aesthetic analysis of what Freud saw in the fine intricacies of Michelangelo's exquisite design. "No piece of statuary", he confessed, "has ever made a stronger impression on me than this" (Freud 1914c: 213). Much psychological speculation has sprung up around Freud's personal "identification" with Moses, and while there may be a great deal of truth in many of these theories, I am not sure they tell us very much about the depth of meaning and special attraction that the figure of Moses had for him. Freud's meditation on the statue amounts to his own character study of the Moses imagined by Michelangelo (*ibid.*: 221). More significantly, I contend that the core insights of this earlier Moses text are most richly illuminated when viewed as a theoretical precursor that anticipates and encapsulates the central thesis of *Moses and Monotheism*. When interpreted within the framework of the later text, "The Moses of Michelangelo" reads like its preview or dress rehearsal, in a highly condensed and concentrated form. Some critics are concerned that Freud's interpretation of this work of art "strays" from the "reality of the Moses statue" by relying on "irrelevant Bible texts" and a series of other "fundamental mistakes" and "gross misinterpretations" (Bremer 1976: 62, 73–5). As important as these concerns may be, they offer little help in grasping the deeper meaning and significance of Freud's text, which can be most fully appreciated when it is read within the context of *Moses and Monotheism*.

I agree with Blum's observation that four dimensions of the Moses figure converge for Freud in this statue: the Moses of history, the Moses of the Bible, the Moses of Michelangelo and the Moses of Freud (Blum 1991: 517). Blum's insight helps to explain the contradictions in Freud's treatment of Moses at times as a figure of history, and at other times as a figure of memory. Freud's analysis of the Moses statue also clarifies Freud's distinction between "material" and "historical" truth, in part because the Moses that Freud sees does not line up with the Moses portrayed in the biblical narrative. The frozen action Freud sees depicted in Michelangelo's Moses represents the triumph of rational self-control over the gratification of blind impulse. Freud's astonishingly detailed examination of the statue shows "not the inception of a violent action but the remains of a movement that has already taken place" (1914c: 229). In contrast, the biblical account portrays Moses as overcome with rage at the Israelites' blasphemous backsliding into idol worship when he witnesses their veneration of the golden calf. Moses comes upon this repugnant scene immediately after having received the laws from God. In his uncontrollable fury at the people's idolatrous behaviour, Moses smashes to the ground the tablets upon which the laws were inscribed. However, Freud's Moses does something quite different. Rather than give in to his violent urge to "spring up and take vengeance and forget the Tables", Freud tells us, *his* Moses restrains himself for the sake of the law (*ibid.*: 229). Interpreted from Freud's psychoanalytic perspective, Michelangelo's sculpture depicts a Moses poised at the psychic crossroads leading to paths either of gratification or renunciation. Despite Moses's intense rage and "pain mingled with contempt" (*ibid.*), he undertakes a massive effort at self-restraint and the renunciation of powerful impulse. In other words, Moses opts to preserve the law. This is the decisive moment that ensures his people will in the future embark on the road towards intellectuality. In his close examination of the Moses statue, Freud detects the profound intensity of the conflict beneath the lines of its face, in the "traces of suppressed movement" apparent in its middle finger, and in an "attitude of projected action" contained in the position of its foot (*ibid.*: 230). Freud's Michelangelo has captured Moses at the apex of his internal battle against his own destructive impulses. The statue embodies the terrible moment of a mind at war with itself, where self-interested desire must ultimately capitulate to the higher demands of other-directed ethical obligation. Intellect triumphs over thoughtless passion in the service of protecting and preserving the moral law.

Freud concludes his essay with the explicit acknowledgment that the imagined Moses of Michelangelo's artistic vision is superior to the "historical or traditional Moses" who acquiesced to the forces of blind impulse when he destroyed the divine law. That Moses gave up, and gave himself up, at least momentarily, by betraying himself, his people and his god. The Moses of Michelangelo and Freud, on the other hand, repudiates the baser demands of unreflected desire for the sake of the moral law, the cornerstone of civilization. Michelangelo's marble figure of Moses fixes for eternity that delicate moment where humanity broke through barbarism to embrace instead the values of justice and truth (Ma'at). The great physical power embodied in this Moses stands as a "concrete expression of the highest mental achievement that is possible in man, that of struggling successfully against an inward passion for the sake of a cause to which he has devoted himself", Freud concludes (1914c: 233). This is the "historical" truth memorialized in the statue of a man who likely never existed, but is remembered to this day as the giver and guardian of the moral law and the initiator of the progress in intellectuality, the highest achievement of humanity and culture. "The Moses of Michelangelo" is unequivocally clear that Moses is indeed, as Assmann would say, a figure of memory, and for Freud a figure of historical truth. The "fact" of his material existence, as Freud consistently maintained, was never the main point.

# FOUR

# Telepathy and the "occult" unconscious

If I had my life to live over again I should devote myself to psychical research rather than to psychoanalysis.　　(Freud in Jones 1957: 392)

The simple truth is that we simply don't know what is going on here.
(Kripal 2010: 26)

## Psychoanalysis and telepathy

In the third and final volume of his biography of Freud, Ernest Jones (1957) devotes a chapter to Freud's interest in "occultism". While Jones's treatment of the subject is on the whole detailed and fair, he does not bother to hide his strong disdain for the "occult". Jones is clear in his expression of contempt for anything to do with occultism, but he also fears that psychoanalysis could in any fashion be associated with it. Jones is especially bothered by Freud's willingness to consider that thought-transference or, as Freud sometimes referred to it, "telepathy", could be a legitimate object of psychoanalytic inquiry. As far as Jones is concerned, the widespread interest in telepathy in his own time was little more than dismal evidence of an immature human tendency to gullibility and "primitive" thinking (*ibid.*: 375). He worried that any serious consideration of "telepathy", or "thought-transference" (*Gedankenübertragung*), as Freud often described it, could only discredit psychoanalysis (*ibid.*: 395) by associating it with the murky world of fraudulent mediums, séances, table-rapping and the conjuring of spirits that so powerfully captivated the popular imagination in *fin-de-siècle* Europe and America (Oppenheim 1985; Owen 2004; Treitel 2004; Saler 2012; Luckhurst 2002). Jones, acutely sensitive to the "strong opposition in Britain to psychoanalysis and quack therapists", was understandably concerned that even the most superficial association between psychoanalysis and the "occult" could seriously damage the credibility of this fledgling science of the mind (Maddox 2006: 166). Being himself "far from convinced of the truth of telepathy", Jones (1957: 393) was alarmed by Freud's views, and he was frankly baffled by "the remarkable fact that highly developed critical powers may co-exist in the same person with an unexpected fund of credulity" (*ibid.*: 375). Not only did he try on numerous occasions to talk Freud out of his "incli-nation to accept occult beliefs" (*ibid.*: 381), he also managed at one point to dis-suade him from presenting his first paper on the subject, "Psycho-analysis and Telepathy" (Freud 1921b) before the Berlin Congress in 1922 (Jones 1957: 392).

In the light of this unresolved tension between Jones and Freud, it is interesting to note that a later version of Jones's Freud biography, edited and abridged by Lionel Trilling and Steven Marcus, omits the chapter on the occult entirely (Jones 1961). This unfortunate exclusion illustrates how the subject of telepathy continues to be treated by many of Freud's commentators to this day. While some critics choose to ignore the subject altogether, others dis-miss it as one of Freud's personality quirks, a primitive superstitious remnant within an otherwise profoundly and naturalistically grounded rational mind. In response to one of Jones's exasperated outbursts at his stubborn insistence that telepathic phenomena were at least worthy of psychoanalytic investigation, Freud retorted, perhaps not without some degree of frustration and impatience himself, "When anyone adduces my fall into sin, just answer him calmly that conversion to telepathy is my private affair like my Jewishness, my passion for smoking and many other things, and that the theme of telepathy is in essence alien to psychoanalysis" (Jones 1957: 395–6). However, the significance of Freud's interest in thought-transference, or telepathy, and its potential as a resource for a fuller understanding of the psychoanalytic unconscious, cannot be dismissively reduced to personal idiosyncrasy alone. Moreover, there are striking parallels between Freud's treatment of the "occult" and of religion. Freud's analysis of the occult is equally nuanced and, as with religion, he is willing to consider its "kernel of truth".

The subject of telepathy as a worthy object of psychoanalytic inquiry is understandably vexing, especially when considered in a historical context where the popular craze for the occult was widely condemned. A number of serious-minded people scoffed that so-called occult phenomena were the prod-ucts of nothing more than chicanery and charlatanism that belonged to vulgar parlour entertainment. Freud, however, made clear and critical distinctions between telepathy and occult phenomena, regarding the former as worthy of scientific investigation, but the latter as nonsense. Telepathy in Freud's view was the occult's possible "kernel of truth", although he tended to vacillate fre-quently between acceptance and rejection, perhaps never fully resolving his own ambivalence towards it (Luckhurst 2002: 272). It is unequivocally clear, however, that Freud did not at any point remotely consider supernatural or spiritualist explanations in his efforts to account for the phenomenon of thought-transference, even though its scientific explanation eluded him. As far as he was concerned, the inability to explain it in fully naturalistic and psychoanalytic terms was a temporary state of affairs until such time as science discovered the mechanisms by which it could occur. Freud regarded telepathy as a mode of affective transfer, a form of unconscious communication between people that occurred outside of ordinary verbal discourse. As Anna Freud explained to Jones, "I never could see that he himself believed in more than the possibility of two unconscious minds communicating with each other without the help of a conscious bridge" (in Gay 1988: 445). Freud's published work on the topic appears to confirm his daughter's view.

Although telepathy was associated with the spiritist fantasies of the occult in popular culture, the meaning of the word itself does not hold supernatural connotations, at least not in the way Freud and a number of his more recent commentators use it. The Greek derivation of the word "telepathy" itself, as Nicholas Royle (1995: 71) points out, refers to both distance (*tele*) and feeling, suffering or a feeling of being touched (*pathein*). Steven Pile explains that in Freud's discussions of telepathy, "we can discern a model of the *circulation* of affects over distance – one that is unconscious yet non-repressed; one that allows the unconscious mind to reach beyond the body" (2012: 46). "Telepathy" belongs to "a family of affect-related terms" suggestive of strong affective experiences occurring between people and involving empathy or antipathy (*ibid.*). Eliza Slavet points out that Freud's concept of thought-transference is "inextricably linked" (2009: 141) both linguistically and theoretically with his theories of both intergenerational transmission of trauma and transference in his use of the same root word – *Übertragung* – for these distinct but related psychoanalytic concepts. These concepts share a focus on the subtle complexities and barely discernible dimensions of the multiple forms of communicative possibilities embedded in emotionally intense relationships between human beings.

We have already seen in the previous discussions of *Totem and Taboo* and *Moses and Monotheism*, with their shared arguments supporting unconscious inheritance of deeply guilt-laden memories across the generations, how psychoanalysis is "saturated with the idea of unconscious transmission from the past to the present, from one generation to another, and from one person to another" (Frosh 2012: 258). From this perspective, it is hardly surprising that the related concept of telepathic communication could emerge as an implicit and explicit theme circulating within Freud's thinking about the nature of the unconscious itself. It is worth seriously considering Nicholas Royle's contention that the concept of unconscious telepathic communication is indeed woven throughout "the foundations of psychoanalysis" itself (1995: 63). Lecia Rosenthal's view, which most closely corresponds to my own, contends that Freud's work on telepathy is "best understood as part of the metapsychological Freud and the continued interest in psychoanalysis as a mode of theorizing the unconscious in its unverifiability" (2010: 125). I further agree with Rosenthal that the whole subject of telepathy should be critically approached as a major aspect of Freud's ongoing efforts to elaborate and work out his theory of the unconscious (*ibid.*: 131). His understanding of telepathy as a "transfer of knowledge" (*ibid.*) between individuals suggests the presence of a more general concept of intersubjectivity that locates individual minds as existing within a "network of exchanges and influences for which no definitive origin or end-point can easily be determined" (*ibid.*: 133).

From Freud's perspective, thought-transference is a property of the unconscious, the psychic and affective medium that is generated, for instance, by the analytic pair – analyst and patient – and which simultaneously envelops them both. The multiple forms of unconscious interaction between analyst and patient is the key factor that facilitates the therapeutic action. Freud understood that hopes for therapeutic success required the analyst to use her own unconscious as a communicative instrument for approaching and connecting with the unconscious of the patient. In an early technical paper, "Recommendations to Physicians Practising Psycho-analysis", Freud advises the analyst to:

> turn his own unconscious like a receptive organ towards the transmitting unconscious of the patient. He must adjust himself to the patient as a telephone receiver is adjusted to the transmitting microphone. Just as the receiver converts back into sound-waves the electric oscillations in the telephone line which were set up by sound waves, so the doctor's unconscious is able, from the derivatives of the unconscious which are communicated to him, to reconstruct that unconscious, which has determined the patient's free associations. (Freud 1912a: 115–16)

The analogy with the telephone is significant, suggesting as it does the activation of a physical process of unconscious communication that becomes possible through the arousal of feelings and affects which originate in the body and whose meanings can be tracked through the patient's free associations. Freud's view can be reframed in contemporary neuropsychoanalytic terms as a "right-brain to right-brain communication from one relational unconscious to another" (Schore 2011a: xxx). Freud maintains at several points throughout his writings that therapeutic work has no chance of success when confined to the exercise of rational intellect and insight alone; it also involves bodily based feelings. Freud's therapeutic recommendation that affective attunement must involve the meeting of the unconscious of both analyst and patient remains a mainstay of analytic theory and clinical practice to this day. Neither Freud nor contemporary psychoanalysis – or neuroscience for that matter – understands exactly how the unconscious operates. Freud did not resort in any measure to supernatural or mystical explanations to fill the gaps in his knowledge about unconscious communication. His line of inquiry did not require them.

One question with which Freud was grappling in respect to thought-transference specifically concerned the ways in which "affect might emerge and flow between bodies over distance" (Pile 2012: 45). As has been pointed out in the course of this book, Freud was preoccupied with the diverse forms of affect transfer that he believed played a significant role in our phylogenetic inheritance. His interest in telepathy belongs to a theoretical inquiry that is much larger than a mere curiosity in the weird details of so called "psychic" or occult phenomena. Freud would almost certainly agree, for example, that in cases where a patient dreams details of her analyst's life, no matter how accurate those details may be, they are in themselves less important than what is affectively and unconsciously transpiring *between* the analytic pair. Explanations of the former belong to the occult, whereas interpretations of the latter belong to psychoanalysis. However, because the complexity and nuance of thought-transference is so easily obscured by the flashy trickery of carnivals, spirit-conjuring and other fakeries, it is understandable that a number of Freud's sympathizers and admirers continue to be stymied and distressed by his readiness to acknowledge the existence of telepathic phenomena. The subject of telepathy at times distressed Freud as well. He held off making his views on telepathy public precisely because he was fully aware of its potential to compromise the legitimacy and scientific credibility of psychoanalysis. These factors undoubtedly help account for the fact that, with respect to scholarly discussions of Freud's theory of religion, the subject of "telepathy" tends to be passed over in silence. Religion does not necessarily embarrass, but telepathy almost certainly does. Those commentators and critics dismayed by Freud's serious interest in the subject may simply not know what to do with it. Certainly, the question of "telepathy" ought to be viewed as embedded within psychoanalysis itself, which Peter Gay indirectly attests to in his observation that "what intrigued [Freud] most, inconclusive though he thought the evidence, was telepathy" (1988: 443).

The very term "occultism", so widely used in the secondary literature in discussions about Freud's consideration of telepathy, is misleading because he accorded so little attention to occult phenomena in general. On those occasions where he did make mention of it, he was addressing the human psychology of the occult, not the occult as such. Freud's response to Nandor Fodor's study of poltergeist phenomena may be regarded as summing up his attitude to the subject in general:

> The way you [Fodor] deflect your interest from the question of whether
> the phenomena observed are real or have been falsified and turn it to the
> psychological study of the medium, including the investigation of his

> previous history, seems to me to be the right steps to take in the plan-
> ning of research which will lead to some explanation of the occurrences
> in question.                                           (Freud in Jones 1957: 396)

In this respect, Freud was not alone in thinking that at least some occult phenomena were worthy of scientific investigation. As Jones and a number of intellectual historians have pointed out, some of the most prestigious scientists and philosophers of the day, including T. H. Flournoy, Charles Richet, Albert von Schrenck-Notzing, William James, Sir William Crookes, Sir Oliver Lodge and F. W. H. Meyers, advocated scientific investigation of "mediumistic and spiritualistic phenomena" (Gyimesi 2012: 132). The first president of the Society for Psychical Research (SPR) was Henry Sidgwick, a professor of moral philosophy at Cambridge. In fact, many of the men and women who belonged to the SPR were part of the "Cambridge intellectual elite", for whom spiritism was "entirely repugnant" (Hacking 1988: 436).

The motivation for psychic research in the late nineteenth and early twentieth centuries was both scientific and modern in its efforts to explore the "depths of human psychological experience" (Treitel 2004: 30) and the unconscious mind. Psychical research was deeply implicated in the new trends emerging within psychology and, inevitably, psychoanalysis (*ibid.*: 47, 48; Owen 2004: 6). The SPR produced "valuable theories" about the psychology of beliefs in and experiences of supernatural events (Gyimesi 2012: 132), and the mental states associated with them. Between 1883 and 1888, the *Proceedings of the Society for Psychical Research* was the "leading scholarly periodical in England" that included articles on the themes of hypnotism and dissociation. Between 1882 and 1900, 39 per cent of its published papers and notes were "devoted" to discussions of "dissociative phenomena", more than appeared in the pages of the *Journal of Mental Science* and *Mind* combined (Sommer 2001: 386–7). Considered in this larger historical and intellectual context, it is not surprising that Freud was a Corresponding Member of the SPR and an Honorary Fellow of its American counterpart. Many of the leading members of these societies "shared a common goal of bringing scientific rigor to the study of the human unconscious", and in this regard there were "many points of contact" between psychoanalysis and psychical research (Treitel 2004: 48). Freud's interest in telepathy, or thought-transference, was shared in the scientific circles of his contemporaries, where it was regarded as a legitimate focus of empirical and theoretical research. Situating Freud's inquiries into the *psychology* of thought-transference within this intellectual context makes it easier to see how it could be considered a part of the larger theoretical landscape of psychoanalysis rather than an unfortunate discordant note. The major psychoanalytic theories pertaining to dreams, the unconscious, unconscious fantasy, transference, introjection, projection and identification are all theories of *communication* within and between individuals. For Freud, psychoanalysis held the key to the mysteries of human communication.

## Telepathy and dreams

Freud (1895, 1915b) had long been aware that the "arrogance of consciousness" (1910b: 39) was blind to the fact that the major portion of mental activity is unconscious. It is "an untenable claim", he writes (1915b: 167), that "whatever goes on in the mind must also be known to consciousness". Freud's contention that mind and consciousness are not identical is widely accepted in the contemporary neuroscientific psychoanalytic literature[1] (Solms 1997; Solms & Turnbull 2002; Bucci 2008; Schore 2011a, 2011b). "At any given moment", Freud (1915b) continues, "consciousness includes only a small content, so that the greater part of what we call conscious knowledge must in any case be for very considerable periods of time in a state of latency, that is to say, of being psychically unconscious" (*ibid.*: 167). As far as Freud is concerned, consciousness is a fleeting, partial and fluid mental state, one where individuals *experience* or *feel* far more of what transpires in the world around them than they consciously perceive. Human beings may be *affectively* and feelingly attuned to what is going on between them and others in ways that remain outside of awareness because of the mundane distractions of daily life. Freud argued that the mind registers and retains far more information and knowledge than is accessible to consciousness at any given moment. Current research into right-brain cognition suggests models of "implicit communications" that operate particularly in affectively intense relationships such as occur in psychotherapy (Schore 2011b: 78).

Freud also thought it could sometimes happen that experiences or knowledge of others not available to waking mental states could be accessed in nocturnal dream states. He writes:

> if there are such things as telepathic messages, the possibility cannot be dismissed of their reaching someone during sleep and coming to his knowledge in a dream. Indeed, on the analogy of other perceptual and intellectual material, the further possibility arises that telepathic messages received in the course of the day may only be dealt with during a dream of the following night. (Freud 1925c: 138)

Freud did not mean to suggest that there are such things as telepathic dreams *per se*. As far as he was concerned, there was no such thing. It must be remembered that in Freud's view, telepathy or thought-transference were forms of non-verbal and non-ordinary communication between individual minds.

While "telepathic" communications picked up outside the parameters of conscious awareness during the day can become manifest in the nocturnal dream state, the dream itself is no less a product of, or subject to, the same processes of the dream work as any other.

One of the most interesting cases reported by Freud of a "telepathic experience in a state of sleep" (1922: 208) concerned a man's dream that his wife had given birth to twins. He later discovered that his daughter from a first marriage had given birth to twins during the night of his dream. He and his current wife had no children of their own. In the course of his analysis of this dream, Freud reiterates his scepticism concerning its telepathic nature, remarking that he has nothing to say that might "throw any light on the problem of telepathy" (*ibid.*: 205). As Freud follows the unconscious processes prompted by the "associative material" to the father's dream, he concludes that the manifest dream is a distortion of an unconscious repressed wish, namely that his daughter, with whom he shared an "intimate bond of feeling" (*ibid.*: 206), ought to have been his second wife. The latent dream work that shaped and transformed the repressed wish resulted in a distorted manifest dream narrative more acceptable to the mind of the dreamer and, it should go without saying, the society in which he lived. In the manifest dream or dream story, the true nature of the father's longing for children with his daughter was concealed behind the dream image of his second wife. Here Freud shifts the focus of inquiry from telepathic communication to a consideration of the dream work itself, where the "dream thoughts" are "reinforced by the [unconscious] wish that no other than the daughter should be the dreamer's second wife, and thus the manifest dream as described to us arises". It is "*simply a dream like any other*", Freud concludes (*ibid.*: 206, emphasis added). The "telepathic" nature of the dream only emerges in the course of interpretation, which in itself says "nothing about the objective reality of the telepathic event" (Freud 1933c: 38). Telepathy *as such* is not the central focus of Freud's investigation. For the sake of argument, Freud insists that even if a telepathic message about the daughter giving birth did reach her sleeping father, it should be considered as part of the dream material "*like any other* external or internal stimulus, like a disturbing noise in the street or an insistent organic sensation in the sleeper's own body" (1922: 207, emphasis added). The so-called telepathic message, combined with the father's already-present repressed wish and its distorted expression through the dream process, indicates that telepathy, even if it exists, has no impact on the dream work itself. Freud reiterates that "the essential nature of dreams consists in the peculiar process of 'dream-work' which, with the help of an unconscious wish", carries elements of the "day's residues" into "the manifest content of the dream" (*ibid.*: 207). He has nothing to say about the fact that the dream occurred on the very night of the birth of the man's grandchildren.

For Freud, the unconscious is the primary mediator of affective communication through which knowledge is transmitted that cannot be conveyed by more ordinary means of verbal expression. "To have *heard* something and to have *experienced* something", he writes, "are in their psychological nature two quite different things, even though the content of both is the same" (Freud 1915b: 176, emphasis added). While Freud does not categorically deny the possibility that a telepathic message may have had something to do with the dream about the birth of the twins, his central focus of interpretation remains psychoanalytic. In this sense, Freud's naturalistic approach is parallel to and consistent with his critique of religious belief: telepathy and other supernatural beliefs, such as in spirits, gods and demons, are all products of the human mind.

Freud applies the same methodology to so-called prophetic dreams, which he illustrates in a "neat little analysis" (Jones 1957: 397) he wrote up in 1899, posthumously published and included as an appendix to *The Interpretation of Dreams*. In "A Premonitory Dream Fulfilled" (Freud 1900a), he tells the story of Frau B, an "estimable woman" who by chance encountered an old family friend, Dr K, at the very location she had dreamed of meeting him the previous night. However, she had forgotten the dream until *after* running into Dr K, at which point she recalled it. As Freud subjected this "prophetic" dream to psychoanalytic inquiry, he discovered that the Dr K of the dream was actually a "screen figure" (*ibid.*: 625) concealing a different Dr K, a lawyer who had been Frau B's lover years before, when her elderly husband was dying. Frau B's associations to the dream while recounting it to Freud revealed that one day twenty-five years prior to the dream, she had been in an intense emotional state of "passionate longing" (*ibid.*: 624) for her lover when he suddenly paid her an unexpected visit.

Freud surmised that, although an elderly woman herself at the time of her "prophetic" dream, Frau B was still in love with the lawyer, who continued to administer her estate over the years subsequent to their affair, and with whom she remained in frequent contact. While their passion had long ago cooled, Freud wondered if the dream of the other, less important Dr K allowed Frau B to become indirectly aware of a nostalgic longing for her former lover that she could not allow herself to experience consciously in the present. Given that she and Dr K had an illicit affair during her husband's terminal illness, her love for him would most certainly have been compromised by feelings of guilt and shame. Assuming that her love and longing for Dr K was never completely extinguished, Freud speculates that Frau B probably had many such dreams of *rendez-vous* with her former lover, most of which she likely repressed or forgot, until the day she ran into the other Dr K, whom she had not seen in a long time. As her family doctor had attended to her dying husband, he, too, was intimately associated with that earlier "happy-unhappy time" in her life, and so was both a logical and benign "cover" for her lover, "also a Dr K" (Freud 1900a: 624).

"We may suppose", writes Freud, "that he had been used in her thoughts, and perhaps in her dreams as well, as a screen-figure behind which she concealed the better-loved figure of the other Dr K" (*ibid.*: 625). The chance meeting with her family doctor may have "revived her recollection of the dream" that was really about her former lover.

Freud conjectures that Frau B probably had a number of dreams about her former lover that she "put aside on waking" (*ibid.*: 625) because it was too painful or difficult for her to think of them. Thus it is most likely that it was her *recollection* of one of these dreams that was distorted, not the dream itself, which had been quite forgotten *until she ran into the "indifferent K"*. Frau B's unexpected encounter with this Dr K aroused both the memory and the feelings still associated with the earlier and unexpected appearance of her lover all those years ago, which in her mind might still have held some residual power of having made a desperate wish come true. The result of all this was that in her mind, Freud concludes, both actual chance encounters with the two Dr Ks, although separated by many years, collapsed into one another in the non-contradictory timelessness that is a hallmark of the dream state. If this is the case, then it is understandable why Frau B believed that she had a "prophetic" dream. The work of the dream censorship allowed Frau B's old longing for her lover to re-emerge through the distorted decoy image of the physician Dr K. What is most important in Freud's interpretations of the two dreams recounted here is his argument that seemingly "occult" phenomena are also susceptible to rational, psychoanalytic explanation. As long as Freud held to the possibility of scientific explanation, whether or not one was presently available, there was no need for him to dismiss the reality of telepathy as a form of "thought-transference" *tout court*. This approach is entirely in line with the view that guides his own work, articulated in his caution against seeking elsewhere "what science cannot give us" (1927: 56).

## Telepathy and technology

Towards the end of "Dreams and Occultism", Freud's last published paper on dreams, he returns yet again to the telephone, the physical medium whereby voices are broken down into electrical impulses at one end, transmitted, and reconstituted into a recognizable voice at the other end (Freud 1933c). "And only think if one could get hold of this physical equivalent of the psychical act!" he declares. Psychoanalysis, "inserting the unconscious between what is physical and what was previously called 'psychical', has paved the way for the assumption of such processes as telepathy", Freud writes (*ibid.*: 55). As he casts about for a scientific explanation of thought-transference that would ultimately elude him, Freud continues his speculations, now wondering if telepathy is a derivative or residue belonging to an "original, archaic method of communication between individuals and that in the course of phylogenetic evolution … has been replaced by the better method of giving information with the help of signals which are picked up by the sense organs". Freud thinks it might be possible that under certain conditions of intense affect, such as occurs in "passionately excited mobs" (*ibid*.), more ancient resources of telepathic transmission might be reactivated, although these resources are now marginalized and displaced by more efficient and sophisticated means of verbal communication commensurate with the modern world.

Freud was not alone in exploring such questions. Lisa Blackman cites the 1916 publication by biologist Charles Bingham Newland of *What is Instinct? Some Thoughts on Telepathy and Subconsciousness in Animals*, where he suggests the possible existence of "complex systems of communication or affective transfer" that could be "shared, transmitted and co-constituted between members of species" (Blackman 2012: xviii). Like Freud, Newland and many other of their contemporaries saw analogies with thought-transference in the new communications technologies, such as the Marconi wireless system, that provided expanded ways of thinking about communication over large distances. It is understandable how, in the context of these novel developing technologies where communication between people could take place over hundreds of miles, the boundaries between "scientific and occult inter-phenomena" (Luckhurst 2002: 79) could blur. The physicist Oliver Lodge linked science and telepathy directly as he speculated upon the relationship between consciousness and the physical brain:

> just as the energy of an electric charge, though apparently on the conductor, is not on the conductor, but in the space all around it … so it may be that the sensory consciousness of a person, though apparently located in the brain, may also be conceived of as also existing like a faint echo in space, or in other brains.                    (In Luckhurst 2002: 79)

In a comment that has nothing to do with the topic of telepathy, but is nonetheless relevant here, psychiatrist and neuro-researcher Iain McGilchrist speculates somewhat similarly to Lodge on the general issue of consciousness and the brain that "it may be that consciousness does not depend on a brain for its existence: just, in the absence of a brain, it is deprived of its expression as that particular mind" (2009: 465 n. 15).

The theorization of telepathy within the multiple intersections of science, technology and psychology is based upon a belief in the possibility that the phenomenon of thought-transference could one day be explained in naturalistic, fully human terms. In the astonishing world of nineteenth-century communication technologies that allowed voices and telegraphic messages to be sent across thousands of miles of geographic space, it was not so unreasonable *at the time* to link telepathy and telecommunication, not only in the popular mind but also in the scientific one. Imagination and science were not rigidly separated in *fin-de-siècle* Britain and Europe. Slavet correctly reminds us that, historically, literary genres such as science fiction imagined "telephony and television long before such tele-technologies became commonplace reality in the late nineteenth and early twentieth centuries" (2009: 147). Freud's repeated references to the telephone, however, were expressed largely on the level of analogies and metaphors that illuminated and gave shape to his own intuitive thinking about the processes of unconscious affective communication between analyst and patient, and with other closely associated individuals.

It is important to remember that when Freud refers to the "telepathic process" as a "mental act", he is thinking of it as a "physical process" as well, where the contents of one mind are transformed and reconstituted in their original terms in the mind of another (1933c: 55). Ironically, in a rhetorical move that was often used by the spiritualists of the time, but with a very different purpose and intent, Freud also appealed to the new communication technologies as providing a "compelling resource" (Noakes 1999: 434) whose epistemology could be seen as partially analogous to that of psychoanalysis. He knew that as voices could not be transmitted over distances without the physical aids of telephones and wires, and as telegrams could not be sent without equipment, neither could the unconscious nor its communications exist without bodies and brains. Although Freud did not understand precisely how the mental emerged out of or specifically related to the physical, he did not hesitate to use the physical images of telephones and wireless technology in order to anchor his arguments within the bounds of natural physical science. Freud writes that "it is a very remarkable thing that the *Ucs* (unconscious) of one human being can react upon that of another, without passing through the *Cs* (consciousness)" (1915b: 194).

Freud hoped that this mental phenomenon would be the subject of further scientific investigation, and it has been with respect to subsequent MindBrain research. In contemporary neuropsychoanalytic terms, this "remarkable thing" may be understood as a "conversation between limbic systems" (Schore 2011a: xxx). Contemporary psychoanalysis, increasingly influenced by neuroscientific theories, accepts that unconscious communication takes place. The point is that unconscious or "implicit" communication bridges distances, weakens boundaries and facilitates intimate connections between minds, which is exactly what any psychoanalyst strives for in the consulting room. The effort to know the mind of another combines intellect with profound affective experience, which in Freud's time might have been seen as a kind of psychic "electricity", with affect providing the emotional "charge" between the analyst and patient. From this perspective, an affective charge between two people might facilitate a form of knowing experienced as *telepathic* communication in a context where neuroscience was still in its very early stage of development. As far as Freud is concerned, telepathy as unconscious communication is the only "kernel of truth" in the otherwise disreputable claims of occult experience (1925c: 136).

In the handful of texts Freud devoted to the subject of telepathy, he was often cautious to the point of inducing confusion in his readers about his own views on the matter. He sometimes insisted that he neither knew nor could say anything about it; on other occasions, he concluded that telepathy does exist. In spite of this vacillating ambivalence, Freud finally accepted that thought-transference, which is "so close to telepathy" that it may be regarded as "the same thing" (1933c: 39), does exist. Despite his steadfast opposition to *supernatural* explanations of these strange human experiences, he nonetheless conceded that minds are capable of communicating outside or beyond conventional modalities. Telepathy raised a host of psychoanalytic questions for Freud, many of which are addressed indirectly and in a variety of different theoretical contexts throughout his writings: the boundaries of consciousness, the permeability of minds, knowledge of and the relationship between self and other, transference, dreams, and the limits of communication, among others. Questions such as these were the real focus of Freud's interest in the possibilities of telepathic knowledge. His clinical experience was also an important factor in leading him to finally conclude that "there remains a strong balance of probability in favour of thought-transference as a fact" (*ibid.*: 43). Freud was always intellectually committed to following the evidence of empirical observation, no matter how inconvenient or contradictory to theory it might be. He wrote some years earlier:

> We have no other aim but that of translating into theory the results of observation, and we deny that there is any obligation on us to achieve at our first attempt a well-rounded theory which will commend itself by its simplicity. We shall defend the complications of our theory so long as we find that they meet the results of observation.
>
> (Freud 1915b: 190)

Paul Roazen (1989) is one of only a few defenders of Freud's willingness to accept that there might be something of scientific value in the study of telepathy. This is not because Roazen professes any personal belief in it himself; instead, he explains Freud's views as consistent with his being an "open-minded rationalist" whose courage in taking the possibility of thought-transference seriously manifested a "temperament that made him able *in the first place* to come up with the daring set of ideas" (*ibid.*: 300, emphasis added) that became psychoanalysis. Long years of clinical practice had taken Freud along many strange and terrifying pathways through "the darkness of mental life" (Freud 1938: 286) with respect to himself as well as others. His treatment of the subject of thought-transference demonstrates both his courage to consider the not-yet-explainable as well as his capacity to hold uncertainty while he struggled to find a coherent and rational explanation for this weird and baffling phenomenon. Freud eventually concluded that in the unsettling affective intensity of the analytic relationship, the fact that experiences can occur that defy explanation does not mean that explanation is not possible.

As psychoanalyst Jessica Benjamin (1986) points out, psychoanalysis is "unique among modern rationalisms" in its efforts to "include the irrational". The irrational constitutes the stock and trade of psychoanalysis. As a theory "of the subject who never knows all that she or he knows", psychoanalysis confronts "the limits of knowledge" (*ibid.*: 487) and reason as it tries to expand them. Freud understood, as contemporary analysts still do, that in fathoming the hidden dimensions of another mind as well as one's own, the analyst must open herself to the other (1912a: 116–17) while maintaining her own identity intact. In this way, the analyst facilitates the emergence of a therapeutic connection mediated by multivalent affective communicational avenues that are generated by both parties. This as yet not fully understood dimension of clinical experience is captured vividly in Lew Aron's description of the ways in which the analyst and patient "feel" the other, and where each gets "under the other's skin, each reaches into the other's guts, each is breathed in and absorbed by the other" (in Schore 2011b: 84). Aron is describing a reciprocal unconscious communicative process that is unsymbolized in language, and that many analysts would recognize as resonating with their own clinical experience. From this point of view, it is easier to comprehend Freud's statement that "thought-transference" occurs when "an idea emerges from the unconscious", as it "passes over from 'primary process' to the 'secondary process'", mentation (1925c: 138). However, it cannot be overstated that this experience must be *affectively charged* to occur. Bodily based affect, not intellect alone, facilitates unconscious communication between individuals.

## Clinical triangles: the curious case of Herr "von Vorsicht"

In 1919, Freud (1933c) was treating a certain Herr P for a limited time until he could rebuild his clinical practice, which had shrunk considerably in the social and economic chaos of the First World War. Having endured years of exhausting personal, financial and professional privations because of the war, Freud could finally look forward to better times with the return of his students and foreign patients. Although Freud reported that his sessions with Herr P were "stimulating and refreshing", he made it clear to his patient from the outset that their time together would cease when his practice was restored. Understandably, Herr P was less than satisfied with a time-limited analysis, but

Freud was adamant. One day, a few minutes prior to Herr P's scheduled session, Dr David Forsyth, a colleague from London University who was of "particular interest" (*ibid.*: 48) to Freud, arrived at his office. Freud had to delay meeting with him until Herr P left. In the session immediately following this visit, Herr P spoke of a young woman he had talked about on previous occasions. Never before had he mentioned to Freud that she used to call him "Herr von Vorsicht". Freud, who was "struck by this information" (*ibid.*: 48) on account of his current preoccupation with the British doctor of the very similar name, began to follow a series of associations in his own mind to explain this strange coincidence. The multiple variations of the name "Forsyth" had particular meaning for Freud with respect to Herr P, who had earlier introduced Freud to Galsworthy's *The Forsyte Saga*. It was only because Herr P had introduced Freud to the British novelist that he knew the name "Forsyte" at all. "The name 'Forsyte', and everything typical that the author had sought to embody in it," Freud remarks, "had played a part of the secret language which so easily grows up between two people who see a lot of each other" (*ibid.*: 50). Noting the close similarities in pronunciation and meaning of the German and English words *Vorsicht*/Forsyth/Forsyte/foresight, Freud concludes that his patient had "selected from his personal concerns the very name with which I was occupied at the same time as a result of an occurrence of which he was unaware" (*ibid.*: 49). As far as Freud is concerned, Herr P's story of being called *von Vorsicht* in the session immediately following Dr Forsyth's visit was not a matter to be explained by mere coincidence.

Once again, Freud tracks the corresponding details of Herr P's story and Dr Forsyth's visit in order to fathom its psychoanalytic meaning (Freud 1933c: 54), which is most significant for him. Thus Freud focuses his attention on what is happening *between* himself and his patient in order to explain its apparently telepathic nature. It is obvious from Freud's account that Herr P, who had a "well-tempered father-transference" to Freud, was far less important to Freud than vice versa. Despite Freud's suggestion "long before" to terminate the analysis, Herr P pressed to continue. As far as Freud was concerned, the case offered little hope of "any therapeutic success". Fully aware that he was acting against "the strict rules of medical practice" (*ibid.*: 48), Freud agreed to conduct the analysis, but only on a temporary basis. A psychoanalytic treatment conducted under circumstances such as these would inevitably be humiliating and disappointing for any patient. In addition, the unfortunate Herr P would be likely to have felt a sustained sense of dread of the certain loss of his father/analyst,[2] which was built into the treatment by Freud from the beginning, before Herr P had a chance to be emotionally ready for it.

The story of Herr P does not show Freud at his clinical best, to be sure. Freud writes candidly enough about his less than professional treatment of this patient that the reader is able to detect traces of Freud's ambivalence, impatience and perhaps even mild sadism towards him. Freud is unequivocally clear to both the reader and to Herr P that the only "Forsyth" of interest to him is his British colleague, whose visit heralded the "promise of better times" (1933c: 48). As Freud continues with the story of this particular session, it becomes evident that Herr P, committed to an analysis with someone who cares so little for him, *feels* what is going on in the absence of conscious awareness of the specific facts of Dr Forsyth's visit. Freud is too astute a clinician not to be well aware of all this as he ponders the meaning of Herr P's self-reference as a "Herr von Vorsicht" in *this particular session* and not an earlier one. Given Freud's rather cavalier treatment of this patient, it is remarkable that he is nonetheless sufficiently attuned to the unconscious affects of jealousy and "melancholy self-depreciation" he detects in Herr P's words: "I'm a Forsyth too; that's what the girl calls me" (*ibid.*: 51). Yet it appears that Freud's attitude to Herr P is even more complex and ambivalent as he recognizes, in a surprisingly moving insight, that what his patient is *really* telling him is something along the lines of, "It is mortifying to me that your thoughts should be so intensely occupied with this new arrival. Do come back to me; after all *I'm a Forsyth too*" (*ibid.*: 51, emphasis added). Freud accepts his patient's jealousy as appropriate under the circumstances, even though he does not speculate upon the existence of a deeper unarticulated humiliation Herr P may feel regarding his inferior status with respect to any number of Freud's associates. Shortly after the session in which Herr P so poignantly tried to persuade Freud that he was "a Forsyth too", the analysis was terminated.

There is a curious history of repeated forgettings, disappearances and omissions that are too detailed to be recounted here in connection with Freud's written notes of this case (Jones 1957; Pierri 2010). This suggests strong ambivalence towards the whole subject of thought-transference or telepathy on Freud's part, as has been pointed out, and on the part of some of his associates, particularly Jones, whose hostility to the subject was undisguised. Freud had planned to present this case of thought-transference, his first writing on the subject, to a small group of colleagues at a meeting in the Harz mountains in 1921, but he mislaid his notes (Freud 1921b: 190). A subsequent version of the text was finally published in 1933, after which it disappeared again, until the original draft was discovered by Maria Pierri (2010). Freud himself attributed his forgetting the notes to "a clear resistance" at the time (1921b: 190), which may have had to do not only with his ambivalence regarding telepathy, but also a sense of unconscious professional shame for his treatment of Herr P. If so, the interlacing of shame in the complex affective therapeutic mix would have generated even more affective intensity between Freud and his patient, resulting in a heightened receptivity on Freud's part to Herr P's "telepathic" insight. This line of thinking is congruent with Freud's own psychoanalytic interpretation of the affectively laden, multiple layers of unspoken communication that passed between him and his patient. Freud is aware of both Herr P's longing to be with him and his own desire to be rid of him.

The unconscious implicit communications between Freud and Herr P can be understood in the context of what Michael Balint describes as a "state of intense positive dependent transference" (1955: 32) on the part of the patient that in this case was not fully appreciated by Freud the analyst. In applying Balint's ideas about "telepathic" occurrences in the clinical setting to this case, it may be considered that in his state of "helpless dependence" on an analyst who kept him at arm's length, Herr P did everything he could to "win the analyst's full attention" through a "desperate means of [telepathic] communication" (*ibid.*) that was conveyed in his story of the girl's nickname for him. Freud's internal process in tracking his own and the patient's associations leads him to the question of *whose* knowledge is revealed in Herr P's associations – the patient's or Freud's? If Freud's, then Herr P somehow had access to the analyst's mind through the affective exchanges in the back-and-forth process between them with its multiple dynamics of desire and rejection. As Freud reviews all the factors that could plausibly explain Herr P having independent "knowledge" of the visit by Dr Forsyth, the fact remains for Freud that Herr P was "receptive to [Dr Forsyth's] presence on the very day of his arrival" and right after his first appearance (Freud 1933c: 53). Herr P in all likelihood would have been exquisitely attuned to Freud's preferences for others over him. Freud's analysis of the session inevitably circles back to Herr P's feelings of longing and jealousy towards him that partially created the affective atmosphere within which the "transference relations *between patient and analyst*" unfolded (*ibid.*: 54). Herr P's poignant declaration, "I'm a Forsyth too", expressed the desperate hope that he also had a place in Freud's mind and that he, too, needed Freud's attention and respect. Although it didn't help Herr P in the end, Freud appears to have received the message.

## The "uncanny": the dark side of narcissism

The existence of the unconscious, and the psychic processes that constitute it, can be inferred primarily, but not exclusively, through dreams. Freud elaborated and altered this concept in various ways throughout his writing, but a detailed technical discussion of the concept and its vicissitudes from a topographical organization *Ucs* (Freud 1915b) to a structural[3] model where it is known as *Id* (Freud 1923b) cannot be undertaken here. Briefly, it connotes a realm of mind not directly accessible to rational conscious experience. It is a complex, dynamic system that includes contents that once were conscious but then subject to repression because of their unacceptability to the ego. It also contains contents that have never been conscious. These latter contents may be phylogenetic in origin, having little to do with the direct experiences of an individual (Laplanche & Pontalis 1973: 475). Freud writes that the "content of the *Ucs* may be compared with an aboriginal population in the mind. If inherited mental formations exist in the human being – something analogous to instinct in animals – these constitute the nucleus of the *Ucs*" (1915b: 195). Large portions of the ego and super-ego, having emerged from within the unconscious, remain unconscious. The biologically based drives (*Triebe*) are mental representations of bodily impulses and cannot become conscious unless they manifest themselves indirectly and obliquely through affects, or become represented in ideas. "If the instinct did not attach itself to an idea or manifest itself as an affective state, we could know nothing about it", Freud says (*ibid.*: 177). There is no sense of linear time or contradiction in the unconscious; there, the socially shared, consciously apprehended reality of daily life has little meaning. The operations of the unconscious show themselves indirectly, in altered mental states such as night dreams or day-dreaming, or in the distortions expressed in the symptoms deriving from the various neuroses (*ibid.*: 187). Often the workings of the unconscious are experienced as "other", as forces not quite belonging to oneself, or at least the self one thinks one knows.

Again, Hans Loewald comes closest to capturing the "uncanny" quality of the Freudian unconscious:

> the power of the unconscious or id is part of myself, and neither is of divine origin nor comes from alien spirits … there is something daemonic about the id, something about the dynamic unconscious that is, as in the Greek idea of *daimon,* neither attributable to the power of a personal god, nor a powerful force of the person *qua* individual or conscious being, but something in between, having an impersonal character. (Loewald 2000: 537)

As with Freud, from whom he takes the idea, Loewald is drawing upon the concept of the *daimon* of ancient Greek religion as, in many respects, an apt metaphor for the ways in which human beings often experience that bewildering, inexplicable and at times frightening unconscious part of themselves that occupies the major portion of mental life. The *daimon* does not designate a "specific class of divine beings", but is rather a "peculiar mode of activity", an "occult power" that "drives man forward where no agent can be named", writes Walter Burkert (1985: 180). The *daimon* is an "unpredictable" force that is felt to be beyond subjective agency, a kind of "driving power", something approximating "fate" with no connection to a visible, discernible source; it is an "uncanny power", the "power of fate, as it were alongside the power of vengeance or the power of the curse" (*ibid.*: 181). Happiness or unhappiness is beyond human control; one either has a good *daimon* (*eudaimon*) or an evil one (*kakodaimon, dysdaimon*) present since birth (*ibid.*).

Freud, who was well versed in classical Greek mythology, uses the concept of the *daimon* in a way that is similar to Burkert's description. The "uncontrolled and indestructible forces" (Freud 1900b: 614) deep within the unconscious can feel like a "daemonic power" when they surface in nocturnal dreams and other altered states of mind, such as hallucinations and visions. The daemonic power also includes the universal, phylogenetic inheritance of the human race, where fantasies, desires and inexplicable impulses are sometimes felt as both part of and alien to oneself. The human psyche combines an "innate disposition" or "constitution" with environmental influences, the product of endowment mixed with chance. "Daimon and Tyche [Endowment and Chance]", Freud (1912b: 99 n. 2) writes, "determine a man's fate – rarely or never one of these powers alone." He goes on to say that the human "constitution itself" is a "precipitate from the accidental effects produced on the endlessly long chain of our ancestors" (*ibid.*: 99, 99 n. 2). In other words, we do not, and perhaps cannot, always experience our minds completely as our own.

Consciousness is merely a *quality*, not the essence of psychic life, "far oftener absent than present", Freud writes (1938: 283). The mind has a tendency to produce "uncanny" experiences that feel as if the individual is *being lived*, or perhaps inhabited, by an alien force, rather than one's own subjective sense of freedom of will. The unconscious or id comprises the "dark, inaccessible part of our personality", (1933b: 73) where "contrary impulses exist side by side" in a "cauldron full of seething excitations", replete with dangerous, forbidden impulses originating in the depths of bodily needs and desires. Freud chooses the impersonal pronoun *das Es*, the "it", to designate this largely unknown and inaccessible portion of the mind because it is "alien to the ego" (*ibid.*: 72) in this *daemonic* sense. Loewald points out that the id is not defined so much by specific mental contents as that it refers to "an earlier, archaic form or level of mentation, an undifferentiated form of experiencing, that characterizes early developmental stages but is operative as well at chronologically later stages" (2000: 539). The id for Freud is both phylogenetic and ontogenetic in character, pertaining to both other and self; given and constructed; us and not us. It is both familiar and foreign, within and beyond, a "class of the frightening which leads back to what is known of old and long familiar", Freud writes in his essay "The 'Uncanny'" (1919: 220).

The unconscious mind for Freud (1915b) is haunted, phylogenetically constituted as it is of "inherited mental formations", memory traces, forbidden longings, ghostly parental introjects and identifications that are stained with the ancient legacies of criminality, guilt and the fear of punishment. The repressed infantile wishes and primitive impulses that are forbidden entry into consciousness by virtue of culture's guardian, the ego, may return in distorted form to haunt our dreams and fantasies. The dissociated mental states that constitute the more fragmented psyches of some individuals have their own twisted narrative structures and incomplete personal histories that sometimes generate a sense of being persecuted, possessed or inhabited by foreign "others" who threaten the emotional stability and psychological survival of the self. These dimly perceived others who inhabit the darkness of the mind are uncanny in their dual nature as both familiar and unfamiliar. They are, Freud says, "*unheimlich*". Freud uses this word "*unheimlich*", or uncanny, because it designates "that class of the frightening which leads back to what is known of old and long familiar", (1919: 220), the me/not-me, the daemonic force that directs one's fate but that can never be fully mastered.

The uncanny also refers to a sense of double-identity or being that hearkens back to the earliest stages of mental development, "long since surmounted" (Freud 1919: 236) but never surpassed or eliminated from the depths of the human mind. It includes the sensation of "involuntary repetition" composed of behaviours that seem "fateful and inescapable when otherwise we should have spoken only of 'chance'", Freud continues (*ibid.*: 237). The frightening, the weird and the strange are uncanny because they contain elements of unconscious familiarity that are felt more than apprehended. The "*unheimlich*" is what was once "*heimlich–heimisch*", familiar; "the prefix '*un*' ['un-'] is the token of repression" (*ibid.*: 245). An experience is uncanny when an "infantile complex" (*ibid.*: 249) has been revived due to an external life circumstance, such as trauma, or when distinctions between internal fantasy and external reality are weakened or dissolved in mental illness, where the thought or wish becomes the deed. The madness of others is an uncanny experience because it evokes the presence of psychotic potential in each of us (*ibid.*: 243). In the uncanny, human beings sense those previously hidden dimensions of their own minds whose origins lie buried within the non-differentiated state of primary narcissism, where awareness of self and other had not yet begun to coalesce. As the mind regresses towards intimations of an earlier, more primitive state of being, the individual is in danger of experiencing himself as two or many or nothing, terrified at the prospect of being divided and lacking cohesion or internal stability. The divided self feels inhabited and possessed by an alien other or "double", a "thing of terror", Freud writes (*ibid.*: 236). Robert Louis Stevenson's novel, *The Strange Case of Dr Jekyll and Mr Hyde*, "highly popular" in the last decades of the nineteenth century, captured the "fin-de-siècle fascination with duality, fragmentation, and disintegration" characteristic of the dual or dissociated personality (Owen 2004: 208).

Freud explores the mystery and terror associated with this weird and frightening dimension of shared human experience by explaining uncanny phenomena in psychoanalytic rather than occult terms. Freud's theory of primary narcissism is further elaborated by Loewald in ways that are particularly helpful to any discussion concerning the psychology of uncanny experiences. Loewald (2000) builds on Freud's theory of primary and secondary narcissism in order to illustrate some of the ways in which the psychic permeability that characterizes the infant–mother field reflects a similar internal permeability within the mind that is most clearly evident in Freud's *The Ego and the Id* (1923). In his later theory, the mental agencies super-ego (*das Über-Ich*) and id (*das Es*) are not as clearly demarcated from the ego (*das Ich*) as they appear to be in his 1915 topographical paper, "The Unconscious". By 1923, it is especially clear that the major portions of the ego and the superego, which themselves emerge from within the id, remain unconscious, as I have noted above. This suggests that unless the distinctions between the mental agencies are hardened into psychic barriers through the work of repression, the conscious and unconscious dimensions of an individual mind continue to remain more fluidly connected with each other through the developmental process as they are simultaneously transformed by it. This set of ordered permeable distinctions *within* the mind is made possible by the creation of psychic links or internal bridges between self-states, which in turn help to foster and underwrite relationships both *within* and *between* individual minds. This helps to explain Freud's view that minds meet through the medium of unconscious communication, where the unconscious of one human being communicates implicitly with another outside of conscious awareness (1915b: 194). Although Freud could not fully explain thought-transference by any means, he was able to point towards what he identified as important clues within psychoanalysis that plausibly suggest, without resort to occult mystifications, how unconscious communication may occur.

## Permeable minds: from narcissism to the differentiated ego

As was discussed more fully in Chapter 2, Freud (1914b, 1917c, 1930a) attempts to theorize the infant mind in terms of "an original libidinal cathexis of the ego" (1914b: 75), or primary narcissism, that expands to take in aspects of the external world while preserving something of its original state. This libidinal energy is drawn back into the infant psyche along with elements of the loved object that are internalized through identifications that enrich and differentiate the infant's developing mental states. Briefly restating Freud's thesis here, we recall that as the child gradually embraces various dimensions of external reality, she takes it in or incorporates elements of it within herself in a gradual process of psychic differentiation. The result is that the original ego, which included "everything", is now able to differentiate itself both from the world and its own internal mental states. This process of internal differentiation is part of the development of the organization of the mind. What we come to experience as our adult "present ego-feeling" is, Freud thought, an echo of a far older, more diffuse, undifferentiated mental state of narcissistic psychic energy floating in a universe without boundaries or distinctions. Under the conditions of a degree of psychological regression, such as Freud thinks occurs in intense religious feelings or mystical states, the mind may recall some sense of the feelings from an earlier, more primitive, less differentiated mental state. Since so little was known about the psychology of early infancy in Freud's time,[4] he could not speculate further about the pre-Oedipal period.

Loewald (2000), however, did carry forward Freud's ideas on primary narcissism in a theory of psychic development that situates this experience of undifferentiated oneness not within an infant–mother relationship, but in a less formulated psychic matrix. Loewald argues that the developing ego's libidinal energies flow not only towards external objects, but are also internally directed, operating within the organization of the psyche, where libidinal forces and processes "establish and maintain the very unity of [one]self" (*ibid.*: 458). Loewald describes the emergent ego in terms of an interplay and intermingling of psychic forces, where the libidinal energies informing the developing object relations are transformed into intrapsychic interactions. This psychic process is a fundamental part of the work of sublimation for Loewald; for him, it is not a *defensive* activity motivated by repression (although it is that in alienated form), but rather a *differentiating* movement that progresses through various, more complex stages towards reconciliation, or differentiated unity. Freud's idea about the originary psychic state of earliest infancy is reformulated by Loewald as a "mother-infant matrix of psychic life" (*ibid.*: 461) that is prior to the mother–child *relationship*. The developing infant's emergent awareness of an other as distinct from self unfolds through sublimating activity, where

> narcissism and object libido, identification and object cathexis, are products of differentiation within primary narcissism … within the mother-infant matrix of psychic life. Sublimation … involves an internal re-creative return toward that matrix, a reconciliation of the polarized elements produced by individuation and … by sexual differentiation. Sublimation thus *brings together what had become separate*.
>
> (Loewald 2000: 461)

This results in the "reconciliation of the subject–object dichotomy" (*ibid.*: 460).

Sublimation is another term for the transformation of primary (earliest) mentation into secondary higher-order mental process that enables language and symbolic thought, whereby passion is converted into "a thirst for knowledge" (Freud 1910a: 74). Intellectual activity and achievement are not the antithesis of passion, but, rather, are nourished and animated by it. For Loewald and for Freud, the creative energies of the primary process are mobilized through the transformations of primary narcissism as it embraces and identifies with external objects, not in a linear, progressive fashion, but rather through a self-differentiating and transmuting activity of "contradiction, conflict, spiraling, reconciliation, a dissolving of achieved reconciliations, [and] new resolutions of dissonances" (Loewald 2000: 448). The result of this developmental process is a higher, individuated psychic unity. Loewald quotes Freud's reminder that "the extirpation of the infantile wishful impulses is *by no means the ideal aim of development*" (Freud 1910b: 53, emphasis added) in support of his own argument. If the sublimatory process is disrupted through the defensive and alienating forces of repression, the internal connections between the various dimensions of psychic experience linking primary and secondary process are broken and distorted. One devastating result of such breakdown is an impaired capacity for symbolic and abstract thought. An individual may then experience these split-off or dissociated parts of her mind as persecutors, monsters, demons or gods against whom she must fight, or appeal to, for survival. As the burden of carrying these psychic monstrosities becomes too much to bear, they are disavowed and projected into the external world and onto others who take on the same terrifying and dangerous qualities. This accounts for the uncanny *(un)heimlich* quality of demons, monsters, spirits or any other manner of frightening supernatural or superhuman entities. Loewald explains that Freud understood how "the sense of the power of early primal forces and experiences (whether for good or evil as to consequences) that dominate life and that, in so far as they are recognized or intimated, convey the sense of the uncanny" (2000: 65). Explanations of the uncanny, the daemonic and telepathy converge in a theory of an originary psyche that does not "reside in a primordial individual self or individual instinctive core but in a *wider 'subjectivity'* that includes the creative-destructive powers of the parental couple" (*ibid.*: 516, emphasis added) and, Freud would add, all the ancestral "parental couples" instantiated in each new generation.

In part, Loewald's argument refines and reformulates Freud's theory of drives in terms of "psychic, motivational forces, [which] become organized as such through interactions within a psychic field consisting originally of the mother–child (psychic) unit" (2000: 127–8). This means that "what is naively called objects plays an essential part in the constitution of the subject … and what is naively called subject plays an essential part in the organization of objects" (*ibid.*: 127) so that there is no such thing as a discrete, bounded or separate individual subject "in here" who encounters an equally discrete and bounded individual object "out there". "Otherness" is part of the constitution of our individual identity, an integral part of who we are, and this internally relational subjectivity is always in the process of becoming through its capacity for receptive openness towards other minds as well as different parts of itself. This is the concept of mind that both underlies and makes possible psychoanalytic clinical phenomena such as transference/counter-transference and projective identification.[5] For Loewald, and for Freud as well (although less optimistically), the clinical goal of fostering emotional and spiritual health involves the reversal of repressive and alienating processes of sublimation that have shattered and broken the connections between primary and secondary processes within an individual's mind (Loewald 2000: 463). The analyst helps the patient re-establish internal bridges between multiple psychic states that can foster healthier connectedness with "others" both within the self and in the world. When this fails to happen, and internal mental states are cut off from each other due to repression, the conditions are set that facilitate uncanny experiences of feeling inhabited by alien "others" or "doubles". As Adam Phillips has written more recently, "To assume that there is an unconscious is to believe that there really are other people, other voices, inside and outside of oneself (that if there is a mind, it has minds of its own)" (2002: xv). Freud emphasizes that the threatening nature of unconscious impulses and desires that are part of the self become perceived as foreign invaders who undermine internal cohesion and emotional stability. In this kind of mental state, the individual is terrorized by a sense of helplessness and vulnerability that can only be located in the daemonic power of inescapable fate.

## Some contemporary psychoanalytic perspectives on the uncanny and telepathy

Loewald's relational and differentiated theory of mind provides a theoretical resource that advances and clarifies Freud's efforts to provide psychoanalytic explanations for so-called telepathic and uncanny phenomena. As has already been discussed in detail, Freud's theory of narcissism attempts to explain the sense of a unitary "oceanic" feeling in terms of a recollection of pre-Oedipal infantile psychic experience. As far as Freud is concerned, a sense of oneness with the external world is a product of the developing mind, and this is the most important point for this discussion. Loewald extends Freud's theory of narcissism with his notion of a "wider subjectivity", where the distinctions between self and other are more permeable than they ordinarily appear. This idea is especially rich in its clinical implications for the possibilities of deeper understanding and communication between the analytic pair. It also goes a long way in offering a psychoanalytic account of the phenomenon of unconscious communication that is again clinically promising. However, none of what Loewald and Freud hypothesize with regard to unconscious communication has been proven by current conventional evidence or methods of empirical validation. This in no way means that unconscious communication does not happen or that there are no strongly plausible arguments to be made in support of its existence. In recent years, psychoanalysts have been more publicly vocal about their own experiences of unconscious communication in the clinical setting (Stoller [1973] 2001; Farrell 1983; Silverman 1988; Marcus 1997; Bass 2001; Mayer 2008). Freud did not attempt to explain fully the detailed mechanisms and precise means whereby unconscious communications transpired between the patient and the analyst (Kantrowitz 2001: 26) and he did not seem overly troubled by it. For Freud, the central focus of psychoanalytic theory is always the unconscious. For him, *all* explanations of occult *experiences* (not phenomena), however weird, must begin with it. It is the home of gods, demons, encounters with the ghosts of the dead and telepathy. The spirits and divinities of all the ages originate and reside in there. Freud did not consider that the internal fantasies, feelings or conflicts resulting in occult experiences could have anything to do with a mysterious reality "out there". Such an idea would fall under what Freud called "the spook complex" (Freud cited in Fodor 1963: 123).

A growing number of contemporary psychoanalysts appear to be more concerned to explain, or perhaps justify, what they believe to be the concrete empirical reality of a whole range of occult experiences that are now collected together under the rubric of "anomalous experiences". By now these include not only unconscious communication, but phenomena that Freud would not have taken into serious account, such as telekinesis, clairvoyance, dowsing or remote viewing (see especially Mayer 2008). Given that psychoanalytic explanations for this wide range of anomalous experiences remain incomplete, some analysts are turning to the reality-bending theories of quantum physics (Mayer 1996, 2002, 2008; Bass 2001; Godwin 1991; Lazar 2001; Altman 2007) to provide the scientific supports they believe can and will legitimate some of what amounts to reconstituted or reconstructed occult claims. What Freud had in mind when he tackled the phenomenon of thought-transference has morphed into quite a different, and at times quasi-spiritual, preoccupation within some areas of contemporary psychoanalysis. Although a full account of this relatively recent interest within psychoanalytic circles is beyond the scope of this chapter, a few remarks are in order by way of conclusion.

One major problem with this growing psychoanalytic appeal to quantum physics (see for example Lazar 2001) is that the field itself offers no conclusive empirical validation for unconscious communication or anomalous experiences. This means that psychoanalysis must proceed with great care as it incorporates its own understanding of contemporary physics within its theorizing. The field of quantum physics is far more complex, complicated, contradictory and contested than it at times appears when represented in the work of some psychoanalysts. Nonetheless, there are analytic writers who do not hesitate to incorporate selected aspects of the diverse range of speculative and highly technical theories of quantum physics – such as Bell's theorem, Heisenberg's Uncertainty Principle, non-locality, entanglement and the quantum hologram – to underwrite their new models of psychic reality (Lazar 2001; Mayer 2008).

I am not arguing that psychoanalysis should not engage with physics in a hermeneutically strategic fashion as a means of deepening and enhancing its own conceptual and theoretical range. As Freud clearly demonstrated with his heavy reliance on a variety of disciplines in his development of psychoanalysis, it is important that psychoanalysis not isolate itself from other epistemological frameworks and conceptual schools of thought. Psychoanalysis should, however, exercise caution in taking a definitive or conclusive stand on internal debates within quantum physics by presuming to evaluate its data and theories.

There are a number of questions in this field in particular that remain to be settled, to say the least. For clinical purposes especially, there is no need to "prove" the existence of thought-transference. Psychoanalysts, after all, are accustomed to uncertainty. Some of the research of disciplines from quantum physics to mirror neurons or meme theory, for example, may be richly suggestive for new paths of psychoanalytic inquiry, and in that respect, ought to be explored. They may also enhance and deepen the way we think about the human mind by interrogating and shifting our perspectives about the way we think and the assumptions we make. At the same time, it cannot be over emphasized that the insights psychoanalysis chooses to incorporate from contemporary physics, however richly suggestive for new and creative ways of thinking about clinical experience, must be held tentatively and lightly.

Elizabeth Lloyd Mayer, whose work is illustrative of a number of analysts who share her views on "anomalous experiences", writes that "the individual boundaried mind and the radically connected mind describe models of the mind that can start to complement each other in new and critically important ways" (2002: 94). As we have seen from the discussion above, Freud's ideas of the mind, especially as elaborated by Loewald, are not incompatible with this view. There may be much important philosophical and experiential truth in her perspective that is worthy of consideration for psychoanalytic theory and clinical practice. But this approach to the mind, however clinically useful and conceptually rich, cannot be "proven" empirically by drawing upon selected theoretical speculations concerning the connectedness of all reality advanced by quantum physics. One problem with invoking the concepts of contemporary physics in support of psychoanalytic theories of the nature of the deep connectedness of human minds is that "there is to date no agreed-upon interpretation of the theory of quantum mechanics" (Appelbaum 2012: 118). Richard Feynman, the Nobel Prize-winning theoretical physicist, remarked that "no one understands quantum mechanics" (in Appelbaum 2012: 118). Moreover, many theories of quantum physics rely to a large extent on mathematical speculations for which there is as yet not a lot of corresponding experimental evidence (*ibid.*: 120).

Although aware of the pitfalls in attempting an "even remotely literal application of changing concepts in science to the ultimately idiosyncratic data of psychoanalysis" (1996: 164), Mayer later did venture into that territory to a fairly significant extent in ways that Freud, for all his interest in the psychology of unconscious communication, would not be likely to endorse. In her subsequent work (2008), Mayer attempts to support her theories of the power of the human mind, and its essential interconnectedness with other minds and the physical world, by appealing to what she sees as the compelling truth claims emerging from researches in extra-sensory perception, remote viewing, telepathy, "distant mental intention" and, of course, quantum physics. She is by no means the first or the last analytic thinker to move in these directions (Devereux 1953; Lazar 2001; Totton 2003).[6] Altman, following a very brief discussion of a few selected ideas from quantum theory, concludes that it supports the idea that "the confluence of mental processes" that occur at times between patient and analyst is "evidence" that this experience emerges from a joint common source" that "transcends" them both (2007: 532). It remains to be seen what the implications of a theory about a unitary relational universe on the subatomic level are for new or altered understandings of reality on the macro level. While Mayer acknowl-edges this point, she concludes that the fact that there is no basis for assuming the existence of correspondences between the subatomic and macro-levels of reality doesn't mean that there isn't one (1996: 188). This may be true, but it can take psychoanalysis no further in explaining these instances of unconscious communication that do occur in the clinical setting.

It is only fair to say that most of the analytic thinkers and clinicians inter-ested in the phenomenon of thought-transference insist they are not concerned with "the domain of occultism", but rather "the occult of psychoanalysis and the psychoanalytic process" (Eshel 2006: 1622). While it cannot be overstated that psychoanalysis remains relevant by engaging with other disciplines to enlarge and strengthen its scope of understanding as a hermeneutics of human being (Ricoeur 1970), there is little at the moment to be gained by trying to account for thought-transference by linking it to the diverse range of occult phenom-ena clustered within the concept of anomalous experience. Unconscious com-munication was a psychoanalytic issue for Freud, not an occult phenomenon. Clinicians know that unconscious communication takes place, and they know something about the conditions that facilitate it, but they don't quite know how. This theoretical uncertainty must be held until such time as neuroscience, quantum physics or some other discipline is able to determine with greater empirical precision how this phenomenon works. The only possible legitimate way that current psychoanalytic theories of permeable mental states and the inherent connectedness of individual minds can be brought into theoretical contact with quantum physics at the moment is by metaphor or analogy, and even that may be questionable. Quantum physics cannot be imported whole-sale into psychoanalysis, lest it become another form of religion, a more diffuse set of spiritual beliefs under the guise of science.

Other analytic thinkers look elsewhere, to the field of neuroscience, for example, and its theory of "mirror neurons" (Rosenbaum 2011), or the intuitive powers of right-brain function (Schore 2011a, 2011b) as they ponder the mysteries of unconscious communication. A similar caution regarding psychoanalytic appropriations of quantum physics applies to the study of the more recently discovered phenomenon of mirror neurons and its corresponding idea of emotional contagion (Mayer 2008: 235). It must be remembered, for example, that "a mirror neuron is but one neuron in a complex network of thousands or perhaps millions of interconnected neurons" (Cozalino 2002: 184). Again, psychoanalysis must proceed with great caution as it attempts to incorporate selected insights from these disciplines. In the end, perhaps the best possible relationship that can exist between psychoanalysis and contemporary science is dialogical, where each contributes something of its imaginative richness to the other in their common effort to envision the world as "open to new possibilities" (Appelbaum 2012: 124) of understanding and meaning. As far as Freud was concerned, there does indeed exist a mysterious universe of widely diverse and strange phenomena. For him, that universe was contained within the biologically based, but not strictly biologically determined, human mind and must be accounted for there.

FIVE

# What's love got to do with it?
# New psycho-mythologies

I myself have always advocated the love for mankind not out of sentimentality or idealism but for sober, economic reasons: because in the
face of our instinctual drives and the world as it is I was compelled to
consider this love as indispensable for the preservation of the human
species.                    (Freud to Romain Rolland, 29 January 1926)[1]

Every psycho-analytic treatment is an attempt at liberating repressed
love ...                                           (Freud 1907b: 90)

Henri Ellenberger captures the challenge of writing about a thinker as capacious
and prodigious as Freud with the astute observation that the vast "profusion
of the literature about him" is so often based on numerous and contradictory
legends that the task can be "exceedingly laborious and unrewarding" (1970:
427). This statement has particular relevance when writing about Freud's critical analyses of religion. The frequent characterization of Freud as aggressively
negative and disdainful towards religion suggests that his views are more often
than not extremely offensive to religious believers. This perspective is succinctly illustrated in the sweeping assertion that "*all* students of psychoanalysis
and religion *agree* that Freud took a dismissive approach to religion because
he was convinced it was delusional" (Anderson 2007: 121, emphasis added).
One could say that Freud's "hostility to religion" (*ibid.*: 122) has itself become
the subject of legend in psychoanalytic circles and beyond. The variety of posi-
tions that assert and attempt to account for this "hostility" to religion are too
diverse and numerous to recount here; instead, my focus in this chapter is on
those commentators who interpret his theory of religion as most lacking an
appreciation of the importance of love in healthy psychological development
and the role of mother-love in particular. The idea that Freudian psychoanalysis
repudiates or is largely devoid of love is a taken-for-granted thesis held by a
number of these critics. That Freud had so little regard for love is seen as key

in accounting for his negativity towards religion. As I will argue here, Freud's psychoanalytic thinking about love is somewhat more complicated than many of these critics acknowledge.

The emergence of object relations theory in psychoanalysis, represented in particular by the Scottish analysts Ian Dishart Suttie (1898–1935) and W. R. D. Fairbairn (1889–1964), is often cited as an important corrective to the quasi-caricature of a loveless Freudian drive theory and its corresponding views of early psychological development. Object relations theory is also credited with providing an opening for a more positive view of religion and its importance to mental health. "With the shift in psychoanalytic theory towards an appreciation for the fundamental psychological value of relationships, a more appreciative model of religion became possible" (Liebman & Abell 2000: 16). Influenced especially by British psychoanalyst D. W. Winnicott's concept of the "transitional object" and "transitional space" (1999), with its positive implications for the creativity of the religious imagination, theologically oriented object relations analysts such as Ana Maria Rizutto assert that human life and its potential for creativity is "impoverished" without religion, which is "an integral part of being human" (1979: 47). Others point to Freud's own personal and psychological conflicts with respect to religion as accounting for his negative attitude. Expressing a view that resonates with Rizutto's in a number of respects, the late psychoanalyst and Jesuit priest W. W. Meissner attributed Freud's critique of religion to both his personal envy towards "the power of religion" as well as the "repressed, unresolved, and ambivalent aspects of his own psychic functioning" (1984: 78).

It is also widely assumed and endlessly repeated that for Freud, the child's desire for the loving protection of the father *alone* and the ensuing "Oedipal relationship" (Aron 2008: xvi) animates the adult's continued need for a father-god. Such assumptions are offered as further evidence that a singular psycho-patriarchal orientation underpins and dominates many of Freud's major theoretical concepts, including the general psychosexual development of the child and the consequent psychic formations of the Oedipus complex and the superego. This reading of Freud has generated an enormous literature that is highly critical of what is taken to be his lopsided focus on masculinity as the sole representative of the full range of human psychological, intellectual, ethical and religious capacity and function. There is certainly no dearth of evidence to support this reading within Freud's work itself. His last paper on women and femininity (1933d), for example, contains a number of troubling statements about female psychosexuality, such as the now infamous idea of "penis envy" and the paucity of women's contributions to culture and ethics. Yet a distinction needs to be made between Freud's analysis of the actual condition of women in Western culture and what he thought it should be.[2] Freud was well aware that in large measure, the so-called intellectual "inferiority" of women had much to do with the restrictions imposed on them by social convention (1908: 198–9) However, there is more that needs to be considered with respect to this particular story.

As is almost always the case with Freud, his ideas are more nuanced, complex and self-questioning than is often acknowledged by his critics. In Steven Pile's view, "one of the most outstanding aspects of Freud's work is his readiness to challenge and reconsider his own presuppositions" (1999: 206). Sometimes Freud does this in the same text, as is well illustrated, for example, in *Moses and Monotheism*. Thomas Ogden makes the very insightful observation that Freud was a writer who thought as he wrote, making:

> no attempt to cover his tracks … his false starts, his uncertainties, his reversals of thinking … and his shelving of compelling ideas for the time being because they seemed to him too speculative or lacking adequate clinical foundation … each of his psychoanalytic writings, from this point of view, is simultaneously an explication of a set of concepts and a demonstration of a newly created way of thinking about and experiencing ourselves. (Ogden 2002: 767)

Ogden's perspective is helpful in understanding the sometimes partial and seemingly paradoxical arguments found in any number of themes throughout Freud's work. Religion is a case in point. Again, Freud says any number of different things about religion in his published texts, depending on the theme he is addressing. This accounts for the sustained respectful curiosity with which he ponders the "oceanic" feeling that is not found in his treatment of religion in *The Future of an Illusion*, for example. Something similar applies to his writing on thought transference. That he took it seriously in no way means that he accepted the supernatural claims commonly associated with occult experiences. His support of Fodor's book on poltergeists was related to Fodor's interest in the psychology of such experiences, not in whether poltergeists actually exist.

Ogden's view also lends support to my contention that Freud's differentiated critique of religion shifts its focus of attention according to what aspect of religious sensibilities, beliefs and their consequences – negative or positive – he is addressing in any given text. Again, the careful attention that is apparent in Freud's discussion of the "oceanic experience" itself belies the charge of a blanket disdain and dismissal of religion on Freud's part. The same is true regarding Freud's theory that the highest cultural achievements of abstract thought, law and morality originate in Egyptian and Jewish monotheism. His hinting at "something further behind" (Freud 1930a) an infantile sense of helplessness in the origin of religion that he cannot account for is an expression of genuine perplexity on his part. When Freud says that the pre-Oedipal world is "wrapped in obscurity" (*ibid.*: 72), he is saying more about the state of psychoanalytic knowledge about this phase of development than he is show-ing any kind of disinterest in it. It is important to note here that Freud is not rejecting the importance of the pre-Oedipal experience; rather, he is admitting his ignorance of it. Freud's *psychoanalytic* inquiry into the psychodynamics of religious belief in the father-god of Christianity and Judaism is not the simple result of a thoughtless exclusion of the maternal dimensions of divine nature or the mother's importance in the psychological and emotional development of her children.

In his posthumously published "Outline of Psychoanalysis", written towards the end of his life, Freud (1940) reiterates the view expressed in a number of places in his work concerning the child's first experiences of an external world encompassed in the maternal breast. The importance of the maternal presence for the developing infant is in Freud's view "unique, without parallel, established unalterably for a whole lifetime as the first and strongest love-object and as the prototype of all later love-relations – for both sexes" (*ibid.*: 188). For Freud, the relationship with the mother underwrites and shapes the individual's love relations over the life span. A little later in the same text, Freud writes that "however long it is fed at its mother's breast, it will always be left with a conviction after it has been weaned that its feeding was too short and too little" (*ibid.*: 189). In this observation, Freud links desire for the mother with desire for knowledge of, and participation in, the larger world. The mother's love and care for the infant's bodily and emotional needs arouses the libidinal energies that ultimately transform and direct the child's desires outwards as a quest for knowledge and connection with others. This theme, taken together with Freud's other partially developed statements and speculations about pre-Oedipal experience and the origins of religion, calls for a reconsideration of the singular exclusivity of the patriarchal god attributed to Freud's theory. While Freud acknowledges the ambivalent nature of the infant–mother experience, he also emphasizes the creative and sustaining significance and power of mater-nal/feminine *love*.

## Love and psychoanalysis in Freud's *Gradiva*

The therapeutic, healing power of love and its potential for psychological resto-ration and repair in clinical and non-clinical relationships is most vividly dem-onstrated in Freud's essay "Delusions and Dreams in Jensen's *Gradiva*" (1907b). Decades before the publication of *Civilization and its Discontents* (1930a), we see Freud turning to archaeological science, one of his favourite subjects, and adapting it in the form of an extended metaphor that illuminates the spatial relationships between the different agencies of the mind. While his topographi-cal and structural theories of mind had yet to be more fully elaborated in his later metapsychology (Freud 1915b, 1923b), several aspects of these concepts are anticipated in the archaeological motif at the heart of the *Gradiva* essay. Archaeology also provides a metaphorical framework for conceptualizing clinical work in Freud's thought: the therapeutic action of psychoanalysis is a form of painstaking excavation and unearthing of the psychical layers of the mind that lie buried and preserved within the unconscious. The deepest recesses of the mind constitute a psychic burial ground created by the forces of repression, which must be undone by clinical work that can illuminate and find meaning in the mind's hidden contents. One of the most remarkable themes at the heart of Freud's interpretation of Jensen's romantic fictional narrative concerns the transformative potential of love in the process of healing one of the most serious psychopathologies: psychotic delusion. Simply stated, Freud's analysis of the *Gradiva* story shows how the love of one human being for another has the potential to overcome psychosis. His examination of love's healing power compels him to explicitly acknowledge the therapeutic limits of the healing potential of psychoanalysis.

It is by now common knowledge that Freud found inspiration for some of his greatest, most important "discoveries" about the human mind in literature and myth. After all, his reading of Greek mythology and drama inspired his single most important concept, the Oedipus complex, that led to his theory of unconscious fantasy and its influence on psychological development. Freud consistently maintained that creative writers possessed insights about the human mind "of which our philosophy has not yet let us dream" (Freud 1907b: 8). The main protagonist of Jensen's *Gradiva*, Norbert Hanold, is a young archaeologist whose devotion to the dead relics of the past displaces and deadens his interest in life to such an extent that he becomes mentally ill. Hanold falls in love with an image of a girl represented in an ancient Roman *bas-relief*. He manages to make a plaster cast of this girl – an image of an image, a representation of a living being twice removed. He hangs the replica of the ancient artefact in his study, where he spends considerable time gazing at what he sees as the girl's charming gait. He names her Gradiva, the one who "steps along" (Freud 1907b: 11). Hanold's obsessive concentration on the girl transforms into a dissociated extended waking dream that allows him to hallucinate Gradiva into existence so that he may pursue and find her. Following a nocturnal dream about Gradiva, whose brief life in Pompeii ended with her death in the volcanic destruction of the town in 79 CE, Hanold mourns her loss.

Eventually, Hanold's compulsive interest in Gradiva sends him to Pompeii. There he encounters a real girl, his forgotten childhood love, Zoe Bertgang. He believes she is Gradiva, the girl in the plaster cast, returned to life. As Hanold struggles to hang on to his remaining shreds of sanity, he cannot decide if the girl is a ghost or a hallucination. It turns out that Hanold had repressed his memories of Zoe Bertgang and his past love because of the weighty demands of his scientific studies. However Zoe, who continued to love Hanold over the years, quickly figures out what is going on. Instead of challenging his delusion or attempting to argue him out of it by reminding him of their childhood friendship, she participates in his hallucination "in order to set him free from it" (Freud 1907b: 21). Zoe's ability to see the kernel of existential truth at the heart of Hanold's delusion allowed her to do what Freud recommends clinicians do when faced with a patient's psychotic delusion: explore its kernel of existential truth. "Even the serious treatment of a real case of illness of the kind could proceed in no other way than to begin by taking up the same ground as the delusional structure and then investigating it as completely as possible" (*ibid.*: 22).

Over time, Zoe's patience pays off and the image of the long dead "Gradiva" eventually resolves itself into the living woman whom Hanold is finally free to love. Freud speculates that as Hanold became engrossed in his studies, he had to repress the memory of Zoe, or more accurately, his erotic *feelings* for her. Hanold fell into the trap of trying to sever emotion from intellect, likely in the all-too-common but mistaken and destructive belief that success in academic work is purchased at the sacrifice of passionate emotion. "What is alone of value in mental life", writes Freud, "is ... feelings" rather than mere cognition. Repression, he points out, is motivated by fear of "feelings which ought not to occur" (Freud 1907b: 49). Hanold's love for Zoe may have been buried by years of repression, but it was not eliminated. The image of the girl in the Roman relief sculpture "aroused the slumbering erotism in him, and made his childhood memories active" (*ibid.*) in a *Gradiva reviva*. The irony, of course, is not lost on Freud that Hanold is an archaeologist who becomes the object of his own profession. He too must undergo an excavation of sorts, a psychic unearthing of the emotional contents buried within his unconscious, if he is to have any hope of getting free of his delusion. Freud writes:

> There is ... no better analogy for repression, by which something in the mind is at once made inaccessible and preserved, than burial of the sort to which Pompeii fell a victim and from which it could emerge once more through the work of spades. Thus it was that the young archaeologist was obliged in his phantasy to transport to Pompeii the original of the relief which reminded him of the object of his youthful love.
>
> (Freud 1907b: 40)

The "ghost" of the dead Gradiva will cease to haunt him only when his memories of the living Zoe and his love for her are revived and restored. Hanold's psychosis may be reframed and understood as the traumatic result of the loss of love in his life.[3] What cures him and restores his sanity is Zoe's love.

Freud's interpretation of the therapeutic power of love has nothing to do with either sentiment or religion (Freud 1921a). Over the course of his psychoanalytic interpretation, love is eventually understood as belonging to a larger, inclusive libidinal energy with its multiple forms of expression in sexuality, friendship, love of parents, family and self. In Freud's view, the capacity for love can expand to embrace "humanity in general" as well as "devotion to concrete objects and to abstract ideas" (*ibid*.: 90). Freud eventually brought these various elements of libidinal energy together in the concept of "Eros" that "coincides" with both the notion of Eros in Plato's philosophy and the love extolled by "the apostle Paul" in his letter to the Corinthians. The libido of psychoanalysis is both a "love-force" (*ibid*.: 91) and a life-force whose creative energy results in the formation of "ever larger unities" (Freud 1920: 43). Included as examples of these "unities" are the reproduction of the human species in sexual activity and the formation of diverse and complex human relationships. Sex, love and friendship are the cornerstones that undergird the creation and shaping of culture in general. Within this conceptual framework, it is possible to interpret Zoe as foreshadowing key elements in Freud's later theory of Eros.

In Freud's interpretation of the narrative, Zoe represents the forces of life and love that counteract Hanold's dangerous, self-destructive drift into psychic disintegration and psychosis that derive from his abandonment of both his own and Zoe's love. Zoe's willingness to accept and share in Hanold's delusion stands as a model for therapeutic action that contrasts sharply with the "coarsening tendencies" of standard psychiatric theories and treatment approaches to psychosis. These, Freud contends, would have misconstrued Hanold's mental state by reducing it and framing it in the more psychiatric terms of "paranoia" and "fetishistic erotomania" because he was "in love with the piece of sculpture" (1907b: 45). Such an understanding of Hanold's psychosis is severely limited by this surface approach that focuses on symptoms while neglecting the underlying existential and psychic truth. By contrast, a psychoanalytic perspective on Hanold's delusion reveals the unconscious psychic conflicts hidden by repression. While Zoe is no psychoanalyst, her capacity to see Hanold's existential predicament allows her to respond to his conflicted and confused *feeling* state. Like any good psychoanalyst, Zoe concentrates on Hanold's feelings, which is the "essence" of therapeutic change:

> But the similarity between Gradiva's [Zoe's] procedure and the analytic method of psychotherapy is not limited to … the making conscious of what has been repressed and the coinciding of explanation with cure. It also extends to what turns out to be the essence of the whole change – to the *awakening of feelings*.     (Freud 1907b: 89, emphasis added)

Freud's interpretation of Zoe's actions suggests that the power of therapeutic action lies in relationship and in love. Effective psychoanalytic work does not and cannot operate on the level of consciousness alone. Freud is very clear that the cultivation of the rational mind is not sufficient to bring about psychological health. As we have seen in Hanold's case, an overemphasis on intellect can be psychologically dangerous. The distorting power and pressure of Hanold's repressed feelings, which erupted in the psychotic delusion precipitated by the image of Gradiva, overpowered his rational intellect honed by long years of scientific study. As the work of repression was incomplete, a psychotic compromise resulted. In similar fashion to Ulysses[4], who had his body strapped to the mast of his ship so that he could experience the pleasure of the Sirens' song without responding to it, so too with Hanold, who could allow himself to feel erotic love, but not for Zoe. Just as his self-imposed physical restraints prevented Ulysses from embracing the Sirens, Hanold's self-imposed psychical restraints paralyzed him with respect to Zoe. By repudiating Eros, both Ulysses and Hanold opt for and embrace existential death. In Hanold's case, he falls in love with death in the form of a dead image of a dead woman who never existed. Yet, somehow, Hanold clings to life by hallucinating his beloved into existence. His love for her, while buried within his unconscious, remains preserved, like a precious ancient artefact. Trapped within the unconscious, deadening conflicts of his own mind, Hanold is haunted by the return of the repressed in the form of a ghost. Cut off from a vital part of himself, Hanold remains cut off from reality. If he can fully access his own feelings, he will be able to reconnect with his love Zoe and thereby regain access to reality through her.

Freud remarks that an analysis of Hanold's delusion offers some insights into the psychology of religious beliefs in spirits and the afterlife. Ghosts and spirits originate in the psychological conflicts of the human mind; they are the signs of the return of the repressed. Freud understands Hanold's belief in Gradiva's ghost as an example of the human tendency to believe in ghosts and the afterlife, representing our willingness "to accept something absurd provided it satisfies powerful emotional impulses". No matter how educated or rational an individual may be, she is ever vulnerable to myriad forms of superstition because of the unconscious needs, motives and conflicts that clamour for satisfaction. Freud cautions:

> It must be remembered, too, that the belief in spirits and ghosts and the return of the dead, which finds so much support in the religions to which we have all been attached, at least in our childhood, is far from having disappeared among educated people, and that many who are sensible in other respects find it possible to combine spiritualism with reason. A man who has grown rational and skeptical … may be ashamed to discover how easily he may for a moment return to a belief in spirits under the combined impact of strong emotion and perplexity.  (Freud 1907b: 71)

Human beings, in short, need ghosts in order to tolerate threatening emotions and explain the unknown.

One of the ego's primary and ongoing labouring activities is to make sense of the unconscious contents of the mind. Culture provides a vast reservoir of literatures, mythologies and religions that help in giving shape to and formulating meaning within the mind's incomprehensible darkness. Hanold's psychosis was just that – an elaborate culturally mediated narrative that gave meaning and coherence to his profound but hidden emotional conflicts. It allowed him to preserve his love for Zoe and tolerate the pain of her loss throughout the years. His psychosis was also the gateway to the restoration of an enlarged, revitalized self that had become shrunken and depleted by his singular devotion to scientific work that excluded feeling and love relations from his life. At the same time, Hanold's delusion contained the alienated psychic truth of his experience. As Freud often reminds his readers, "There is a grain of truth concealed in every delusion, there is something in it that really deserves belief, and this is the source of the patient's conviction, which is therefore to that extent justified" (Freud 1907b: 80).

Freud's reading of the Gradiva story also forces him to acknowledge the limits of psychoanalysis as a clinical therapy. Zoe's "treatment" of Hanold parallels a psychotherapeutic approach that remains as close as possible to the experience of the patient. She takes Hanold's delusion seriously because, like Freud and any other experienced clinician, she perceives the grain of truth within it. Zoe remembers the shared childhood love with Hanold, and she gently coaxes him to health as she helps him connect with his repressed memories. The advantage that Zoe has over the clinician, Freud points out, is that *her* "therapeutic procedure" need not be limited to "making conscious … what has been repressed" but can extend to reviving Hanold's feelings for *her* (Freud 1907b: 89). Zoe's love for Hanold helps him remember his love for her, further helping to resolve his delusions and restoring him to psychic health. Zoe, as the living symbol of the return of the repressed, facilitates the reawakening of Hanold's repressed desire and love, which heretofore had been partially manifested in the distortions of psychotic symptoms (*ibid.*: 90). The curative aim of the therapeutic process "is accomplished in a relapse into love" that is only *temporarily* directed at the analyst in the transference. For the patient to live a richer, more satisfying life, his love *must* eventually be redirected to someone or something other than the analyst, an outcome that is by no means guaranteed. Herein lie the limits of psychoanalysis, and Freud is well aware of it.

Zoe has far more success than any analyst could. Once awakened, Hanold's love for her can be acted upon, as can hers for him. Restricted by the ethics of her profession, the analyst cannot – must not – offer the fullness of love to the patient that Zoe could offer Hanold. As the "object" of Hanold's repressed love, she "was able to return the love which was making its way from the unconscious into consciousness" (Freud 1907b: 90). Like Zoe, the analyst too must become an object of the patient's love in the process of liberating that love from repression. Unlike Zoe, the analyst cannot return the patient's love fully. Freud did not approve of any form of sexual contact with patients, as is clear in his caution to his friend and colleague Sandor Ferenczi against kissing his patients (Jones 1957: 163–5). Nonetheless, in a poignant and moving passage, Freud acknowledges that the analyst is of necessity a "stranger, and must endeavour to become a stranger once more after the cure; he is often at a loss what advice to give the patients he has cured as to how in real life they can use their recovered capacity to love" (1907b: 90).

While Freud was well aware of the potential transformative healing power of love in the therapeutic process, he never idealized it. Instead, he attempted to analyse and understand the complexity and contradictory nature of its creative and destructive possibilities. Familial relations of love can provide the stability and strength for subsequent enriching love relationships throughout the human lifespan; incestuous love cannot. Freud has a differentiated concept of love that locates it within a multiplicity of dynamic components that constitute Eros, the life force motivated by desire not only for sexual gratification and reproduction of the human species, but by the desire for connection and unity with specific concrete others and the surrounding world. While Freud believed that human beings are capable of love, tenderness and devotion from the earliest stages of life, he dismissed sentimentalized idealizations of love as championed in the Christian command to love the neighbour, as we have seen in Chapter 2. Freud's rejection of an ethics of love for an empty abstraction in no way means that he was blind to the constructive power of love between people, as his account of Zoe and Hanold attests. Genuine meaningful love for another person is motivated partly by the recognition of oneself in the other, which has its psychic roots in narcissism but is not necessarily cynically solipsistic. For Freud, there are healthy and diseased forms of narcissism. As we have seen, the movement of primary to secondary narcissism involves the "taking in" of aspects of beloved others who contribute to the organization and emotional enrichment of the growing child's inner world.

The analyst's love in clinical work is motivated by an acceptance of the patient's suffering that is based on a willingness to stay as close as possible to the truth of his experience, no matter how unsettling or even frightening it may be. Freud's understanding of the common humanity shared by the analyst and patient informs his consistently expressed view that mental illness is part of a dimensional psychic continuum rather than a separate categorical phenomenon. Freud (1940) explains that his analyses of dreams yielded a lifelong conviction that "it is not scientifically feasible to draw a line of demarcation between what is psychically normal and abnormal". Such distinctions for Freud possessed merely "conventional value", revealing very little of the nature of the mind and its potential for psychopathology. For Freud, knowledge of neuroses allows for "an understanding of the normal life of the mind" (*ibid.*: 195). The vicissitudes of human experience over the course of a life, and their impact on psychological health, affect the analyst and neurotic alike. That psychoanalytic theory and practice is about human beings and their relationships with each other, as well as with different parts of themselves, was abundantly clear to Freud. Loewald describes analytic love in a way Freud could accept, as Loewald appears to be aware of himself, when he writes:

> It is impossible to love the truth of psychic reality, to be moved by this love as Freud was in his lifework, and *not to love and care for the object whose truth we want to discover* ... Our object, being what it is, is the other in ourselves and ourself in the other. To discover truth about the patient is always discovering it with him and for him as *well as for ourselves and about ourselves.*          (Loewald 2000: 297, emphasis added)

Although it seems clear that Freud shared such a view of analytic love, he does not lose sight of its necessary limits. In light of all this, there is a need to revisit the widespread view of Freud as a theorist whose work is devoid of love and holds scant appreciation of the vital importance of the mother–child relationship in the fostering of psychological health. There may be a number of understandable reasons for this general attitude, some more compellingly argued than others. However, one of them involves traces of a lingering Christian bias against "Jewish" psychoanalysis that remain hidden yet active within contemporary theory.

## The Christian anti-Judaism of Ian Dishart Suttie

In recent years, the psychotherapist Ian Dishart Suttie has become increasingly recognized as one of the most important representatives of a distinctively Scottish psychoanalysis with an interest in revising "traditional Christian doctrines in order to provide a rational, non-fideistic religion suitable for the modern world" (Miller 2008: 38). Suttie's repudiation of Freudian theory is increasingly considered to be an important early antidote and "relational alternative" to a psychoanalysis understood to privilege sex, aggression and envy over love, and instinctual gratification over connectedness (Shaw 2003: 260). Whereas Freud is simplistically interpreted as positing a world strictly populated by atomized, innately aggressive individuals locked in death-dealing struggles against each other,[5] Suttie and his followers are seen as envisioning an alternative world of Christian-inspired communities founded upon their adherents' innate capacity for love. Although largely neglected during his own lifetime, and for years afterwards, Suttie is now credited with inaugurating object relations theory, which postulates the need for relationships as a primary directive of psychological development. His influence continues to shape psychoanalysis to this day (Gerson 2009; Shaw 2003; Cassullo 2010; Aron 1996; Homans 1989; Brown 1963). Peter Rudnytsky goes so far as to declare that Suttie's only book, the posthumously published *The Origins of Love and Hate* (1966), is not only a "classic" text but "contains virtually every idea" (Rudnytsky 1991: 6) subsequently elaborated by object relations theorists. Howard Bacal (1987: 82) asserts that Suttie's ideas anticipate the self psychology tradition later founded by Heinz Kohut. Even more recently, Graham Clarke (2011) has persuasively demonstrated that the much better known Scottish object relations theorist W. R. D. Fairbairn derived some of his most important and enduringly influential ideas directly from Suttie's book. Clarke's discovery of Suttie's strong influence on Fairbairn casts a new and modifying light on statements such as Hoffman's that "the religious narratives that influenced Fairbairn" contributed "ultimately" to the "relational turn" (2004: 771) in contemporary psychoanalysis. If Hoffman and others are correct in such observations, then the distilled traces of Suttie's religiosity, which stands behind Fairbairn's, must inevitably be present in contemporary relational psychoanalysis as well.

In the context of the putative significance and continuing impact of Suttie's thought on subsequent developments in psychoanalysis, it is necessary to examine more carefully the main outlines of Suttie's criticisms of Freud. Some of Suttie's harshest comments on Freud are most clearly contextualized in his contrasting portraits of Christianity and Judaism, which frame his critique. Briefly, Suttie's sharpest repudiations of Freud are based not only on a narrow reading of his ideas, but also on some serious simplifications of Freud's thought that are expressed in terms of the superiority of a love-based, "maternal" Christianity over a loveless, patriarchal Judaism. Eli Zaretsky (1998: 35) goes so far as to describe Suttie's depiction of Freud's emphasis on the father as having "overtones of anti-Semitism", although he does not elaborate. The discussion of Suttie presented here reflects the general argument, advanced in previous chapters, that Freud's texts on religion and culture tend to be narrowly interpreted as little more than hostile atheistic tracts. In the particular case of Suttie, his repudiation of Freudian theory brings into the field of psychoanalysis a disturbing, persistent and very old Christian theological tradition of anti-Judaism.[6] Although in many respects long severed from their conscious and explicit anti-Judaism theological sources, echoes of this ancient Christian religious bias nonetheless reverberate in arguments that castigate Freud's negative attitude to religion and religious spirituality. Suttie's critique of Freud is squarely rooted in and informed by this Christian prejudice. Later writers influenced by Suttie have implicitly and inevitably incorporated some of these traces of Christian anti-Judaism into their own work. This becomes especially apparent in the uncritical acceptance of Suttie's charge that Freudian theory champions a "taboo on tenderness" that refuses to acknowledge that love is a primary motivator in psychological development. Most unsettling is that writers since Suttie continue to account for Freud's putative repudiation of tenderness by referring to the patriarchal Jewish elements assumed to reside in his personality and thought (Wright 2006: 174). The idea seems to be that Judaism is devoid of love.

Suttie, despite his former "blind devotion to Freud" (1966: 194), scathingly denounces his entire theory on the grounds that it is "correlated with a pessimism and aggressive attitude which, in fact, we find in *all* Freud's writings" (*ibid.*: 196, emphasis added). His numerous accusations against Freud include charges that he negates love "for its own sake" (*ibid.*: 201); that Freud "sees no positive drives whatever in life" and, most strikingly, that "Freudian theory is *based on hate – a denial of love*" (*ibid.*: 205, emphasis added). For Suttie, this means that any psychoanalytic theory that denies love cannot result in therapeutic success – not, on the face of it, an unreasonable assumption.

However, Suttie's charge that psychoanalysis promotes hatred can hardly be taken seriously as applying to Freud, as my earlier discussion of his analysis of the *Gradiva* narrative makes clear. Suttie attributes Freud's "denial" of love to a "grudge against mothers and a mind-blindness for love" (1966: 189). He partially grounds his argument on a historical anthropological assumption that matriarchal societies based on justice and love preceded and were supplanted by patriarchal rule based on aggression and hatred. He postulates the existence of a pre-Christian "Pagan Teutondom of northern Europe" (Suttie 1932: 290) that was religiously organized around a "predominance of female divinities" and gender relationships characterized by heterosexual complementarity and social companionship (*ibid.*: 290, 295). Suttie believed that an older matriarchal ethics of justice, care and love persisted long after the establishment of patriarchal power, resurfacing in the "new ethical theory" and "social psychology" introduced by Jesus. Early Christianity ushered in a "new conception of God [and] his relation to man" that held revolutionary implications for the "purpose and value of human lives". This "salient departure from the parent faith", Judaism, is summed up in Suttie's formulation: "Good fellowship is good service to God, and the law is for the good of mankind. Love, not law, is the basis of social life, and transgressions can and ought to be forgiven" (*ibid.*: 296).

As Suttie understands the religious and cultural dynamics of first-century Palestine, the new love religion of early Christianity supplanted the "Semitic sense of sin" and lightened the burden of "guilty apprehension that characterizes Judaism" (*ibid.*: 296). The "repressive and propitiary" legacy of Judaism (*ibid.*: 298) within psychoanalysis could only be countered by a shift in focus on the innate reciprocal love of mother and child that displaces and refutes the authoritarian law of the father, which accords with Christian teaching (Suttie

1966: 116). In a "thoughtful" (Shaw 2003: 260) review of *The Origins of Love and Hate*, William Alanson White repeats (without critical comment) Suttie's view that "Freud, being a Jew and therefore brought up in the beliefs and traditions of his race, which are essentially patriarchal in character, has naturally and unconsciously emphasized the significance of the father to the exclusion of the mother" (White 1937: 458) in his psychoanalytic theory. In a more recent article by Kenneth Wright (2006) that explicitly acknowledges Suttie's influence on contemporary psychoanalysis, we find that the binary formulation that sets "Judaism/Law" over "Christianity/Love" is carried over intact: "Paternal religion wants the Law (the Ten Commandments, for example) to reign supreme", says Wright; "Jesus, a more maternal advocate, wanted to replace this love of the Law with an empathic love of one's neighbour" (*ibid*.: 176).

Wright appears to follow Suttie in assuming that "patriarchal" Judaism is also devoid of empathy and group solidarity. Christianity, on the other hand, emphasizes the sociality of communion, which is what Suttie believes. For Suttie, the value of maternal love for Christianity is evidenced by the "cult of the Virgin Mother", whose earlier antecedents derive from the "Holy Ghost" (1966: 129). In Suttie's Christian view, there is ample evidence that "the main concern of the Christian teachings" is "the cultivation of love as the basis of happiness, mental stability and social harmony" (*ibid*.: 127). It is clear to him that Christianity "is addressed to, and meets the needs of, more developed minds than those to which the older father cult appeals" (*ibid*.: 130). The Christian message of love and good fellowship fosters higher intellectual development and promotes mental health in comparison with the anxious adherence of less developed Jewish minds to the more primitive and authoritarian patriarchal divinity of Judaism. The argument put forward by Suttie and accepted by some later psychoanalytic writers influenced by him of Christianity as a maternal religion of love amounts to little more than a "polemical mirror image of [Suttie's] distorted picture of Judaism". Most New Testament scholars today would concur that Suttie's portrayal of early Christianity and first-century Judaism "represents a profound misunderstanding of them both".[7]

The anti-Judaism bias that underlies Suttie's repudiation of Freud is part of an ancient but stubbornly persistent supercessionist and triumphalist Christian theological tradition that is not uncommon in New Testament scholarship, particularly that of the nineteenth and early twentieth centuries (Tyson 1999; Sanders 1999). The argument supporting Christianity's displacement of Judaism is based on a longstanding and "historically incorrect view" (Tyson 1999: 217) that paints the religious ethos of first-century Judaism as obsessed with strict adherence to worn-out legalisms and deadening ritual practice. In his influential and important book *Das Wesen des Christentums* (*What is Christianity?*), the respected early twentieth-century New Testament scholar Adolf von Harnack wrote that the Pharisees[8] had "darkened" and "distorted" the "good and holy" within the law by "choking" it with the "sand and dirt" of ritual practice and legalistic imperatives; Jesus came to change all that by liberating the purity and clarity of the law's truth with his message of love (in Tyson 1999: 229–30). Von Harnack's view belongs to a "consensus" (*ibid.*: 228) within New Testament scholarship that has long portrayed the father-god of Judaism as "distant and estranged" (*ibid.*: 224), a deity possessing neither love nor mercy but insisting only on a rigid adherence to his laws. On this account, Judaism degenerated into a hypocritical religion devoted to strict observance of a deadening enslavement to external ritual. Judaism had become estranged from love and mercy in its obsession with the rules of obedience and punishment. Apparently, this attitude is carried over in Freudian psychoanalysis.

The arrival of Jesus, as the story goes, ushers in a new religiosity of justice, mercy and love that emphasizes instead a more psychologically based dispositional ethics (Tyson 1999: 230). New Testament scholar Ed Sanders describes this psychological Jesus as a theological construct that was developed and nurtured in the long tradition of New Testament scholarship and its "subordinating polemic" (Sanders 1999: 276) towards Judaism. The purpose of such theologically-interested scholarship is to discredit and displace Judaism in order to prove the religious and moral superiority of Christianity. This "malignant religious polemic" (*ibid.*: 283–4) within Christian theology paints Judaism as devoid of love, mercy and grace. This depiction has been increasingly challenged, to be sure, within more contemporary New Testament studies. In Sanders's view, theological Christian anti-Judaism not only bears scant resemblance to the reality of first-century Judaism, it also demonstrates ignorance and inadequate knowledge of the "Jewish sources" (*ibid.*: 284). In its full-fledged form, this theologically biased portrayal of first-century Judaism (and by inevitable association, modern Judaism) is an invention of "nineteenth-century Protestant scholars" (*ibid.*: 285) who were partly concerned to build a case that Judaism is the now surpassed religious antithesis of Christianity.

## Freud and object relations theory

Unfortunately, a good deal of Suttie's critique of Freud is skewed by this biased understanding of both Judaism and Christianity. If Suttie's views were not considered to have such an important place in subsequent developments in psychoanalytic theory, particularly object relations theory, they might be more easily dismissed or ignored outright. The commonly held assumption that object relations theory and its later psychoanalytic derivatives[9] emerged in order "to bring love back into psychoanalytic discourse" (Lothane 1998: 37) is problematic on any number of grounds; three, however, stand out. The first is that the origins of this move are associated with a Christian theological bias against Judaism that derives in large part from Suttie's ideas, as I have demonstrated above; the second relates to distorted and/or oversimplified interpretations of Freud's idea of love; and the third is that Freud had a monological conception of the internal world of human beings that does not include or value the importance of relationships with others in the course of psychological development. Since the first and second have already been discussed, I will now examine this third misapprehension in more detail. It is often assumed in contemporary psychoanalysis that Freud's view of human development is motivated primarily – if not solely – by the need to satisfy bodily based impulses (drive theory) that pretty much excludes or minimizes the need for relationships, especially with the mother. This interpretation is open to significant critical challenge when read against one of Freud's most important and remarkable papers, "Mourning and Melancholia". This paper clearly can be read as formulating and anticipating some key ideas that are now more exclusively associated with later object relations theory. I also agree with Thomas Ogden's even stronger observation that some of the basic concepts contained in this essay have "played a major role in shaping psychoanalysis" ever since (Ogden 2002: 768).[10]

In "Mourning and Melancholia" (1917d), Freud describes and analyses the emotional devastation that can occur following the loss of a beloved other person. Such an experience is not only confined to the loss of another, but could involve an ideal that has "taken the place of one", such as patriotism or liberty (*ibid*.: 243). The psychic characteristics of both mourning, understood as grief, and melancholia, understood in contemporary terms as depression, involve a range of painful feelings. These include the loss of interest in the world around one and the capacity for love that are often accompanied by guilty self-reproach and sometimes by expectations of punishment. What distinguishes the temporary grief of mourning from the longer-term or even permanent debilitating effects of melancholia is the loss of "self-regard" that can find no consolation in ultimately accepting that the object is lost forever. Eventually, Freud thinks, the work of mourning will result in a "respect for reality" (*ibid*.: 244) based on the full realization that the beloved other is never to return, and that life can and must go on. The love for the other that has been withdrawn in acquiescence to the hard necessity of circumstance can eventually find another object. The mourner will then be able to emerge from a state of lethargic disinterest associated with grieving to embrace the world once more with a renewed and enlivened sense of hope for the future. As Freud observes, "when the work of mourning is completed the ego becomes free and uninhibited again" (*ibid*.: 245).

Melancholia or depression, on the other hand, represents something of a different psychological phenomenon from mourning, despite its many shared features (Freud 1917d: 244). While the mourner is always conscious of what she has lost, the melancholic is not; she knows *who* is lost, but not *what*. "This would suggest", writes Freud, "that melancholia is in some way related to an object-loss which is withdrawn from consciousness, in contradistinction to mourning, in which there is nothing about the loss that is unconscious" (*ibid.*: 245). The melancholic is entirely absorbed by loss such that his "self-regard" or ego becomes "extraordinarily" depleted and diminished "on a grand scale" (*ibid.*: 246). While the mourner feels the world to be empty and meaningless for the duration of the grieving process, the melancholic experiences an impoverishment and emptiness of self that may be so severe as to lead to suicide. The melancholic is beyond consolation; any attempt on the part of the analyst to give comfort that challenges the patient's profound self-loathing or strong sense of worthlessness only exacerbates the problem, leaving him feeling even more misunderstood, ashamed and isolated. If the analyst cannot understand the patient, then no one can. While there may be no apparent justification for the melancholic's severe "self-abasement", Freud nonetheless understands that he is expressing "a *correct description of his psychological situation*" because, in his mind, he has a "*good reason* for this" (*ibid.*: 247, emphasis added): what the melancholic has lost is not another person or object, but a vital aspect of his very *self*, or ego.

In order to account for the disparity between what the depressed person feels himself to be and what others see, it is necessary to bear in mind Freud's concept of ambivalence. Love for Freud is always alloyed with its opposite, hate, and in the case of the melancholic, his self-reproaches represent the displacement of negative feelings towards an object onto himself. Whereas the mourner has been able to successfully resolve his ambivalent feelings towards the loved object, the melancholic cannot, likely because of a repressed trauma or traumatic set of experiences or emotional injuries connected with the lost object; Freud gives the example of a jilted lover (1917d: 245). The disparities between the "self-accusations" of the melancholic, and who others take him to be, reveal the "key to the clinical picture: we perceive that the self-reproaches are reproaches against a loved object which have been shifted away from it on to the patient's own ego" (*ibid.*: 248). What Freud detects in the melancholic's litany of examples attesting to his worthlessness is a concealed protest originating in a "mental constellation of revolt" that has "by a certain process" become "crushed" in melancholia (*ibid.*). Freud's careful exploration and elaboration of this "certain process" throughout the rest of his essay builds upon and extends his 1914 theory of narcissism and his later discussion of the oceanic feeling.

Here it should be recalled that Freud characterizes the primary narcissism of earliest infancy as a libidinal or (to use his later term) *erotic* life energy whose initial object is the primitive ego. As a result of the infant's needs-based motivations that direct these ego-libidinal energies outward, where they find satisfying maternal responsiveness, primary narcissistic identification transforms into a secondary narcissistic object tie. If this movement unfolds within an emotionally and physically sustaining infant–mother psychic matrix, as Loewald calls it, the developing child's emerging sense of self consolidates and coalesces around identifications and internalizations involving external others. In this relational context, the child is able to invest the external world with libidinal energies that foster a growing sense of self (as self-in-other) and other (as other-in-self). The loving, supportive and nurturing infant–mother relational field supports the outward investment of psychic energies, which in turn facilitates and enriches the child's capacity for knowledge and mutually satisfying relationships. The child's "original attachment" (Freud 1914b: 87) to "the persons who are concerned with [his] feeding, care, and protection" form the basis of later object choices, particularly those involving a sexual partner. The child grows into an adult whose identity and emotional stability are organized around his capacity for relationships of love and reciprocal recognition.

These narcissistic and attachment-type relationships roughly develop side by side in healthy mental functioning. However, infant development can go drastically wrong as a result of a variety of environmental and biological privations, especially those involving repeated trauma and sustained neglect. Melancholia may arise following a "disturbance in early narcissistic development" where the melancholic "in infancy and childhood was unable to move successfully from narcissistic object-love to mature object-love involving a person who is experienced as separate from himself" (Ogden 2002: 775). Thus, in the face of object loss, severe disappointment or serious narcissistic injury, the melancholic proves incapable of separating from the lost object and instead regresses to a state of primitive narcissistic identification with it, thereby evading the agonizing pain of loss (*ibid.*). In other words, melancholic depression is the devastating result of love that is lost combined with the ensuing despair that it cannot ever be restored. Freud writes: "An object-choice, an attachment of the libido to a particular person, had at one time existed; then, owing to a *real slight or disappointment coming from this loved person, the object-relationship was shattered*" (1917d: 248–9, emphasis added).

The melancholic is left with no alternative but to withdraw and relocate love back into the ego through narcissistic identification. From then on, the ego languishes under "the shadow of the object", and a "special" psychic agency, which later becomes known as the super-ego, turns its ruthless judgement against the ego as if it were "the forsaken object. In this way an object loss is transformed into an ego-loss", Freud writes (1917d: 249). Through the process of regressive identification of the ego with the other, the original conflict between them is transformed into a "cleavage" between the critical agency of the ego and "the ego as altered by identification" (*ibid.*: 249). Narcissistic identification substitutes for the previous erotic or loving investment in the other so that, despite the conflict with it and its resulting loss, the love relationship itself "need not be given up" (*ibid.*). Although the relationship between the melancholic and the loved object is complicated by unconscious struggles involving multiple sources and forms of ambivalence, one thing is clear: the need to preserve love, even after the object is gone. "[B]y taking flight into the ego love escapes extinction" (*ibid.*: 257), Freud writes. The conscious barrage of self-reproaches with which the melancholic torments himself, no matter how vicious, is a way of unconsciously preserving love for the now abandoned object. "After this regression of the libido the process can become conscious", Freud writes, "and it is represented to consciousness as a conflict between one part of the ego and the critical agency" (*ibid.*).

For Freud, melancholia or depression is the outcome of the shattering impact of some version of the loss of love and the inability to mourn it. In all likelihood, the melancholic response to object loss in adulthood has its roots in impaired childhood relationships that undermined the developing child's capacity to move from primary to secondary, more mature, forms of narcissistic object love for others experienced as separate from oneself. As Ogden astutely points out, Freud presents here an *object relations theory* of early development to account for the "narcissistic nature of the melancholic's personality [that] renders him incapable of maintaining a firm connection with the painful reality of the irrevocable loss of the object" (2002: 775). In fact, as far as Ogden is concerned (and on this point I agree with him completely), the entire argument presented in "Mourning and Melancholia" develops "a line of thought which later would be termed 'object-relations theory'... [that] has played a major role in shaping psychoanalysis from 1917 onwards" (*ibid.*: 768).

If the roots of object relations theory can properly be traced back to Freud, it is no longer imperative to establish it or any other later developments in psychoanalytic theory as either entirely *new* or as *superseding* Freud. This is not to deny the important and transformative theoretical advancements and enhanced clinical effectiveness achieved by psychoanalysis in a variety of areas after Freud. But there is little need to account for this by attributing views to Freud he did not hold, or by ignoring the presence of some of his most important ideas throughout later psychoanalytic traditions. As Ricoeur points out, Freud's notion of desire is profoundly "intersubjective" (1970: 387). Suttie was blind to this "profound truth" of Freudian theory (*ibid.*). Analytic writers who unquestioningly accept Suttie's arguments repudiating Freud need to be aware of his prejudicial Christian religious agenda and its reconstituted anti-Jewish theology. Suttie used what he regarded as the superior vantage point of his personal religious faith to denounce, rather than critically analyse, Freud's theories. As this dangerous aspect of Suttie's work goes unacknowledged, it becomes an uncritically assumed and endlessly repeated misconception that circulates deeply within and throughout subsequent developments in psychoanalytic theory. Love itself, and its importance in infant and early psychological development and healthy mature mental functioning, is not at issue here; it has been established beyond doubt in attachment theory through its unfolding in John Bowlby (1971, 1998), the object relations theory of paediatric psychoanalyst D. W. Winnicott (1990, 1999), Peter Fonagy (2001), and the empirical studies of infant research conducted by Daniel Stern (1985) and his colleagues. The basis of Suttie's denunciation of Freud's psychoanalytic theory on the alleged grounds of its hatred and exclusion of maternal love originating in a moribund, law-obsessed patriarchal Judaism, is a serious problem that must be faced by those who see themselves as influenced by or indebted to Suttie's thought. While Suttie's specific religious prejudices with respect to Freud may have been repressed, forgotten or ignored in later psychoanalytic thinking, the echoes of his religiously based prejudice continue to reverberate within it.

Freud was hardly oblivious to the importance of relationships with others in the developing human psyche; nor did he trivialize or dismiss the power of love and its role in fostering and recovering mental health, as has been demonstrated in the discussion of his *Gradiva* paper. More to the point is that Freud thinks about these things *differently* than Suttie and those who follow him. Freud understood that before they are mothers, women are children and sexual human beings. Like all human beings, women also struggle with their own internal conflicts, fantasies, repressed desires and ambivalences towards those they love, including their children. It is certainly true that Freud gives far more prominence and attention to the presence and role of fathers in the psychosexual, intellectual and moral development of (mostly male) children, especially with respect to his idea of the Oedipus complex. Freud admitted that he understood men better than women. This certainly cannot excuse some of his views about women, such as their feeble capacity for justice or interest in political life (Freud 1933d).

There is no dearth of important feminist perspectives criticizing Freud's treatment of women and mothers. Inevitably, some are more nuanced than others. Madelon Sprengnether takes a subtle approach to Freud on the subject of women, making important observations concerning the "persistent, though suppressed" maternal presence that inhabits Freud's work (Sprengnether 1990: 2). Diane Jonte-Pace (1996, 2001) argues persuasively that themes of maternal love and desire are not absent in Freud, but rather form a "counter-thesis" to his "Oedipal master thesis". While there may be much truth in analyses such as these, Juliet Mitchell makes an even more compelling and accurate observation that Freudian psychoanalysis is "not a recommendation *for* a patriarchal society, but an analysis *of* one" (1974: xiii). Her view, compatible with my own, is that psychoanalysis calls us to examine how we acquire our ideas, attitudes, moral values, religious beliefs and views of human society "within the unconscious mind, or, to put it another way, the unconscious mind *is* the way in which we acquire these laws" (*ibid.*: xiv). When Freud writes about the intimate connections between love and hate or the Oedipal fantasies that underlie and give rise to religion, he is not advocating that this is how things *should* be, but rather how he thinks they *are*. With respect to mothers and love, Freud inquired into the destructive *and* positive features of both. A brief discussion of his study of Leonardo da Vinci will further illustrate some of these points.

## Maternal love and Eros divine in Freud's Leonardo da Vinci

Freud's Leonardo study explores the source of genius in the sensuous bonds of love between the infant and his mother in the formative years of early child-hood. Although there is scant historical evidence supporting Freud's assumption that da Vinci lived alone with his mother for the first five years of his life (Armstrong 2005: 65), this weakness in Freud's account is secondary to a stronger interest in the connections between infantile sexuality, artistic creation and religion. Although there is no coherent or sustained theory of sublimation in Freud's work, his treatment of Leonardo may nonetheless be considered as the fullest expression of the concept in his thinking. Freud's psychoanalytic inquiry into the importance of infantile sexuality in the formation of Leonardo's creative abilities derives from a mistranslation of an early memory recounted by da Vinci of a vulture putting its tail in his mouth. What the infant Leonardo encountered in his cradle was in fact a kite (in Italian, *nibbio*), not a vulture (in German, *Geier*) as Freud thought. This detail, however important, is ultimately beside the point in the context of Freud's general psychoanalytic arguments. Freud thinks that behind Leonardo's fantasy, with its connotations of fellatio, lies a deeper "reminiscence of sucking – or being suckled – at his mother's breast, a scene of human beauty that he, like so many artists, undertook to depict with his brush, in the guise of the mother of God and her child" (1910a: 87). On the basis of the mistranslation of "kite" as "vulture" that generated in Freud's mind a series of associations between mothers and vultures in ancient Egyptian language and myth, Freud determines that Leonardo's sexual awaken-ing due to maternal seduction symbolized in the vulture fantasy was the source of his "instinct for research" (*ibid.*: 74, 132). Freud describes Leonardo's "thirst for knowledge" as a "divine spark which is directly or indirectly the driving force – *il primo motore* – behind all human activity" (*ibid.*: 74).

Freud conjectures that Leonardo left his mother's home at the age of five when he entered the household of his father and stepmother. His early experi-ences of maternal love and nurturing had an indelible impact on his internal world (*ibid.*: 92), forming the originary basis of his lifelong love of (mother) nature and his intense desire to explore her secrets. The early years spent under the primacy of maternal care fostered within Leonardo a capacity for inde-pendence of thought and judgement that attenuated the formation of his more purely intellectual power within the patriarchal family he was to encounter later. In Freud's view, Leonardo's creative genius and artistic and scientific accomplishments were nourished in the soil of maternal love and cultivated by the light of paternal authority. Leonardo had learned to "do without his father" (*ibid.*: 123) in the first years of his life, spent alone with his mother. As a result, his mind was not restricted by excessive reliance on paternal authority as is so common with "most other human beings" (*ibid.*: 122); "only Leonardo could dispense with that support", Freud writes (*ibid.*: 123). The foundation of Leonardo's psychological strength was established within a mother–infant field of gratifying love grounded in his experience of the mother's body and nurturing breast. The energy of infantile sexuality unfolding within the relational dynamics of maternal care gradually embraced the world in a non-repressive sublimatory process. Leonardo's heightened capacity for abstract intellectuality was the result of his "general urge to know" (*ibid.*: 132).

Freud writes that Leonardo's "later scientific research, with all its boldness and independence, presupposed the existence of infantile sexual researches uninhibited by his father, and was a prolongation of them with the sexual element excluded" (*ibid.*: 123). Freud points out that the crucial importance of both parental imagoes does not negate his theory of religion's origins in the Oedipal longing for a protective father. Whatever Leonardo's private religious beliefs may have been, they exerted no authority over his thinking (*ibid.*: 124). As far as Freud can tell from Leonardo's writings, there is nothing to suggest that his thinking was "led astray in the slightest degree" by reliance on scripture or that he had any interest in a "personal relation" with "divine power" despite his admiration for the "Creator" of nature (*ibid.*: 124). Rather, Leonardo's research suggests strongly that he had "removed himself far from the position from which the Christian believer surveys the world" (*ibid.*: 125). With this view of Leonardo, we see further evidence of Freud's central and most important objection to religion: its insistence on inhibiting and forbidding independent critical thought. In Freud's account of Leonardo, it is the early relationship with the *mother* that creates the conditions for the development of an inquiring, rebellious and independent mind.

Freud's discussion of Leonardo da Vinci, like *Totem and Taboo* or *Moses and Monotheism*, has far less to do with historical record than with psychoanalysis. His speculations about Leonardo's psychosexual development and the trajectory of his artistic and scientific growth provide Freud with a theoretical scaffolding for further exploration of multiple intersections of sexuality and creativity, Eros and culture, and body and spirit. Although Freud had great admiration for the genius and accomplishments of Leonardo da Vinci, he appears to be almost more interested in how he represents or exemplifies the potential of a universal psychic process of successful sublimation. Leonardo is a vivid example of Freud's larger "awareness" that "authentic transcendental experiences and insights ('spirituality') are anchored in the individual's personal life history and its instinctual roots" (Loewald 2000: 416).

Loewald's choice of the word "spirituality" accurately reflects an aspect of Freud's thought that is often overlooked with respect to his theory of religion. Freud never denied the existence or value of the human spirit; rather, he understood it as located in biologically based human experience. Body and spirit for Freud were intimately connected. Under good enough familial circumstances, infantile sexual energy becomes transformed into intellectual activity within an uninhibited or non-repressive process of sublimation. When sexuality is repressed and severed from intellect, spiritual impoverishment is the result. There is "convincing evidence", Freud writes in a passage that universalizes Leonardo's childhood experience, "that originally the genitals were the pride and hope of living beings; they were worshipped as gods and transmitted the divine nature of their functions to all newly learned human activities. As a result of the sublimation of the basic nature there arose innumerable divinities". At some point within the development of culture, this connection became severed through repression, with the result that "so much of the divine and sacred was ultimately extracted from sexuality that the exhausted remnant fell into contempt" (Freud 1910a: 97). More precisely, it was the mother and female sexuality that "fell into contempt" under the hegemony of patriarchal religions. What is especially important here is Freud's insight that intellectuality of the kind achieved by Leonardo da Vinci is empowered and driven by its connection to, not severance from, its origins in infantile sexuality and the maternal bond.

However one may interpret Freud's treatment of mothers – as a "spectral", "suppressed presence" (Sprengnether 1990); as a subversive, non-Oedipal "counter-thesis" (Jonte-Pace 1996, 2001); or as standing in direct contradiction to the "patriarchal aspect of Freud's thought" (Armstrong 2005) – the fact remains that the Oedipal paradigm is not a seamless hegemonic concept in Freudian theory. Nor does it provide a complete picture of the origins of religion, as Freud hinted at in his reference to its possible pre-Oedipal roots (1930a: 72). Suttie's (1966: 56) sarcastic retort to Freud's speculation about the "something else" of religious desire as being opaque only to *him* – "There *is* something else 'behind this,' namely the child's need for the *mother's* love" falls flat when we attend to what Freud actually wrote. The mother–infant relationship "is in the nature of a completely satisfying love-relation, which not only fulfils every mental wish but also every physical need", representing "one of the forms of attainable human happiness" in this world (Freud 1910a: 117). Freud also understood that the psychic intensity of the infant–mother bond is rooted in bodily experience. That Freud acknowledged the "biological–archaic roots of man's existence" (Loewald 2000: 415) as the source of potential transcendence and spirituality within human life in no way undermines or denigrates the higher creative or ethical achievements of individuals and culture. Claims such as "Freud emphasized the importance of sex [whereas] Suttie emphasized the significance of love" (Brown 1963: 64), or that Suttie recognized the importance of human sociality and the "primordial communion" of the mother–child relationship while Freud did not (Miller 2008: 40; 45), cannot be supported by a wider reading of Freud's texts.

Perhaps the greatest difference between Freud's ideas of maternal love, the nature of the mother–infant bond and the idealized picture offered by Suttie, has something to do with Freud's recognition of the ambivalence that is inherent in love. Ambivalence infuses the psychic depths of the internal worlds of human beings. Mothers are associated with birth and sustaining of life, but also with death, as Freud (1913a) points out in his discussion of King Lear. There are "three inevitable relations that a man has with a woman", which are: "the mother herself, the beloved one who is chosen after her pattern, and lastly the Mother Earth who receives him once more" (*ibid.*: 301). For Freud, these are the three faces and functions of the maternal found in a diverse multiplicity of literary and mythical themes that preserve the discarded feminine within the nature and origins of divinity. In this sense, the maternal embodies and signifies the primal contradictions of existence and human experience, not as sex *versus* love, as life *versus* death or as body *versus* spirit, but as a *both/and* relationship. Freud insists that just as the human spirit has its originary roots in biology and concrete personal biography, so too does religion. He writes:

> We do not share the belief that myths were read in the heavens and brought down to earth; we are more inclined to judge … that they were projected on the heavens after having risen elsewhere under purely human conditions. *It is in this human content that our interest lies.*
>
> (Freud 1913a: 292, emphasis added)

# Epilogue

On 28 August 1930, Sigmund Freud was awarded the Goethe Prize for Science and Literature by the city of Frankfurt. Previously bestowed upon cultural luminaries such as the poet Stefan George, Albert Schweitzer and the philosopher Leopold Ziegler, the prestigious prize highlighted not only Freud's contribution to science, but to philosophy and aesthetics. In addition to Freud's scholarly achievements, the award recognized the humanistic and cultural value of his work – psychoanalysis – and its contribution to understanding and healing "the driving forces of the soul" (in Gay 1988: 571). Not surprisingly, Freud's work had a profound influence on the early "Frankfurt School" critical theorists (Hewitt 2012), providing one of the foundation stones (*Bildungsmächte*) of their philosophy. Throughout this book I have emphasized the philosophical, ethical, creative and deeply humanistic nature of Freud's psychoanalytic theory that was recognized and acknowledged long ago, not only by the city of Frankfurt and the critical theorists, but by a number of others since. As I have attempted to demonstrate, Freud's writings on religion are especially expressive of these qualities.

Freud describes the contradictory, conflictual and painful nature of what it means to be human without the consolation of sentimentality or compromising illusion. While he is relentless in exposing the darkness of the human mind and its destructive impulses to aggression and hatred, he is not oblivious to our capacity for love, creativity and noble cultural achievements, some of which come into being by way of religion. With Freud, psychoanalysis is a ruthless critique that is integral to the cultivation of an ethical capacity to take responsibility for the whole of our mental life. As is clear in his letter to Binswanger, cited at the beginning of this book, Freud was supremely aware that the loftiest productions of culture, such as religion, have their origins in the darkest recesses of the unconscious mind. Perhaps for many critics it is this steady conviction, which informs all his thinking and writing on religion, that is unforgiveable. In the spirit of his remarks to Binswanger, it may well be that a more realistic understanding of religion requires that we, like Freud, find the courage to spend more time in the basement.

# Notes

## Introduction

1. As will become apparent throughout the course of this book, the subsequent theoretical developments within which I situate Freud include British and American object relations theory and the more current relational and intersubjective theories. These latter have become globally prevalent and influential throughout the analytic world. This focus is crucial to the arguments advanced here that refute and/or heavily modify a number of endlessly repeated and pervasive misconceptions about Freud that have by now uncritically hardened into unquestioned psychoanalytic doctrine. Especially with respect to religion, a number of adherents of these psychoanalytic perspectives tend to establish and/or legitimate themselves in opposition to a Freud who is either misinterpreted or did not exist. Furthermore, but for different reasons, my treatment of Freud on religion does not include the French or Continental analytic traditions as reflected in the indisputably important work of theorists such as Jacques Lacan or Julia Kristeva. A comparative examination of the reception of Freud by Anglo-American and European psychoanalytic thinkers would involve a different kind of theoretical study than the one offered here.

## 1. Psychoanalysis as a critical theory of religion

1. It is important to bear in mind, at the risk of repetition, that by religion, all three thinkers refer primarily to Christianity, and in Freud's case, primarily the Catholicism of late nineteenth- and early twentieth-century Austria (Freud 1927: 38; 1933a: 169).
2. Symptoms, for Freud, emerge as highly distorted derivatives of unconscious impulses for wish-fulfilment; they create a "substitute" for the "frustrated satisfaction by means of a regression of the libido to earlier times" (1917b: 360, 365). Symptoms represent a "return of the repressed" that comes about through a compromise between repressed and repressing ideas (Laplanche & Pontalis 1973: 398).
3. Meissner (1984) provides a good example of faith-based responses to Freud's critique of religion that sees "a pressing urgency for efforts in the psychology of religion to be informed by astute and informed theological opinion" (ibid.: 19).

4. By historical truth, Freud does not mean literal or concrete truth, which he calls "material truth." This crucial distinction will be more fully elaborated in the chapters dealing with *Totem and Taboo* and *Moses and Monotheism*, where it plays a crucial role in his analysis of religion.

## 2. "The mind is its own place, and in itself/Can make a Heaven of Hell, a Hell of Heaven"

1. Freud's theory of narcissism is far too complex and at times ambiguous (1923b: 63–6) to discuss fully here. My discussion of narcissism is limited to its relevance *in so far as it illuminates an explanation of the oceanic feeling* associated with religious experience.
2. In a single paragraph, Freud states both views: that aggression is "an original, self-substituting instinctual disposition in man", while a few sentences later he describes aggression as "the derivative and main representative of the death instinct" (1930a: 122).
3. While Freud is fully aware that an infant cannot distinguish the gender of each parent, he nonetheless for purposes of simplicity in his discussion of the ego-ideal makes the father the representative of the parents, or "parental agency". He also uses the male model of psychosexual development in his discussion of the Oedipus complex, partly for simplicity's sake, but also because he did not fully understand the more complicated nature of female psychosexual development.
4. For an ethnographic anthropological explanation arguing for the universality of the Oedipus complex, see Melford E. Spiro's *Oedipus in the Trobriands* (1982).

## 3. Crime, punishment and the return of the repressed: the triumph of the intellectual and the moral mind

1. For a fuller and very interesting account of Freud's "Lamarckism" and a critical response to it, see Yerushalmi (1991) and Bernstein (1998), respectively.
2. *Geistigkeit* is difficult, if not impossible, to translate into English. The German *Geist* combines the meanings of spirit, intellect or mind. This is the sense in which I use "intellectuality" in the course of this chapter. In English intellect often carries a sense of dry rationality divorced from and/or opposed to passion and imagination. In this respect "intellect" lacks the dynamic power and depth of the German *Geist*. The English "spirit" or spirituality, on the other hand, often carries anti-intellectual overtones. It tends to be a vague, meaningless term that carries more theoretical weight than it can properly bear. *Geistigkeit* combines spirit and mind, which is how Freud understood the Jewish ethical and intellectual tradition.

## 4. Telepathy and the "occult" unconscious

1. The journal *Neurospychoanalysis* is a fine resource and guide to the field.
2. I want to thank Dr Joshua Levy for drawing this very important clinical fact to

my attention (personal communication, 2013). It further demonstrates important aspects of the painful and ambivalent relationship that must have existed between Freud and his patient.

3. Freud's conception (*Auffassung*) of the mind is better understood as organizational rather than structural. The English "structure" collapses a number of different terms used by Freud. It also conveys an overly rigid or fixed quality of mind that is belied by Freud's dynamic, messier and more fluid concept of mental life, where consciousness emerges out of the unconscious. Thus, "structure" is better understood metaphorically rather than concretely. Ornston's (1985) detailed discussion of the problems associated with Strachey's use of this term is extremely helpful here.

4. Contemporary infant research firmly rejects the idea that infants ever experience a period of complete fusion, or undifferentiated oneness, with their environment. See for example Daniel N. Stern's *The Interpersonal World of the Infant* (1985). He argues that the idea that infants experience an autistic- or symbiotic-type phase at any point is an imaginary attribution of infancy from the perspective of adulthood, and is without empirical basis. My discussion of Freud's theories of early infancy is intended to explain how they illuminate his ideas about the uncanny in mental life.

5. For example, Herbert Rosenfeld's idea of projective identification as a form of non-verbal *communication* whereby the patient is able to convey his unformulated and unconscious experience by inducing the analyst to "feel and understand his experiences" so that the analyst may contain and interpret them back to the patient, is relevant here (Rosenfeld 1988: 121)

6. Dialogue with modern physics belongs to the history of psychoanalysis itself, as Carl Jung's friendship and correspondence with the early quantum theorist Wolfgang Pauli demonstrates. Pauli's work influenced Jung's concept of synchronicity (Jung 2008).

## 5. What's love got to do with it? New psycho-mythologies

1. Published in E. L. Freud (1961: 365).

2. For a comprehensive and nuanced critical discussion of Freud and female psychosexual development, see Mitchell (1974).

3. The connection between psychosis and the impairment of the capacity for love and its absence in an individual's life is affirmed by a number of psychoanalytic thinkers to this day. See for example the work of R. D. Laing (1965) and Bertram Karon (2003).

4. See the psychoanalytically informed discussion of Ulysses' encounter with the Sirens in *Dialectic of Enlightenment* (Horkheimer & Adorno 2002).

5. In Freud's view there is neither pure hate nor pure love. Rather, human relationships are characterized by and imbued with both love and hate, which is what Freud means by his important concept of "ambivalence", which is discussed later in this chapter.

6. The term "anti-Judaism" should be distinguished from "anti-Semitism" because while they may be often related, they are not necessarily identical. I use "anti-Judaism" to refer to a Christian set of attitudes and assumptions that rejects Judaism

on religious and theological grounds, whereas anti-Semitism expresses antipathy to Jewish people on racial grounds. For a fuller theological and historical account of the development of the *adversus Judaeos* tradition within Christian theology, see Rosemary Radford Ruether's *Faith and Fratricide* (1974). For a variety of views concerning this tradition in the Gospels and Christian New Testament scholarship, see also the collection of essays in William R. Farmer's *Anti-Judaism and the Gospels* (1999).

7. John Kloppenborg, personal communication, January 2013.

8. The Pharisees were a politically active and influential reform group of observant Jewish religious leaders in ancient Palestine concerned with preserving Jewish identity and religious traditions associated with the Covenant with God.

9. These later developments include object relations theory, interpersonalist theory, self psychology and relational psychoanalysis. For an excellent overview of the emergence of object relations theory and its later derivatives, see Greenberg and Mitchell (1983) and Mitchell and Black (1995).

10. The discussion of "Mourning and Melancholia" advanced here is largely in agreement with, but not identical to, Thomas Ogden's (2002) reading of Freud's paper.

# Bibliography

Altman, N. 2007. "Integrating the Transpersonal and the Intersubjective". *Contemporary Psychoanalysis* 43: 526–35.

Anderson, J. W. 2007. "Harmful vs Beneficial Religion: A Psychoanalytic Perspective". *Annual of Psychoanalysis* 35: 121–36.

Appelbaum, J. 2012. "Science and Theory in Modern Physics and Psychoanalysis". *International Forum of Psychoanalysis* 21: 117–24.

Armstrong, R. H. 2005. *A Compulsion for Antiquity*. Ithaca, NY: Cornell University Press.

Aron, L. 1996. *A Meeting of Minds: Mutuality in Psychoanalysis*. Hillsdale, NJ: Analytic Press.

Aron, L. 2008. "Foreword". In *Repair of the Soul: Metaphors of Transformation in Jewish Mysticism and Psychoanalysis*, K. E. Starr, ix–xviii. Relational Perspectives Book Series 38. London: Routledge.

Assmann, J. 1997. *Moses the Egyptian: The Memory of Egypt in Western Monotheism*. Cambridge: Cambridge University Press.

Atran, S. 2002. *In Gods We Trust: The Evolutionary Landscape of Religion*. Oxford: Oxford University Press.

Bacal, H. A. 1987. "British Object Relations Theorists and Self-Psychology: Some Critical Reflections". *International Journal of Psychoanalysis* 68: 81–98.

Balint, M. 1955. "Notes on Parapsychology and Parapsychological Healing". *International Journal of Psychoanalysis* 36: 31–5.

Bass, A. 2001. "It Takes One to Know One; or, Whose Unconscious Is It Anyway?" *Psychoanalytic Dialogues* 11(5): 683–702.

Benjamin, J. 1986. "Comment on 'When Interpretation Masquerades as Explanation'". *Journal of the American Psychoanalytic Association* 34(2): 483–7.

Bernstein, R. J. 1998. *Freud and the Legacy of Moses*. Cambridge: Cambridge University Press.

Bernstein, R. J. 2002. *Radical Evil: A Philosophical Interrogation*. Cambridge: Polity.

Blackman, L. 2012. *Immaterial Bodies: Affect, Embodiment, Mediation*. London: Sage.

Blass, R. B. 2004. "Beyond Illusion: Psychoanalysis and the Question of Religious Truth". *International Journal of Psychoanalysis* 85: 615–34.

Blass, R. B. 2006. "The Role of Tradition in Concealing and Grounding Truth: Two Opposing Freudian Legacies on Truth and Tradition". *American Imago* 63: 331–53.

Blum, H. P. 1991. "Freud and the Figure of Moses: The Moses of Freud". *Journal of the American Psychoanalytic Association* 39: 513–35.

Boehm, C. 1999. *Hierarchy in the Forest: The Evolution of Egalitarian Behavior.* Cambridge, MA: Harvard University Press.

Bowlby, J. 1971. *Attachment.* Harmondsworth: Pelican.

Bowlby, J. 1998. *Loss.* London: Pimlico.

Boyer, P. 2001. *Religion Explained: The Evolutionary Origins of Religious Thought.* New York: Basic Books.

Boyer, P. 2004. "Out of Africa: Lessons from a By-Product of Evolution". In *Religion as a Human Capacity*, T. Light & B. C. Wilson (eds), 27–43. Leiden: Brill.

Brabant, E., E. Falzeder & P. Giampieri-Deutsch 1993. *The Correspondence of Sigmund Freud and Sandor Ferenczi,* P. T. Hoffer (trans.), vols 1–2. Cambridge, MA: Belknap Press.

Bremer, R. 1976. "Freud and Michelangelo's Moses". *American Imago* 33: 60–75.

Brown, J. A. C. 1963. *Freud and the Post-Freudians.* London: Cassell.

Bucci, W. 2008. "Pathways of Emotional Communication". *Psychoanalytic Inquiry* 21(1): 40–70.

Burkert, W. 1983. *Homo Necans: The Anthropology of Ancient Greek Sacrificial Ritual and Myth*, P. Bing (trans.). Berkeley, CA: University of California Press.

Burkert, W. 1985. *Greek Religion.* Cambridge, MA: Harvard University Press.

Burkert, W. 1996. *Creation of the Sacred: Tracks of Biology in Early Religions.* Cambridge, MA: Harvard University Press.

Capps, D. 2001. *Freud and Freudians on Religion: A Reader.* New Haven, CT: Yale University Press.

Carroll, M. P. 1987. "Moses and Monotheism Revisited: Freud's 'Personal Myth'?" *American Imago* 44: 15–35.

Cassullo, G. 2010. "Back to the Roots: The Influence of Ian D. Suttie on British Psychoanalysis". *American Imago* 67(1): 5–22.

Chapais, B. 2008. *Primeval Kinship: How Pair-Bonding Gave Birth to Human Society.* Cambridge, MA: Harvard University Press.

Clarke, G. S. 2011. "Suttie's Influence on Fairbairn's Object Relations Theory". *Journal of the American Psychoanalytic Association* 59(5): 939–59.

Cozalino, L. 2002. *The Neuroscience of Psychotherapy: Building and Rebuilding the Human Brain.* New York: Norton.

Dawkins, R. 1989. *The Selfish Gene.* Oxford: Oxford University Press.

Dawkins, R. 2006. *The God Delusion.* Boston, MA: Houghton Mifflin.

Derrida, J. 1995. *Archive Fever: A Freudian Impression*, E. Prenowitz (trans.). Chicago, IL: University of Chicago Press.

Devereux, G. (ed.) 1953. *Psychoanalysis and the Occult.* New York: International Universities Press.

Edmunson, M. 2003. Introduction in *Sigmund Freud: Beyond the Pleasure Principle and Other Writings*, J. Reddick (trans.) vii–xxx. London: Penguin.

Ellenberger, H. 1970. *The Discovery of the Unconscious.* New York: Basic Books.

Eshel, O. 2006. "Where are You, My Beloved? On Absence, Loss, and the Enigma of Telepathic Dreams". *International Journal of Psychoanalysis* 87: 1603–27.

Falzeder, E. 2007. "Is there Still an Unknown Freud? A Note on the Publications of Freud's Texts and on Unpublished Documents". *Psychoanalysis and History* 9: 201–32.

Farmer, W. R. (ed.) 1999. *Anti-Judaism and the Gospels*. Harrisburg, PA: Trinity Press International.

Farrell, D. 1983. "Freud's 'Thought-Transference', Repression, and the Future of Psychoanalysis". *International Journal of Psychoanalysis* 64: 71–81.

Feuerbach, L. 1957. *The Essence of Christianity*, G. Eliot (trans.). New York: Harper & Row.

Fodor, N. 1963. "Jung, Freud, and a Newly-Discovered Letter of 1909 on the Poltergeist Theme". *Psychoanalytic Review* 50B: 119–28.

Fonagy, P. 2001. *Attachment Theory and Psychoanalysis*. New York: Other Press.

Fonagy, P., G. Gergely, E. L. Jurist & M. Target 2002. *Affect Regulation, Mentalization, and the Development of the Self*. New York: Other Press.

Forrester, J. 2006. "Introduction". In *Interpreting Dreams*, S. Freud, J. A. Underwood (trans.), vii–liv. London: Penguin.

Freud, E. L. (ed.) 1961. *Letters of Sigmund Freud 1873–1939*, T. & J. Stern (trans.). London: Hogarth Press.

Freud, S. [1961] 2001. *The Standard Edition of the Complete Psychological Works of Sigmund Freud (SE)*, 24 vols, J. Strachey (trans.). London: Vintage/Hogarth Press.

Freud, S. 1895. "Project for a Scientific Psychology". *SE* vol. 1, 295–397.

Freud, S. 1900a. "A Premonitory Dream Fulfilled". *SE* vol. 5, 623–5.

Freud, S. 1900b. *The Interpretation of Dreams*. *SE* vols 4–5.

Freud, S. 1905. "Psychical (Or Mental) Treatment". *SE* vol. 7, 283–302.

Freud, S. 1907a. "Obsessive Actions and Religious Practices". *SE* vol. 9, 117–27.

Freud, S. 1907b. "Delusions and Dreams in Jensen's *Gradiva*". *SE* vol. 9, 7–95.

Freud, S. 1908. "'Civilized' Sexual Morality and Modern Nervous Illness". *SE* vol. 9, 179–204.

Freud, S. 1909. "Notes upon a Case of Obsessional Neurosis". *SE* vol. 10, 155–249.

Freud, S. 1910a. "Leonardo da Vinci and a Memory of his Childhood". *SE* vol. 11, 63–137.

Freud, S. 1910b. "Five Lectures on Psychoanalysis". *SE* vol. 11, 9–55.

Freud, S. 1911. "Formulations on the Two Principles of Mental Functioning". *SE* vol. 12, 218–26.

Freud, S. 1912a. "Recommendations to Physicians Practising Psycho-analysis". *SE* vol. 12, 111–20.

Freud, S. 1912b. "The Dynamics of Transference". *SE* vol. 12, 99–108.

Freud, S. 1913a. "The Theme of the Three Caskets". *SE* vol. 12, 290–301.

Freud, S. 1913b. *Totem and Taboo*. *SE* vol. 13, 1–161.

Freud, S. 1914a. *On the History of the Psychoanalytic Movement*. *SE* vol. 14, 7–66.

Freud, S. 1914b. "On Narcissism: An Introduction". *SE* vol. 14, 69–102.

Freud, S. 1914c. "The Moses of Michelangelo". *SE* vol. 13, 211–38.

Freud, S. 1915a. "Parapraxes". *SE* vol. 15, 15–79.

Freud, S. 1915b. "The Unconscious". *SE* vol. 14, 166–215.

Freud, S. 1915c. "Thoughts for the Times on War and Death". *SE* vol. 14, 275–300.

Freud, S. 1916. "Transference". *SE* vol. 16, 431–47.

Freud, S. 1917a. "A Difficulty in the Path of Psycho-analysis". *SE* vol. 17, 137–44.

Freud, S. 1917b. "The Paths to the Formation of Symptoms". *SE* vol. 16, 358–77.

Freud, S. 1917c. "The Libido Theory and Narcissism". *SE* vol. 16, 412–30.

Freud, S. 1917d. "Mourning and Melancholia". *SE* vol. 14, 243–58.

Freud, S. 1918. "From the History of an Infantile Neurosis". *SE* vol. 17, 7–122.

Freud, S. 1919. "The 'Uncanny'". *SE* vol. 17, 219–52.

Freud, S. 1920. "Beyond the Pleasure Principle". *SE* vol. 18, 7–64.

Freud, S. 1921a. "Group Psychology and the Analysis of the Ego". *SE* vol. 18, 69–143.

Freud, S. 1921b. "Psycho-analysis and Telepathy". *SE* vol. 18, 177–93.

Freud, S. 1922. "Dreams and Telepathy". *SE* vol. 18, 197–220.

Freud, S. 1923a. "A Seventeenth-Century Demonological Neurosis". *SE* vol. 19, 72–105.

Freud, S. 1923b. *The Ego and the Id*. *SE* vol. 19, 3–66.

Freud, S. 1925a. "An Autobiographical Study". *SE* vol. 20, 3–74.

Freud, S. 1925b. "Negation". *SE* vol. 19, 234–9.

Freud, S. 1925c. "Some Additional Notes on Dream-Interpretation as a Whole". *SE* vol. 19, 127–38.

Freud, S. 1927. *The Future of an Illusion*. *SE* vol. 21, 5–56.

Freud, S. 1930a. *Civilization and its Discontents*. *SE* vol. 21, 59–145.

Freud, S. 1930b. "Preface to the Hebrew Translation of *Totem and Taboo*". *SE* vol. 13, xv.

Freud, S. 1933a. "The Question of a Weltanschauung". *SE* vol. 22, 158–82.

Freud, S. 1933b. "The Dissection of the Psychical Personality". *SE* vol. 22, 57–80.

Freud, S. 1933c. "Dreams and Occultism". *SE* vol. 22, 31–56.

Freud, S. 1933d. "Femininity". *SE* vol. 22, 112–35.

Freud, S. 1935. "An Autobiographical Study: Postscript". *SE* vol. 20, 71–4.

Freud, S. 1937. "Analysis Terminable and Interminable". *SE* vol. 23, 211–53.

Freud, S. 1938. "Some Elementary Lessons in Psycho-analysis". *SE* vol. 23, 281–6.

Freud, S. 1939. *Moses and Monotheism*. *SE* vol. 23, 7–137.

Freud, S. 1940. "An Outline of Psychoanalysis". *SE* vol. 23, 141–207.

Frosh, S. 2012. "Hauntings: Psychoanalysis and Ghostly Transmission". *American Imago* 69(2): 241–64.

Gay, P. 1987. *A Godless Jew: Atheism, and the Making of Psychoanalysis*. New Haven, CT: Yale University Press.

Gay, P. 1988. *Freud: A Life for Our Time*. New York: Norton.

Gerson, G. 2009. "Culture and Ideology in Ian Suttie's Theory of Mind". *History of Psychology* 12(1): 19–40.

Godwin, R. W. 1991. "Wilfred Bion and David Bohm: Toward a Quantum Metapsychology". *Psychoanalysis and Contemporary Thought* 14: 625–54.

Granqvist, P. 2006. "On the Relation between Secular and Divine Relationships". *International Journal for the Psychology of Religion* 16: 1–18.

Greenberg, J. R. & S. A. Mitchell 1983. *Object Relations in Psychoanalytic Theory*. Cambridge, MA: Harvard University Press.

Grubrich-Simitis, I. 1986. "Reflections on Sigmund Freud's Relationship to the German Language and to Some German-Speaking Authors of the Enlightenment". *International Journal of Psychoanalysis* 67: 287–94.

Grubrich-Simitis, I. 1987. "Metapsychology and Metabiology". In *Sigmund Freud: A Phylogenetic Fantasy*, I. Grubrich-Simitis (ed.), A. & P. T. Hoffer (trans.). Cambridge, MA: Harvard University Press.

Grunbaum, A. 1987. "Psychoanalysis and Theism". *The Monist* 79: 152–73.

Gyimesi, J. 2012. "Sándor Ferenczi and the Problem of Telepathy". *History of the Human Sciences* 25: 131–48.

Hacking, I. 1988. "Telepathy: Origins of Randomization in Experimental Design". *Isis* 79(3): 427–51.

Harvey, V. A. 1997. *Feuerbach and the Interpretation of Religion*. Cambridge: Cambridge University Press.

Hewitt, M. A. 2008. "Attachment Theory, Religious Beliefs, and the Limits of Reason". *Pastoral Psychology* 57(1–2): 65–75.

Hewitt, M. A. 2012. "Dangerous Amnesia: Restoration and Renewal of the Connectins between Psychoanalysis and Critical Social Theory". *Contemporary Psychoanalysis* 48: 72–99.

Hoffman, M. 2004. "From Enemy Combatant to Strange Bedfellow". *Psychoanalytic Dialogues* 14: 769–804.

Homans, P. 1989. *The Ability to Mourn: Disillusionment and the Social Origins of Psychoanalysis*. Chicago, IL: University of Chicago Press.

Horkheimer, M. 1972. "Thoughts on Religion". In *Critical Theory: Selected Essays*, M. J. McConnell *et al.* (trans.), 129–31. New York: Continuum.

Horkheimer, M. & T. W. Adorno 2002. *Dialectic of Enlightenment: Philosophical Fragments*, E. Jephcott (trans.). Stanford, CA: Stanford University Press.

Hughes, A. 2006. "Haven't we Been Here Before? Rehabilitating 'Religion' in Light of Dubuisson's Critique". *Religion* 36: 127–31.

Jacoby, R. 1975. *Social Amnesia: A Critique of Contemporary Psychology from Adler to Laing*. Boston, MA: Beacon Press.

James, W. [1902] 2004. *The Varieties of Religious Experience: A Study in Human Nature*. New York: Barnes & Noble.

Jones, E. 1957. *The Life and Work of Sigmund Freud, vol. 3: The Last Phase*. New York: Basic Books.

Jones, E. 1961. *The Life and Work of Sigmund Freud*, abridged edn (L. Trilling & S. Marcus, eds). New York: Basic Books.

Jonte-Pace, D. 1996. "At Home in the Uncanny: Freudian Representations of Death, Mothers, and the Afterlife". *Journal of the American Academy of Religion* 64(1): 61–88.

Jonte-Pace, D. 2001. *Speaking the Unspeakable: Religion, Misogyny, and the Uncanny Mother in Freud's Cultural Texts*. Berkeley, CA: University of California Press.

Jung, C. 1963. *Memories, Dreams, Reflections*, R. & C. Winston (trans.). New York: Vintage.

Jung, C. 2008. *Synchronicity: An Acausal Connecting Principle*. London: Routledge.

Kandel, E. R. 1998. "A New Intellectual Framework for Psychiatry". *American Journal of Psychiatry* 155: 457–69.

Kantrowitz, J. L. 2001. "The Analysis of Preconscious Phenomena and Its Communication". *Psychoanalytic Inquiry* 21: 24–39.

Kaplan, G. & W. B. Parsons 2010. "Framing Freud on Religion". In *Disciplining Freud on Religion: Perspectives from the Humanities and Social Sciences*, G. Kaplan & W. B. Parsons (eds), vii–xiii. Lanham, MD: Lexington.

Karon, B. P. 2003. "The Tragedy of Schizophrenia without Psychotherapy". *Journal of the American Academy of Psychoanalysis* 31: 89–118.

Kirkpatrick, L. A. 1999. "Attachment and Religious Representations and Behaviour". In *Handbook of Attachment*, J. Cassidy & P. R. Shaver (eds), 803–22. New York: Guildford Press.

Kirkpatrick, L. A. 2005. *Attachment, Evolution, and the Psychology of Religion*. New York: Guilford Press.

Kirkpatrick, L. A. & P. R. Shaver 1990. "Attachment Theory and Religion: Childhood Attachments, Religious Beliefs, and Conversion". *Journal for the Scientific Study of Religion* 29: 315–34.

Knauft, B. 1991. "Violence and Sociality in Human Evolution". *Current Anthropology* 32(4): 391–428.

Kripal, J. J. 2010. *Authors of the Impossible: The Paranormal and the Sacred*. Chicago, IL: University of Chicago Press.

Kroeber, A. L. 1971. "Totem and Taboo in Retrospect". In *Psychoanalysis and History*, B. Mazlish (ed.), 45–9. New York: Grosset & Dunlap.

Laing, R. D. 1965. *The Divided Self*. Harmondsworth: Pelican.

Laplanche, J. & J. B. Pontalis 1973. *The Language of Psychoanalysis*, D. Nicholson-Smith (trans.). New York: Norton.

Lazar, S. G. 2001. "Knowing, Influencing, and Healing: Paranormal Phenomena and Implications of Psychoanalysis and Psychotherapy". *Psychoanalytic Inquiry* 21: 113–31.

Lear, J. 2005. *Freud*. New York: Routledge.

Lewis-Williams, D. & J. Clottes 2007. "Paleolithic Art and Religion". In *A Handbook of Ancient Religions*, J. R. Hinnells (ed.), 7–45. Cambridge: Cambridge University Press.

Liebman, S. J. & S. C. Abell 2000. "Reconstructing the Sacred: Evolving Conceptualizations of Religious Faith in Psychoanalytic Theory and Practice". *Journal of Contemporary Psychotherapy* 30(1): 7–25.

Loewald, H. 2000. *The Essential Loewald: Collected Papers and Monographs*. Hagerstown, MD: University Publishing Group.

Lothane, Z. 1998. "The Feud between Freud and Ferenczi over Love". *American Journal of Psychoanalysis* 58: 21–39.

Luckhurst, R. 2002. *The Invention of Telepathy*. Oxford: Oxford University Press.

Maddox, B. 2006. *Freud's Wizard: Ernest Jones and the Transformation of Psychoanalysis*. Cambridge, MA: Da Capo.

Marcus, D. M. 1997. "On Knowing What One Knows". *Psychoanalytic Quarterly* 66: 219–41.

Marcuse, H. 1970. *Five Lectures: Psychoanalysis, Politics, and Utopia*, J. J. Shapiro (trans.). Boston, MA: Beacon Press.

Marx, K. 1975a. "Contribution to the Critique of Hegel's *Philosophy of Law: Introduction*". In his *Collected Works*, vol. 3, 175–87. New York: International Publishers.

Marx, K. 1975b. "Economic and Philosophic Manuscripts of 1844". In his *Collected Works*, vol. 3, 229–346.

Marx, K. 1976. "Ideology in General, German Ideology in Particular". In his *Collected Works*, vol. 5, 28–93.

Mayer, E. L. 1996. "Changes in Science and Changing Ideas about Knowledge and Authority in Psychoanalysis". *Psychoanalytic Quarterly* 65: 158–200.

Mayer, E. L. 2002. "Freud and Jung: The Boundaried Mind and the Radically Connected Mind". *Journal of Analytical Psychology* 47: 91–9.

Mayer, E. L. 2008. *Extraordinary Knowing: Science, Skepticism, and the Inexplicable Powers of the Human Mind*. New York: Bantam.

McCauley, R. N. 2004. "Is Religion a Rube Goldberg Device?" In *Religion as a Human Capacity*, T. Light & B. Wilson (eds), 45–64. Leiden: Brill.

McCutcheon, R. T. 1995. "The Category 'Religion' in Recent Publications: A Critical Survey". *Numen* 42: 284–309.

McGilchrist, I. 2009. *The Master and his Emissary: The Divided Brain and the Making of the Modern World*. New Haven, CT: Yale University Press.

Meissner, W. W. 1984. *Psychoanalysis and Religious Experience*. New Haven, CT: Yale University Press.

Meissner, W. W. 2005. "On Putting a Cloud in a Bottle: Psychoanalytic Perspectives on Mysticism". *Psychoanalytic Quarterly* 74: 507–59.

Miller, G. 2008. "Scottish Psychoanalysis: A Rational Religion". *Journal of the History of Behavioural Science* 44(1): 38–58.

Mitchell, J. 1974. *Psychoanalysis and Feminism: Freud, Reich, Laing and Women*. New York: Vintage.

Mitchell, S. A. & M. J. Black 1995. *Freud and Beyond: A History of Modern Psychoanalytic Thought*. New York: Basic Books.

Mithen, S. 1996. *The Prehistory of the Mind: The Cognitive Origins of Art, Religion, and Science*. London: Thames & Hudson.

Mithen, S. 1999. "Symbolism and the Supernatural". In *The Evolution of Culture: An Interdisciplinary View*, R. Dunbar, C. Knight & C. Power (eds), 147–72. New Brunswick, NJ: Rutgers University Press.

Noakes, R. J. 1999. "Telegraphy is an Occult Art: Cromwell Fleetwood Varley and the Diffusion of Electricity to the Other World". *British Journal for the History of Science* 32(4): 421–59.

Ogden, T. H. 2002. "A New Reading of the Origins of Object-Relations Theory". *International Journal of Psychoanalysis* 83: 767–82.

Oppenheim, J. 1985. *The Other World: Spiritualism and Psychical Research in England, 1850–1914*. Cambridge: Cambridge University Press.

Ornston, D. 1985. "Freud's Conception is Different from Strachey's". *Journal of the American Psychoanalytic Association* 33: 379–412.

Owen, A. 2004. *The Place of Enchantment: British Occultism and the Culture of the Modern*. Chicago, IL: University of Chicago Press.

Panksepp, J. & L. Biven 2012. *The Archaeology of Mind: Neuroevolutionary Origins of Human Emotions*. New York: Norton.

Parsons, W. B. 1999. *The Enigma of the Oceanic Feeling: Revisioning the Psychoanalytic Theory of Mysticism*. New York: Oxford University Press.

Paul, R. A. 1987. "Interpretation in Psychoanalytic Anthropology". *Ethos* 15(1): 82–103.

Paul, R. A. 1991. "Freud's Anthropology: A Reading of the 'Cultural Books'". In *The Cambridge Companion to Freud*, J. New (ed.), 267–86. Cambridge: Cambridge University Press.

Paul, R. A. 1994. "Freud, Sellin, and the Death of Moses". *International Journal of Psychoanalysis* 75: 825–37.

Paul, R. A. 1996. *Moses and Civilization: The Meaning Behind Freud's Myth*. New Haven, CT: Yale University Press.

Paul, R. A. 2010. "Yes, the Primal Crime did take Place: A Further Defense of Freud's *Totem and Taboo*". *Ethos* 38(2): 230–49.

Penner, H. & E. A. Yonan 1972. "Is a Science of Religion Possible?" *Journal of Religion* 52: 107–33.

Phillips, A. 2002. "Introduction". In *Sigmund Freud: Wild Analysis*, A. Bance (trans.), vii–xxv. London: Penguin.

Pierri, M. 2010. "Coincidences in Analysis: Sigmund Freud and the Strange Case of Dr Forsyth and Herr von Vorsicht". *International Journal of Psychoanalysis* 91: 745–72.

Pile, S. 1999. "Freud, Dreams and Imaginative Geographies". In *Freud 2000*, A. Elliott (ed.), 204–34. New York: Routledge.

Pile, S. 2011. "Distant Feelings: Telepathy and the Problem of Affect Transfer Over Distance". *Transactions of the Institute of British Geographers* 37(1): 44–59.

Preus, J. S. 1987. *Explaining Religion: Criticism and Theory from Bodin to Freud*. New Haven, CT: Yale University Press.

Rempel, M. H. 1997. "Understanding Freud's Philosophy of Religion". *Canadian Journal of Psychoanalysis* 5: 215–42.

Ricoeur, P. 1970. *Freud and Philosophy: An Essay on Interpretation*, D. Savage (trans.). New Haven, CT: Yale University Press.

Rizutto, A. M. 1979. *The Birth of the Living God*. Chicago, IL: University of Chicago Press.

Rizutto, A. M. 1998. *Why did Freud Reject God? A Psychodynamic Interpretation*. New Haven, CT: Yale University Press.

Roazen, P. 1989. "Review of 'A Godless Jew', P. Gay". *Psychoanalytic Review* 76: 300–303.

Robert, M. 1976. *From Oedipus to Moses: Freud's Jewish Identity*. New York: Anchor.

Rose, J. 2004. "Introduction". In *Mass Psychology and Other Writings*, S. Freud, J. A. Underwood (trans.), vii–xlii. London: Penguin.

Rosenbaum, R. 2011. "Exploring the *Other* Dark Continent: Parallels between Psi Phenomena and the Psychotherapeutic Process". *Psychoanalytic Review* 98(1): 57–90.

Rosenfeld, H. 1988. "The Psychopathology of Psychotic States: The Importance of Projective Identification in the Ego Structure and the Object Relations of the Psychotic Patient". In *Melanie Klein Today: Developments in Theory and Practice*, E. B. Spillius (ed.), vol. 1, 117–37. London: Routledge.

Rosenthal, L. 2010. "Fictions of Possession: Psychoanalysis and the Occult". In *Freud and Fundamentalism: The Psychical Politics of Knowledge*, S. Gourgouris (ed.), 125–37. New York: Fordham University Press.

Royle, N. 1995. *After Derrida*. Manchester: Manchester University Press.

Rudnytsky, P. 1991. *The Psychoanalytic Vocation: Rank, Winnicott, and the Legacy of Freud*. New Haven, CT: Yale University Press.

Ruether, R. R. 1974. *Faith and Fratricide: The Theological Roots of Christian Anti-Semitism*. New York: Seabury Press.

Saler, B. 1993. *Conceptualizing Religion: Immanent Anthropologists, Transcendent Natives, and Unbounded Categories*. Leiden: Brill.

Saler, B. 2004. "Towards A Realistic and Relevant 'science of Religion'". *Method and Theory in the Study of Religion* 16: 205–33.

Saler, M. 2012. *As If: Modern Enchantment and the Literary Prehistory of Virtual Reality*. Oxford: Oxford University Press.

Sanders, E. P. 1999. "Reflections on Anti-Judaism in the New Testament and in Christianity". In *Anti-Judaism and the Gospels*, W. R. Farmer (ed.), 265–86. Harrisburg, PA: Trinity Press International.

Santner, E. L. 2001. *The Psychotheology of Everyday Life: Reflections on Freud and Rosenzweig*. Chicago, IL: University of Chicago Press.

Schore, A. N. 2011a. "Foreword". In *The Shadow of the Tsunami and the Growth of the Relational Mind*, P. M. Bromberg, ix–xxxvii. New York: Routledge.

Schore, A. N. 2011b. "The Right Brain Implicit Self lies at the Core of Psychoanalysis". *Psychoanalytic Dialogues* 21: 75–100.

Segal, R. 2006. "Dubuisson's *The Western Construction of Religion*". *Religion* 36: 131–8.

Shaw, D. 2003. "On the Therapeutic Action of Analytic Love". *Contemporary Psychoanalysis* 39: 251–78.

Silverman, S. 1988. "Correspondences and Thought-Transference during Psychoanalysis". *Journal of the American Academy of Psychoanalysis* 16: 269–94.

Slavet, E. 2009. *Racial Fever: Freud and the Jewish Question*. New York: Fordham University Press.

Smith, J. Z. 1998. "Religion, Religions, Religious". In *Critical Terms for Religious Studies*, M. C. Taylor (ed.), 269–84. Chicago, IL: University of Chicago Press.

Solms, M. 1997. "What is Consciousness?" *Journal of the American Psychoanalytic Association* 45: 681–703.

Solms, M. & O. Turnbull 2002. *The Brain and the Inner World*. New York: Other Press.

Sommer, A. 2001. "Professional Heresy: Edmund Gurney (1847–88) and the Study of Hallucinations and Hypnotism". *Medical History* 55: 383–8.

Spiro, M. E. 1966. "Religion: Problems of Definition and Explanation". In *Anthropological Approaches to the Study of Religion*, M. Banton (ed.), 85–126. London: Tavistock.

Spiro, M. E. 1982. *Oedipus in the Trobriands*. Chicago, IL: University of Chicago Press.

Spiro, M. E. 1987. "Collective Representations and Mental Representations in Religious Symbol Systems". In *Culture and Human Nature: Theoretical Papers of Melford E. Spiro*, B. Kilborne & L. L. Langness (eds), 161–84. Chicago, IL: University of Chicago Press.

Spiro, M. E. & R. G. D'Andrade 1958. "A Cross-Cultural Study of Some Supernatural Beliefs". *American Anthropologist* 60(3): 456–66.

Sprengnether, M. 1990. *The Spectral Mother: Freud, Feminism, and Psychoanalysis*. Ithaca, NY: Cornell University Press.

Stepansky, P. E. 1986. "Feuerbach and Jung as Religious Critics – with a Note on Freud's Psychology of Religion". In *Freud: Appraisals and Reappraisals*, P. E. Stepansky (ed.), 215–39. Hillsdale, NJ: Analytic Press.

Stern, D. N. 1985. *The Interpersonal World of the Infant: A View from Psychoanalysis and Developmental Psychology*. New York: Basic Books.

Stoller, R. [1973] 2001. "Telepathic Dreams?", E. L. Mayer (ed.). *Journal of the American Psychoanalytic Association* 49: 635–52.

Strachey, J. [1961] 2001. "Editor's Note". In *The Standard Edition of the Complete Psychological Works of Sigmund Freud*, vol. 23, 3–5. London: Vintage/Hogarth Press.

Suttie, I. D. 1932. "Religion: Racial Character and Mental and Social Health". *British Journal of Medical Psychology* 12(4): 289–314.

Suttie, I. D. 1966. *The Origins of Love and Hate*. New York: Julian Press.

Taves, A. 2006. "Comments on Dubuisson's 'The Western Construction of Religion'". *Religion* 36: 138–40.

Totton, N. (ed.) 2003. *Psychoanalysis and the Paranormal: Lands of Darkness*. London: Karnac.

Treitel, C. 2004. *A Science for the Soul: Occultism and the Genesis of the German Modern*. Baltimore, MD: Johns Hopkins University Press.

Tyson, J. B. 1999. "Anti-Judaism in the Critical Study of the Gospels". In *Anti-Judaism and the Gospels*, W. R. Farmer (ed.), 216–51. Harrisburg, PA: Trinity Press International.

van IJzendoorn, M. H. & A. Sagi 1999. "Cross-Cultural Patterns of Attachment: Universal and Contextual Dimensions". In *Handbook of Attachment*, J. Cassidy & P. R. Shaver (eds), 713–34. New York: Guilford.

Wallace, E. R. 1983. *Freud and Anthropology: A History and Reappraisal*. New York: International Universities Press.

Werman, D. S. 1986. "On the Nature of the Oceanic Experience". *Journal of the American Psychoanalytic Association* 34: 123–39.

White, W. A. 1937. "Ian D. Suttie, *The Origins of Love and Hate*". *Psychoanalytic Review* 24: 458–60.

Whitebook, J. 1995. *Perversion and Utopia: A Study in Psychoanalysis and Critical Theory*. Cambridge, MA: MIT Press.

Whitehouse, H. 2004a. *Models of Religiosity: Cognitive Theory of Religious Transmission*. Walnut Creek, CA: Altamira Press.

Whitehouse, H. 2004b. "Why Do We Need Cognitive Theories of Religion?" In *Religion as a Human Capacity*, T. Light & B. C. Wilson (eds), 65–88. Leiden: Brill.

Winnicott, D. W. 1990. *The Maturational Processes and the Facilitating Environment*. London: Karnac.

Winnicott, D. W. 1999. *Playing and Reality*. London: Routledge.

Wright, K. 2006. "Preverbal Experience and the Intuition of the Sacred". In *Psychoanalysis and Religion in the 21st Century*, D. M. Black (ed.), 173–90. London: Routledge.

Yerushalmi, Y. H. 1991. *Freud's Moses: Judaism Terminable and Interminable*. New Haven, CT: Yale University Press.

Zaretsky, E. 1998. "Melanie Klein and the Emergence of Modern Personal Life". In *Reading Melanie Klein*, L. Stonebridge & J. Phillips (eds), 33–48. New York: Routledge.

# Index

and affective transfer  87
and communication technologies  95–6
and contemporary psychoanalysis  11,
    109–12
and definition  87
and dreams  11, 91, 92–4
and foundations of psychoanalysis  87
and the unconscious  88
totemism  49–50

*Über-Ich*  25, 45, 105; *see also* super-ego
uncanny  101–2, 104, 107
unconscious  101, 102, 103, 105, 108, 117,
    118
  and affective impressions  72
  and memory  31, 63, 66, 68, 69, 71, 74,
    79
  and neuroscience 91, 96; *see also*
    unconscious communication

and origin of gods, demons, ghosts
    109
and return of the repressed  72, 80
and transmission  87
and unconscious communication  10,
    11, 87, 89, 96, 97, 98, 105, 108, 109,
    111, 112; *see also* neuroscience
and wishes  51

von Harnack, A.  126–7

Whitehouse, H.  4
White, W. A.  126
Winnicott, D. W.  114, 132
Wright, K.  126

Yaweh religion  68, 77

Zaretsky, E.  124; *see also* Suttie, I. D.